Capturing Institutional Change

'This excellent work explains how "ideas" help us move to an information society from a society otherwise clothed in public secrets. It shows how State–society "epistemic networks" help negotiate the dialectics of secrecy and openness. This provides a nuanced analysis of ways in which "ideational" and "State churning" together seek to provide non-linear law and policy gateways for social change (both as a space for governance reform and normative retrogression). This deep analysis of the everyday and the extraordinary enables both a structural and functional grasp of change towards new horizons of the global human rights revolution.'

—Upendra Baxi, Emeritus Professor of Law,
University of Warwick, UK, and University of Delhi, India

'In this persuasively argued book, Himanshu Jha cuts a distinctive and original path in a field that is rich in research studies. He shows the incremental causality of ideas that have their origins within the State, rather than in society, and that finally reached a tipping point early in this century. I highly recommend *Capturing Institutional Change* as an important contribution to work on institutional change.'

—John Harriss, Professor Emeritus,
Simon Fraser University, Canada

'A compelling story about how the world's largest democracy recognized the public's right of access to government records.'

—Alasdair Roberts, Professor,
University of Massachusetts Amherst, USA

'From democratic complacency to institutional change, Jha's intersectional analysis of the Right to Information movement and the power of information is invaluable.'

—Aruna Roy, Social Activist and Founder Member,
Mazdoor Kisan Shakti Sangathan, and National Campaign
for People's Right to Information

INSTITUTIONS AND DEVELOPMENT IN SOUTH ASIA SERIES

SERIES EDITORS

Rahul Mukherji, Subrata K. Mitra, and Raghbendra Jha

Institutions are a central facet of development in South Asia. They can promote competition, spur democracy, and engender citizen well-being. They can equally be the harbingers of monopolies, authoritarianism, and social inequities. Institutions embody norms that influence the behaviour and lives of citizens in South Asia. How do democratic institutions succeed and fail in South Asia? This question is central to the exploration of the mechanisms of South Asian development.

Citizen well-being and economic growth within a sustainable framework are equally constitutive of the process of South Asian development. Economic growth often requires regulated market systems that promote internal and global competition. How can regulated competitive capitalism be promoted in South Asia? Can regulations structure markets to create a sustainable future? Can the State in South Asia ensure a dignified life for the average South Asian citizen?

In seeking answers to these questions, this series will interrogate the interplay of global and local forces within and outside the State that create and perpetuate norms that spur and deter South Asian development.

Rahul Mukherji is Professor and Head, Department of Political Science, South Asia Institute, Heidelberg University, Germany.

Subrata K. Mitra is Emeritus Professor of political science at Heidelberg University, Germany.

Raghbendra Jha is Professor of Economics, Arndt-Corden Department of Economics, and Executive Director, Australia South Asia Research Centre, Australian National University, Canberra.

INSTITUTIONS AND DEVELOPMENT IN SOUTH ASIA SERIES

Capturing Institutional Change

The Case of the Right to Information Act in India

Himanshu Jha

OXFORD
UNIVERSITY PRESS

OXFORD
UNIVERSITY PRESS

Oxford University Press is a department of the University of Oxford. It furthers the University's objective of excellence in research, scholarship, and education by publishing worldwide. Oxford is a registered trademark of Oxford University Press in the UK and in certain other countries.

Published in India by
Oxford University Press
22 Workspace, 2nd Floor, 1/22 Asaf Ali Road, New Delhi 110002, India

First Edition published in 2020

ISBN-13 (print edition): 978-0-19-012478-6
ISBN-10 (print edition): 0-19-012478-4

ISBN-13 (eBook): 978-0-19-099122-7
ISBN-10 (eBook): 0-19-099122-4

Typeset in Adobe Garamond Pro 11/13.5
by The Graphics Solution, New Delhi 110 092
Printed in India by Rakmo Press, New Delhi 110 020

To
Rahul, Ma, and Babuji

Contents

Tables, Box, and Figures

Tables

Box

Figures

Abbreviations

ADB	Asian Development Bank
ADMK	Anna Dravida Munnetra Kazhagam
AGM	annual general meeting
AIFB	All India Forward Bloc
AINEC	All India Newspaper Editors Conference
AIR	All India Radio
ASEAN	Association of Southeast Asian Nations
BDO	block development officer
BEAG	Bombay Environmental Action Group
BGVS	Bharat Gyan Vigyan Samiti
BJP	Bharatiya Janata Party
BPL	below poverty line
CAG	Comptroller and Auditor General of India
CBI	Central Bureau of Investigation
CERC	Consumer Education and Research Centre
CGG	Centre for Good Governance
CHRI	Commonwealth Human Rights Initiative
CM	chief minister
CMP	Common Minimum Programme
CoS	Committee of Secretaries
CPDR	Committee for Protection of Democratic Rights
CPI	Communist Party of India
CPI-M	Communist Party of India-Marxist
CPIA	Country Policy and Institutional Assessment
CPR	Centre for Policy Research
DMK	Dravida Munnetra Kazhagam

DoPT	Department of Personnel and Training
DoT	Department of Telecommunications
DRPSC	department-related parliamentary standing committee
DRPSC-HA	Department-Related Parliamentary Standing Committee on Home Affairs
EPW	*Economic and Political Weekly*
FoI	freedom of information
GoI	Government of India
GoM	group of ministers
HC	high court
IAS	Indian Administrative Services
IDA	International Development Association
IDRC	International Development Research Centre
IFI	international financial institution
IFSMN	Indian Federation of Small and Medium Newspapers
IIPA	Indian Institute of Public Administration
IMF	International Monetary Fund
IPC	Indian Penal Code
IPD	Initiative for Policy Dialogue
JP	Jayprakash Narayan
KSSP	Kerala Sastra Sahitya Parishad
LBSNAA	Lal Bahadur Shastri National Academy of Administration
MEA	Ministry of External Affairs
MGNREGA	Mahatma Gandhi National Rural Employment Guarantee Act, 2005 (originally National Rural Employment Guarantee Act)
MHA	Ministry of Home Affairs
MISA	Maintenance of Internal Security Act, 1971
MKSS	Mazdoor Kisan Shakti Sangathan
MP	member of parliament
MPPP	Ministry of Personnel, Public Grievances and Pensions

NAC	National Advisory Council
NCPRI	National Campaign of People's Right to Information
NDA	National Democratic Alliance
NF	National Front
NGO	non-governmental organization
NUJ	National Union of Journalists
NUS	National University of Singapore
OSA	Official Secrets Act, 1923
O&M Division	Organisation and Methods Division
PCI	Press Council of India
PDS	public distribution system
PIL	public interest litigation
PM	prime minister
PMO	Prime Minister's Office
PRIA	Society for Participatory Research in Asia
PTI	Press Trust of India
PUCL	People's Union for Civil Liberties
PUCLDR	People's Union for Civil Liberties and Democratic Rights
RaaG	RTI Assessment and Advocacy Group
RSS	Rashtriya Swayamsevak Sangh
RTI	Right to Information
SAP	structural adjustment program
SASP	South Asian Studies Programme
SC	Supreme Court
SDM	subdivisional magistrate
SEWA	Self Employed Women's Association
SP	Samajwadi Janata Party
SWRC	Social Work and Research Centre
TDP	Telugu Desam Party
ToI	*Times of India*
UDHR	Universal Declaration of Human Rights
UF	United Front
UK	United Kingdom

UN	United Nations
UNESCO	United Nations Educational, Scientific and Cultural Organization
UNICEF	United Nations Children's Fund
UPA	United Progressive Alliance
USA	United States of America
WB	World Bank
WTO	World Trade Organization
WWF	World Wide Fund for Nature

Foreword

This serious piece of scholarship contributes to a growing body of literature that suggests that social scientists should pay sincere attention to the State and the ideas that come to dominate it to understand governance. Comparative politics following the Weberian and the structural Marxist traditions has paid significant attention to the State. In Indian politics, however, there is much greater scholarly engagement with class and party systems than with the State as a way of exploring the nature of institutions that govern citizens. *Capturing Institutional Change* fills that gap.

The State in India is decried both by liberals and Marxists. Both liberal and Marxist scholarship opine that the action really lies in class conflict or the conflict among diverse interest groups. The State as an actor becomes largely epiphenomenal for both the strands of scholarly thought. The left has only hesitatingly come to accept the role of the State in redistributive politics.

This book on the right to information (RTI) in India demonstrates the importance of ideation within the State. This right owes a lot to how the weight of ideas within the State shifted in favour of transparency and accountability over time. It did not matter whether the Janata Party, the Bharatiya Janata Party (BJP), or the Congress Party were in power. Even the BJP under Prime Minister (PM) Vajpayee had prepared a draft Act. The Congress Party that legislated the Act had opposed it for a long time in the past. The book argues powerfully and persuasively that the norm of secrecy was gradually overtaken by the norm of transparency within the State. This involved movements within the legislature, the bureaucracy, and the judiciary. The State also learned from experiments carried out by non-governmental organizations (NGOs) such as the Mazdoor Kisan Shakti Sangathan (MKSS; Association for the Empowerment of Workers and Peasants).

The book also demonstrates the gradual nature of institutional change in India, likening it to a layered tipping point. Layering occurs when a new norm is allowed to grow along the edges of the old norm. Over time, the new norm gains a certain momentum to reach a threshold, from where the system tips unequivocally in the direction of the new norm. The manuscript is a product of painstaking research that shows how the norm of transparency was allowed to evolve on top of the secrecy norm over time. The RTI Act, 2005, is considered the tipping point from where the new norm of transparency came to dominate the relationship between the citizen and the State.

It is only fitting that Oxford University Press's series titled Institutions and Development in South Asia is inaugurated by a volume that explains the trajectory of democratic politics through the prism of the RTI in India. The volume brings the State, and ideation within it, back into an understanding of democratic politics in India. This volume will hopefully inspire scholars to take the State more seriously when trying to understand institutions and institutional change. The manuscript suggests the importance of ideation within the State, often after taking into account social initiatives and developments at the global level. Such ideation could be critical for understanding the State's capacity to govern either within existing institutions or by changing them.

Professor Rahul Mukherji
Chair, Department of Political Science
South Asia Institute
Heidelberg University
Germany, 22 July 2020

Preface and Acknowledgements

The seeds of this research were sown during my close involvement with the development sector in India prior to my academic association. This coincided with the time of considerable socio-economic and political change in India. On the one hand, the country was experiencing growth, while on the other, a plethora of legally mandated social rights were being extended to the citizens. These changes in many cases were institutional. Citizens' rights represented a marriage between the directive principles of State policy and the fundamental rights enshrined in the Constitution of India. Moving beyond the schemes and programmes, citizens' well-being was now legally enforceable through Acts of parliament. For example, right to work promulgated as National Rural Employment Guarantee Act, 2005, was also part of right to life (or live). Similarly, high economic growth was a cumulative result of the fundamental overhauling of economic institutions in 1991. My own work (especially between 2004 and 2011) focused on monitoring the institutions of governance. I argued that institutions are vehicles that carry the governance agenda forward and, therefore, it was important to monitor their performance. On numerous occasions, as a practitioner, I would also engage with these emerging legal regimes and put into practice these rights. One of these was the RTI—to procure crucial information from the State. In fact, I recall that at one point of time, I co-organized a workshop of RTI users from across the country to listen to and to learn from their fascinating experiences. RTI had clearly emerged as a powerful tool for accountability and citizens' right. This work always kept taking me back to the source of these changes. It is at this stage that I started thinking deeply about how these institutional changes occurred in the first place. There were settled explanatory narratives. Dominant narratives suggested that these social rights were a result of the bottom-up pressures and demands. For instance, it was somewhat of a settled subject that social movement was consequential in the promulgation of RTI. I finally gave into my intellectual curiosity and embarked on what seemed, at that point, a rather daunting, behemoth, mountain-like challenge staring me in the face. I decided to give up my rather settled life in Delhi and go back to the academic drawing board to dig deeper in the hope of contributing to the existing narratives. The origins of this book can be traced back to these events—intellectual curiosity being the usual suspect.

This book examines the process of institutional change through the lenses of transformation in the 'information regime' in India by tracing the passage of the RTI Act, 2005. Institutional change in the information regime in India presents a research puzzle where, prior to the RTI Act, details and the process of governance were shrouded in secrecy, limited to the corridors of public authorities, and governed by laws that weakened the citizens' right to know from the State (public authorities). The legal system did not favour citizens' right to transparency and accountability during the pre-RTI period. What explains this move towards institutional change? Why and how did the State decide to turn the page on a legal regime that had persisted since colonial times and that was consolidated towards secrecy in the aftermath of the Indo-China conflict (1962) and Indo-Pak war (1965)? I try to capture the why and how of institutional change in order to unravel this puzzle. In doing so, this book seeks to contribute conceptually to the emerging literature on institutional change by presenting a nuanced and an alternative perspective on the evolution of the RTI Act.

This volume is the product of a strong ideational collaboration between my academic mentor and myself. Hence, first and foremost, I would like to extend my heartfelt thanks and gratitude to Rahul Mukherji. I would have been lost in this long, arduous journey but for Rahul's constant guidance, encouragement, thought-provoking questions, and comments on numerous drafts of my writing. His interventions injected both a sense of adventure and spirit in the process of research and writing.

I must also express my deep gratitude to Professor Vineeta Sinha, the former head of the South Asian Studies Programme (SASP) at the National University of Singapore (NUS). She was always generous and forthcoming in providing the right kind of support, advice, and encouragement. I am grateful to Professor Yong Mun Cheong, also the former head of the SASP, for encouraging me as a newly minted doctoral scholar.

This research would not have been possible without the generous support of the NUS. The NUS has been more than magnanimous in providing research scholarships, field trip grants, and conference funding. I am thankful to my current academic home at the South Asia Institute, Heidelberg University (HU), in Germany. Surrounded by the scenic beauty of Heidelberg and motivated by the intellectual legacy of HU, I was inspired to publish parts of this work as journal articles and eventually complete the book manuscript. Parts of this work were further refined and improved upon following presentations in various seminars, conferences, and invited talks. Feedback and comments received in these forums enabled me to address some of the glaring gaps. I am thankful to them all.

I would be failing in my duty if I did not extend my gratitude to the people who supported me during my fieldwork and over the course of my research development. I will start by thanking Professor Shekhar Singh who invited me into his home and, over numerous cups of *lopchu* tea, shared the nitty-gritty of the RTI story. His inputs clarified many doubts and at the same time stimulated me into asking some puzzling questions, which I have tried to address in this book. Apart from that, Professor Singh was kind enough to share with me RTI-related material in his possession, which turned out to be a great source of empirical 'ammunition' for my arguments. He put me in touch with the main actors of the RTI story. Without his facilitation, it would not have been possible to interview these important people. I must also thank Aruna Roy, Nikhil Dey, and Shankar Singh for opening the doors of the MKSS and inviting me in, and sharing their stories with me in Devdungri (Rajasthan). Several people took time out of their busy lives and provided valuable and insightful comments. I would specifically like to acknowledge Manjusha Nair, Arun Kumar Thiruvengadam, Alasdair Roberts, Andrew Wyatt, John Harriss, Aseema Sinha, Wajahat Habibullah, A.N. Tiwari, T.N. Chaturvedi, Venkatesh Nayak, Sudhir Kumar Rakesh, Ashish Ranjan, Subramanian Swamy, E.M.S. Natchiappan, Naresh Minocha, Venkitesh Ramakrishnan, Irfan Waheed Usmani, and Jayarethnam Pillai. I also appreciate the support of those sympathetic actors from within the State whose names, as they had requested, remain anonymous. Finally, I would like to acknowledge and thank my numerous co-travellers who critically engaged with parts of this book, providing valuable support and guidance. It is not possible to name all of you here but once you read this, you will know I am talking about you.

Last but not the least, I would like to express a deep sense of gratitude to my family. Pranjala, without your unflinching support this journey would have been a lonely one. I am thankful to you for tolerating my academic swings, the ups and the downs. Thanks to Mummy and Papa (in law) for their constant support and for keeping a close tab on my progress. Above all, thank you, Ma and Babuji, for believing in me.

Introduction

In 2014, I met Mazloom Nadaf, resident of Machdi village located in Jhanjarpur block of Madhubani district in the eastern Indian state of Bihar (a state notorious for its nexus of bureaucracy, corrupt politicians, and dominant class and caste groups; a governance crisis; and a law-and-order problem). Mazloom is a rickshaw puller. By the government's definition of poverty, Mazloom is below the poverty line and, therefore, eligible for the Indira Awas Yojana—a government programme that aims to lend money to the rural poor to build a house. Although the local government office listed Mazloom as a beneficiary, he was asked to pay a bribe of INR 5,000. Mazloom could not afford it and was made to run around for five years. In 2005, the RTI Act was promulgated to provide citizens a legal regime to access information that was earlier under the control of public authorities (RTI Act, 2005).[1] In 2006, about a year after the RTI Act was enacted, a local lawyer advised Mazloom to file an RTI application, and helped him ask the concerned department to explain

- why he was not allotted a house under the Indira Awas Yojana;
- list the beneficiaries of the scheme for the previous five years; and
- certify that he was economically better off than beneficiaries in his village.

Even before he received the information sought, the block development officer (BDO) came to his village and handed him the

[1] For legal scope and operation of RTI, see Naib 2011; 2013.

cheque for the first instalment of his loan.[2] Later, in 2009, he was given an award for showcasing how the RTI Act benefits the poor. Mazloom told me, 'Neither my award nor my RTI made me rich; I am still poor. However ... it made me "Mazloom Bhai" overnight.' It seemed that seeking accountability from the State gave Mazloom a sense of empowerment, entitlement, and dignity.

Prior to the RTI Act, Mazloom could not have approached the BDO to seek such accountability—it would have been unthinkable and even illegal. The RTI Act presents a contrasting 'before' and 'after' picture, a valid case of institutional change.

This book captures the processual dynamics and nature of institutional change[3] in the information regime in India by examining the RTI Act. I seek to offer an alternative perspective on the evolution of the RTI Act. In doing so I contribute conceptually to the emerging literature on institutional change. At the outset I should state that this book does not examine the implementation of the RTI Act. The stage after institutional change should be treated as being a distinct one of institutional progression and as related to the implementation of the law (on institutional progression of the RTI Act, see Jha 2018a).[4] This book solely focuses on providing a causal story of the institutional change in the information regime in India.

[2] Mazloom did not follow up on this RTI application as he received the first instalment of the loan, which was the objective of his filing the RTI application in the first place.

[3] We define institutional change as drastic rearrangements in 'norms' (North 1990) or changes in the 'rules of the game' (North 1990), whereby new institutions replace the path-dependent old institutions. This definition is elaborated within this introduction.

[4] Admittedly, there are a number of studies primarily published around 2009–10 which examine the implementation of the RTI Act and highlight numerous problems in implementation: lack of awareness among citizens, barriers to the use of law, bureaucratic indifference, rejection of appeals, rising pendency, and the nature of RTI use (Roberts 2010; RTI Assessment and Analysis Group [RaaG] and National Campaign for People's Right to Information [NCPRI] 2009;).

The Puzzle

Institutional change in the information regime presents a research puzzle. Prior to the RTI Act, the details and processes of governance were shrouded in secrecy. Laws such as the Official Secrets Act, 1923 (OSA); Civil Services Conduct Rules, 1964; and the Indian Evidence Act, 1872 (Sections 1, 2, and 3) as well as manual and office procedures of the Government of India (GoI) had weakened the citizens' right to know (Deva 1977; Shrivastava 2009). The logic of, and demand for, transparency and accountability was on the fringes during the pre-RTI period, and the institution of 'secrecy' was 'locked in' within the State at all systemic levels. In contrast to this past, transparency and accountability have truly taken centre stage in the governance discourse of today. Why did the State decide to initiate institutional change in the legal regime persisting since the colonial times, and even strengthened it in 1967 after the Indo-China conflict (1962) and Indo-Pak war (1965)? The puzzle deepens. The Indian State is viewed to be one captured and dominated by a nexus of vested interests (for such views, see Bardhan 1984; Chandra 2004; Kohli 1987, 2012; Lakshman 2011). Why would the State, so deeply penetrated by vested interests, initiate a change in the legal framework of the information regime, which would be used, variously, to highlight and expose the very nexus said to govern its institutions?

Indeed, the RTI Act has been used to expose corruption both 'grand' and 'petty'. Instances of grand corruption exposed by the RTI Act include the Delhi Commonwealth Games scam 2010 (Garg 2012), Adarsh Nagar housing scam (Katakam 2010), and the 2G spectrum scam (Swamy 2011). It has also been used to ensure public service delivery at the grassroots and make public authorities accountable to citizens. RTI has also been used extensively at the national and sub-national levels. A report by Transparency India International (2017) estimates that 24.4 million RTI applications were filed between 2005 and 2016. Admittedly, some segments of the State are still reluctant to share official information, and implementation has been imperfect. Regardless, the dominant interest-based nexus, which purportedly connived to engage in corruption, were exposed due to the RTI Act.

I pose two central questions to unravel the above-mentioned puzzle:

1. What explains institutional change?
2. How did it come about?

By tracing the journey from ideas to a concrete institutional arrangement, the first question will unravel the evolutionary aspect of institutional change and, in turn, describe the nature of change and explain why the State brought it about. By addressing how institutional change is brought about, the second question will reveal the political and social processes that led to the change. In exploring these questions, I introduce four arguments.

First, I argue that the RTI Act was the culmination of an incremental, slow-moving process of 'ideas'—that emerged endogenously from within the State—developing into a 'layered tipping point' (Jha 2018b; Mukherji 2013, 2014a) of institutional change, from the norms and policies of 'secrecy' to those of 'openness'. In this model of institutional change, the incremental weight of endogenous ideas is, on achieving an appropriate critical mass, consequential in 'tipping' the institution to change. This is a long-drawn, gradual process, endogenous in nature, where ideas play an instrumental role in shaping the state's interests and policy preferences.

Second, I establish that ideas of openness emerged from within the State, and that the political power of ideas and the resultant State thinking played a crucial role in the incremental push towards institutional change. Moving beyond linear, societal-based explanations of institutional change, I show that the processes within the State as well are significant to explain change.

Third, I explore State–society complementarity, but in terms of 'epistemic networks' with ideational linkages. I propose to move beyond existing explanations—in terms of social or people's movement, middle-class elite network, public sphere, or symbolic capital—and argue instead for a nuanced understanding, by engaging with arguments that show that the State and society constitute each other in a mutually empowering relationship.

Fourth, I show that global norms had both demonstrative and operative influence on the ongoing institutional change in India. I argue that global norms need to be placed within the broader context of the emerging discourse at the national level.

Establishing Institutional Change

Why should the RTI Act be treated as a case of institutional change? At the outset it is important to define institutions to answer this question. Institutions[5] have been variously defined as norms in terms of

- interrelated rules and routines that define appropriateness in actions (March and Olsen 1989);
- standard operating procedures (Hall 1986); or
- informal–formal rules of the game (North 1990).

Scholars point towards the 'stickiness' of institutions as stubbornly persisting on the historical landscape. Institutions suffer from path dependence; and this nature of institutions renders them resistant to change, because history matters and it is cost-ineffective to exit from the status quo (Boettke, Coyne, and Leeson 2008; Mukherji 2013, 2014a; North 1990; Page 2006; Pierson 2000). As institutions tend to persist, the related political processes and social behaviours persist as well. The institution of secrecy in this case was a colonial legacy, the path dependence of which was informed by laws established in the colonial period, such as the OSA, strengthened and sustained by the accompanying laws in the post-colonial period. Hence, the institution of secrecy was persisting on the historical landscape and the institution was locked in within the State in a self-perpetuating loop of network of externalities and learning, rendering change from

[5] For our purpose, one of the most comprehensive definitions is provided by North (1990: 3): institutions 'are the rules of the game in a society, or more formally, are the humanly devised constraints that shape human interaction', as opposed to organizations. Institutions 'reduce uncertainty by providing a structure to everyday life', and include 'both formal rules such as laws and constitutions, and informal constraints such as conventions and norms'.

within the existing institutional structure difficult and the adoption of an alternate institutional arrangement impossible (North 1990: 94–100; Pierson 2000).

In this light, I define institutional change as drastic rearrangements in norms or changes in the rules of the game, whereby new institutions replace old institutions suffering from path dependence. Hence, the RTI Act, enacted on 12 October 2005, presents a valid and substantive case of institutional change on three counts.

First, on the basis of the definitions of institutions discussed earlier, the RTI Act represents rearrangements in norms, standard operating procedures, or rules of the game—it enables citizens to access information under the control of public authorities. The RTI Act replaced the locked-in and persisting institutional arrangement that perpetuated secrecy within the State. A rearrangement of the existing norms by unlocking the persisting institutional gridlock represents a regime shift, that is, from secrecy to openness. Section 22 of the RTI Act completes the institutional change by stating the supremacy of the Act in case of direct conflict with OSA and other such Acts.[6]

Second, unlike other rights-based legislation, the RTI Act does not represent policy continuity; instead, it marks a complete departure from the previous policy regime. For instance, continuity can be seen between the Mahatma Gandhi National Rural Employment Guarantee Act (MGNREGA; 2005) and previous policies/schemes such as Jawahar Rozgar Yojana (1989) and Food for Work Programme (2004); or the Right of Children to Free and Compulsory Education Act (2009) can be seen emanating from earlier policy programmes such as the Sarva Shiksha Abhiyan (2002). On the other hand, prior to the RTI Act, there was not even a single policy that allowed access to information from state/public authorities.

[6] Section 22 of the RTI Act says: 'The provisions of this Act shall have effect notwithstanding anything inconsistent therewith contained in the Official Secrets Act, 1923, and any other law for the time being in force or in any instrument having effect by virtue of any law other than this Act' (RTI Act, 2005, available at: righttoinformation.gov.in/webactrti.htm [accessed 12 February 2020]).

Third, the RTI Act is justiciable. Thus, citizens' access to the information of public authorities, which was a legal offence in the pre-RTI Act regime, is now a justiciable right under the new regime. This is different from other rights-based legislation that represent a crossover between directive principles and fundamental rights, where the formerly non-justiciable has now become justiciable. In the case of the RTI Act, the shift is not from non-justiciable to justiciable, but significantly institutional, where what was formerly a legal offence is now a justiciable right. The RTI Act is both a statutory law and a fundamental right. In this case, the scope of fundamental rights provided in the Constitution of India has been expanded and redefined. This, in turn, redefines state–citizen linkages in the sense that the RTI Act is statutory and a constitutional right as well. Hence, it is not the case that the state is the benevolent provider of this right; it is a constitutionally provided fundamental right, and citizens can demand it. The change is de jure.

Admittedly, the state on numerous occasions has attempted to dilute the legal provisions of the RTI Act, ostensibly to weaken the law. The most recent is the RTI Act amendment bill of 2019, which seeks to change the provisions of the appointment and salaries of the information commissioners at the central and the state levels. Do these dilutions reverse institutional change? I argue that the institutional change is irreversible on two counts. First, any government in power cannot withdraw this constitutionally granted legal right. Second, a right that was non-existent prior to 2005 was systemically instituted with the promulgation of the RTI Act. To illustrate this, I will draw on another case of institutional change—the 1991 economic reforms (see Mukherji 2013, 2014a). The uneven progress and performance of the Indian economy does not reverse the institutional change of 1991. The norm changes that were instituted in 1991 have fundamentally changed domestic economic policies. Likewise, moves to dilute the RTI Act have neither deterred the citizens from using this right, nor has it reversed the norm change from secrecy to openness. At this juncture it is not possible to ascertain the impact of the 2019 RTI amendment. Assessing a moving target falls beyond the ambit and objective of this book, which seeks to explain institutional change by examining the case of the RTI Act. Having stated that, I will further elaborate on the issue of the 2019 RTI amendment in the Conclusion.

Existing scholarly literature provides alternative arguments to explain this institutional change. In the following section, I will discuss the relevant literature.

Alternative Explanations of Institutional Change: Existing Literature

The mainstream literature examines the evolution of the RTI Act through a number of vantage points.

The first cluster of explanations of institutional change in the information regime in India posits the primary role to the 'People's or Social Movement' (Baviskar 2007; Mander and Joshi 1998; Mishra 2003; Pande 2014; Roy and Dey 2001; Roy and the MKSS Collective 2018; Shrivastava 2009; Singh 2010). The mainstream view of the literature is that the state yielded to popular demand in the form of protests or amplified political contestation, which led to institutional change; the literature on social movements supports this view. Initially, most of this literature emanated from actors who were involved in or familiar with the social mobilization spearheaded by the MKSS and were part of the National Campaign of People's Right to Information (NCPRI), a citizen's platform to demand RTI. The people's movement narrative was accepted beyond question and carried forward in the post-RTI Act scholarship, for which the epicentre of the demand for RTI in India was the MKSS movement in the Indian state of Rajasthan (Jenkins and Goetz 1999; Peisakhin and Pinto 2010; Roberts 2006; Sarangi 2012). The law was seen to be 'drafted by the civil society itself' and a result of 'struggle by the civil society, NGOs and media' (Ashraf 2008). This resulted in the scholarly conviction that 'the real movement for the right to information originated from the grass-roots level. The right to information was demanded in a similar way … the origins of the RTI movement lie in Devdungri' (Naib 2013: 41).

In locating the focus within the social movement argument, recent scholarship on the subject has provided a nuanced understanding.

Pande (2014) points towards the significance of a multi-scaled activism that negotiated with a 'differently layered' state. This was achieved through the Habermasian 'public sphere' of *jan sunwayi*s (public hearings) or Bourdieu's 'symbolic capital' of eminent activists (Pande 2014).

Problematizing the social movement narrative, the second cluster of scholarship explores the role of elite networks (Sharma 2015). It is argued that the post-liberalization climate has resulted in the retreat of the state and the changing nature of the bureaucratic order—the elite who dominated the bureaucracy have moved to other spaces, such as the private sector. The greater democratization of higher bureaucracy, and the support to the RTI Act of the urban, well-educated, high-caste elite, which was no longer vested in the state, was consequential in rendering the political climate conducive for the promulgation of the RTI Act (Sharma 2015: 146–51). This process, which led to the RTI Act, is understood in terms of a dense interpersonal network of members of the middle-class elite with similar backgrounds (such as a common alma mater or professional background, such as the Indian Administrative Services [IAS]). Arguments for the enactment of the RTI Act are located in the nature of leadership embedded in the ruling elite (Sharma 2015). This view can be categorized within the scholarship-of-elite argument, or that the demand for a rights-based development was led primarily by the network of middle-class elites that represents 'two contending projects of Indian democracy—one which is liberal and the other social democratic' (Corbridge, Harriss, and Jeffrey 2013). Similarly, economic reforms in India in the early 1990s are seen to emanate from the 'elite revolt' against the dirigiste state, especially those aspects of policy framework that constrained the interests of business groups and the urban middle class (Corbridge 2009; Corbridge and Harris 2000).

Yet another view posits primacy to broad-based civil society coalitions or alliances that play an instrumental role. With their connections and access to the political and permanent executive, this coalition took advantage of political opportunity and pushed for the RTI Act (Baviskar 2007).

More recent scholarship 'broadens' the narrative: Mathur (2015) holds that several factors cumulatively shaped policies, providing 'a policy environment—a context—in which such a change is perceived as acceptable and legitimate'. This argument holds that the interaction between ideational processes and institutions led to policy change. It proposes several factors, such as the role of domestic politics—where the United Progressive Alliance (UPA) regime thought it to be politically prudent to enact the RTI Act and international influence in the form of policy diffusion 'embedded in an international context'—or the policy compulsions that came with the new public management as India embarked on the path of liberalization from the 1990s onwards.

Thus, the different strands of literature provide significant direction in understanding institutional change in the information regime in India in the form of the RTI Act. However, there are some nagging gaps and, therefore, considerable scope for nuance. In the following section I will discuss some of these gaps and add to the existing corpus of scholarly literature by proposing alternative arguments.

Taking the Scholarship Forward: Presenting Alternative Arguments

To understand the process of transition from the norm of secrecy to the norm of openness, it is pertinent to define the point of departure. The arguments in the mainstream literature are ambiguous about the point of departure, possibly because these tend to cluster the RTI Act with other rights-based legislations promulgated during the same period, that is, the post-liberalization phase of the early 1990s. The argument that '*it was in the 1990s* [my emphasis] when various people's movements, most prominent among them being the MKSS, put concerted and sustained pressure to build up such an institution' is symptomatic of this view (Naib 2013: x). Further, the literature discussed earlier does not discuss the RTI Act directly in terms of institutional change. It alludes to it tangentially. I argue that the RTI Act is different from other rights-based legislation as it marks a complete departure from the previous regime, and that the OSA should be treated as both the starting point and the point of departure. To provide a causal explanation of institutional change it is important to trace the institutional path. This allows for delineation and identification of small, interlinked processes or sequences leading to an outcome. Hence, both institutional persistence and change should be treated as part of this causal story.

Redefining the starting point and the point of departure allows for the examination of historical evidence that scholars have ignored, and provides us with evidence to add nuance to existing explanations. In this light, I explore the twin processes of 'emergent ideas' and the resultant 'ideational diffusion' within the state to explain that the trajectory of institutional change is 'path-dependent'. This line of argument is consistent with the scholarship on institutional change, which assigns the primary role to ideas and ideational churning in shaping state's preferences (for such ideational accounts of institutional change, see Baker 2015; Béland 2007; Blyth 2002, 2013; Blyth, Helgadottir, and Kring 2016; Carstensen and Schmidt 2016; Culpepper 2008; Greif and Laitin 2004; Hall 1993; Jha 2018b; Mukherji 2013, 2014a; Quirk 1988). Since the norm of secrecy can be traced to the OSA, the ideas on openness and access to information have their origin in the 'nested' norm of secrecy; for example, I will establish in subsequent chapters that, in the parliament, opposition parties challenged the ruling party and permanent executive's privilege of access to official information, and demanded an extension of this privilege. Additionally, the Constitution of India provided the ideational basis for institutional change. By exploring this aspect I will show that, starting from the early 1950s, judicial verdicts shaped the ideas around openness by providing constitutional interpretation, starting from ensuring 'citizens' (fundamental) rights to free speech and expression' to 'right to know and information' as integral to the freedom of expression and speech, provided for in Article 19 (1) (a) of the Constitution.

Second, was institutional change a one-way process of societal interests (or demands) that played a consequential role in determining and guiding the state's policy preferences? Did the dense interpersonal network of the middle-class elite play an instrumental role (Sharma 2015)? Or did the 'symbolic capital' of eminent activists with its multi-scaled activism result in institutional change (Pande

2014)? Clearly, existing explanations place their point of enquiry primarily in the societal realm, where societal interests are consequential in shaping the state's policy choices. I present an alternative view by arguing that the causality for institutional change was multi-layered, and not limited only to the existing causal explanations discussed earlier. I capture institutional change by suggesting a process of a layered tipping point.

Layered Tipping Point of Institutional Change

First, by engaging with new and ignored historical material, I will reveal a significant layer that is conspicuous by its absence and treatment in the mainstream literature. I argue that *institutional change in the case of RTI in India is an incremental and gradual process of ideas emerging from within the state*. I will trace the crucial role of the state and the emerging ideas from within its different segments to capture the incremental shift in policy processes and preferences. The evidence examined casts light on the role of the state and emergent ideas within it, rather than societal interests singularly, as a significant variable to explain institutional change. In doing so, I challenge the claim that 'there was little effort by the government to institutionalize, and set up a legal framework to exercise the right to information' (Naib 2013: x). In this sense, this book fills a significant gap in the existing literature by bringing ideas and 'the state back in' (Skocpol 1985).

Admittedly, in broadening the mainstream narrative, Mathur (2015) alludes to the multi-layered process of the evolution of the RTI and points towards the interaction of ideas and institutions, but does not elaborate on the argument. Additionally, Sharma (2015) points towards the role of judicial pronouncements, reformist elements within the bureaucracy, and individuals from both state and society pushing the boundaries; but argues that suggesting the role of multiple factors 'does not quite answer the political questions lurking just beneath the surface of this process' (126). However, I argue that it is precisely these multiple factors that explain the undercurrent of processes consequential in institutional change.

Similarly, change in political regime (from the National Democratic Alliance [NDA] led by the BJP to the UPA led by the Indian National Congress [hereafter, Congress]) providing political opportunity (Baviskar 2007) or widening of social base in the post-Congress polity starting with the National Front (NF) government in 1989 (Ruparelia 2013) is insufficient to explain the institutional change. On the contrary, the evidence presented in the book shows that the incremental progression of ideas gained enough political power to tip the system over in 2005. This persuades me to adopt an ideational argument, where ideas played a pivotal role in causing institutional change.

I show that the 'ideational churning' around the norm of openness had started right since Independence, and that this long-drawn churning of ideas had an incremental impact on state thinking. The existing literature argues that social pressures played a consequential role in legislation. Based on archival material, internal government papers, primary and secondary material, and in-depth interviews, I present an alternative argument. I hold that the state, and the gradual evolution of ideas within it, played a key role in tipping the information regime towards transparency. I argue that the institutional change was layered processes leading to a tipping point—the culmination of a slow-moving process driven substantially, and endogenously, by the increasing political power of ideas (for similar accounts of tipping points, see Culpepper 2008; Hall 1993; Jha 2018b; Mahoney and Thelen 2010; Mukherji 2013, 2014a; North and Weingast 1989; Thelen 2004). What constitutes a tipping point? The tipping point has three distinct characteristics. First, the changes are evolutionary, gradual, and largely endogenous. Second, by carefully tracing the institutional path one should be able to delineate small, interlinked changes incrementally accumulated over time. Third, the changes will continue to evolve over time until they reach a threshold (Jha 2018b; see also, Mukherji 2013, 2014a). This is somewhat like an earthquake, which is caused when tectonic shifts over time reach critical mass (Mukherji 2014a). What seems sudden, like an earthquake, is actually a culmination of the process of slow-moving ideas emerging initially on the fringes, gradually moving to the policy centre stage, and incrementally reaching a tipping point. One cannot identify the exact threshold when the tipping point is reached, but if a considerable critical mass of ideas is reached and results in change, the system can be said to have tipped over. Scholars examining institutional change using a historical institutional lens often use critical junctures to provide a causal explanation (Acemoglu and Robinson 2012; Capoccia 2016; Capoccia and Kelemen 2007; Crawford 2018; Krasner 1984). This argument follows the 'punctuated equilibrium' model and suggests that exogenous shocks alter the path of a historically persistent institution resulting in institutional change.[7] Critical junctures are short-term and sudden shocks leading to institutional change are followed by a long-term impact of institutional persistence. On the contrary, I provide a historical–institutional account of a slow-moving endogenous institutional change where ideas play a consequential role. This change is neither sudden, nor is there any punctuation to alter the institutional path.

This endogenous movement of ideas towards a tipping point was a layered process. In this 'layering', a new norm emerges on the edges of the existing institutional structure and, eventually, wears it out (for 'layering' see, Béland 2007; Falleti 2004; Jha 2018b; Mukherji 2009; Thelen 2004). In the evolution of the new transparency regime of the RTI Act, I demonstrate, layering occurred in two steps. In the first layer, the norm of openness sprouted on the fringes of the nested secrecy regime. The pro-secrecy regime was primarily of the ruling party and mainstream bureaucracy. In the second layer, ruling-party support brought the idea of openness into the mainstream gaining enough critical mass to reach a tipping point in 2005. In establishing

[7] In their 1972 paper, palaeontologists Niles Eldredge and Stephen Jay Gould proposed the 'punctuated equilibrium' model, which held that 'the great majority of species appear with geological abruptness in the fossil record and then persist in stasis until their extinction'. In other words, the evolutionary path was characterized by long periods of relative stasis (equilibrium), which were altered, interrupted, or redefined (punctuated) by a revolutionary period or a decisive, path-altering shock. The model challenges—and marks a departure from—the mainstream, gradual, evolutionary theory of species postulated by Charles Darwin.

the layered tipping point of institutional change, I will challenge the viewpoint that efforts prior to 1989 were 'small talk, but no action' and that 'despite such lofty exhortations ... precious little changed in practice' (Sharma 2015: 11–112). I establish that, instead, these early ideas were instrumental in the long-drawn process of institutional change. It was the incremental weight of these ideas that created the critical mass to tip over the state's thinking from secrecy to openness.

It is pertinent to note that I acknowledge the role of social network and non-state social actors especially during the final stages of the promulgation of the RTI Act. Hence, this process is treated as part of the second layer. However, had the ideas within the state not moved favourably towards the norm of openness, the state would have dealt with the same social actors differently.

Elaboration on the Concept of State Engaged in This Work

Since I am arguing that the counter-norm of openness emerged incrementally from various segments of the State and accumulated enough power to reach a tipping point in 2005, it is important to elaborate on the concept of State that has been engaged with in this book. I present a variegated concept of State represented by its various arms such as the legislature, the political and the permanent executive, the judiciary, and State institutions. The State has been a much-debated concept in previous literature. However, from the nebulous concept, some scholars have identified specific institutions, which they equate with the State. To provide an example, for Milner (1991) the State is diffused, with no single hierarchy of authority—so given the issue, the executive, the Supreme Court (SC), the Congress, and the states[8] are all treated as representing the State. I engage with the concept of State in this scholarly tradition. I move away from the State as a unitary concept and present a disaggregated-pluralist view of State. I postulate that the State is not a monolith; neither do I call for its reification. Instead, different segments within the State such as the legislature,

[8] To differentiate between the State and the sub-national state we have used upper-case S to denote macro state and lower-case s to represent the sub-national state.

executive, and the judiciary are treated as significant arenas where the ideas on openness emerged, became powerful, and eventually gained enough political traction to tip the institution over. Hence, this is a structural argument, where structure is more important than the agency. I argue that the degrees of autonomy and the capacity of the State need to be seen in the light of pursuing certain ideas, such as the norm of openness. State thinking, then, is contingent upon these ideas. This pluralist view of the State is different from the 'everyday' State that citizens experience in their constant interaction with State agencies (Corbridge et al. 2005), or an alternate view that society and the State constitute each other in a dynamic process of policymaking (Chopra 2011), or finally that the state is an autonomous actor distinct from society (Bardhan 1984).

Conceptual Broadening of Institutions and Institutional Change: Arguments for an Indian Case

At this point, it is equally pertinent to flag some conceptual issues on the existing literature on institutional change. First, scholars explaining institutional change have primarily engaged with the advanced economies of the West. Barring few exceptions (see Falleti 2010; Levitsky and Murillo 2009, 2013; Mukherji 2013, 2014a), this scholarship has ignored examining similar changes in the emerging economies of the developing world. The literature is relatively sparse in this area and is especially glaring in the case of India. However, as a standalone scholarly work, this is addressed in Mukherji's (2013, 2014a) account of India's economic reforms, which demonstrates how ideas favouring globalization proliferated in the Indian policy environment since 1975. Over time, these ideas became more powerful, and finally tipped over in 1991 to embrace globalization.

Second, scholars capture sociopolitical and economic change in India from varied explanatory lenses such as elite agency (Corbridge and Harriss 2000; Sharma 2015; Varshney 1998), political regimes (Chhibber and Nooruddin 2004; Kohli 2012), social movements (Hasan 2018; Roy and the MKSS Collective 2018), caste- and class-based explanations (Bardhan 1984; Chandra 2004; Lakshman 2011), electoral incentives (Auerbach 2017; Thachil 2014), and reforms through stealth (Jenkins 1999). These accounts of change have not directly engaged with either historical institutionalism or ideas.

In this light, the book fills a significant gap at two levels—first, by bringing in a case from a developing world it contributes to the larger corpus of literature on institutional change. Second, by engaging with historical institutionalism and ideas the book provides an alternate lens to explain the case of institutional change in India.

Second, the literature predominantly focuses on explaining institutional changes in economic policy paradigms. Admittedly, there have been few exceptions such as the institutional change in the rights-based approach in India (Mukherji 2014b) and on healthcare reforms in Brazil (Falleti 2010). In this context, the book contributes to the existing literature by examining a rather thinly discussed case of institutional change in the social policy paradigm in India.

Additionally, scholarly work on institutions in India is 'by and large' parsimonious. This sparse and scattered literature examines institutions in the context of their mandated powers, functions, and performance. For instance, recently a group of scholars has paid attention to the institutions, not as norms but as complex organizations. They have focused on economic and political institutions such as the presidency, the parliament, the SC, the Reserve Bank of India, the civil services, and the Election Commission of India to name a few (Kapur, Mehta, and Vaishnav 2017). This body of work is primarily concerned with the inner workings of institutions as organizations and their performance in governance delivery—examining the what and how of institutional working, mapping the changes and continuities, identifying gaps, and providing a policy road map for future reforms (Kapur, Mehta, and Vaishnav 2017). This book, on the other hand, pays attention to another sparsely treated dimension of institutions—explaining the why and how of institutional change in India. Furthermore, moving beyond the focus on economic and political institutions, I provide a causal explanation for change in a social-policy paradigm. I hold that while it is important to evaluate the inner workings of institutions, it is equally significant to capture the process of institutional change with some explanatory rigour.

This in turn provides us with a deeper understanding of sociopolitical processes, their workings and inter-linkages, and the institutions themselves. Institutions are important arenas where these changes occur in the form of ideas and counter-ideas or new nascent norms coming in conflict with the old nested norms. Therefore, institutions are the epicentre for such churning, which this book will show, and they play an important part in institutional change. Hence, institutions in this causal explanation are not static organizations with mandated functions and expected performance, but are a significant part of institutional change itself. In the following section, I interrogate the social movement narrative relevant for the case of the RTI Act and present an alternative view.

Refining the Social Movement Narrative

To understand the process of institutional change it is pertinent to problematize the singular–linear narrative which suggests that societal interests are instrumental in influencing the State's policy thinking and in effecting institutional change. By examining State–society interactions, I propose a nuanced understanding of the process and propose two arguments.

The first argument demonstrates that 'progressive' actors from both the State and society forged linkages, complemented and constituted each other, removed the 'locked-in' political and policy uncertainty, and finally effectuated institutional change. I draw upon literature that acknowledges the State–society complementarity and the idea that these constitute each other in a mutually reinforcing power relationship (Evans 1997; Migdal 1988, 2001; Migdal, Kohli, and Shue 1994).

The second argument will establish the significance of ideational linkages in the formation of an epistemic network from both within and outside the State realm, which intensified the policy movement around the RTI. Haas (1992: 3) defines an 'epistemic community' as 'a network of professionals with recognised expertise and competence in a particular domain and authoritative claim to policy relevant knowledge within that domain or issue area'. I will establish that actors from both the state and society—bound by progressive ideas on openness, transparency, and access to information—came together to pursue a 'common goal'. Each node of this 'epistemic network' had their own set of epistemic characteristics, which played a consequential role in the final stages of institutional change. This argument is based on the large body of literature dealing with 'networks' (for discussions on networks, see Elke 2005; Jenkins-Smith and Sabatier 1994; Keck and Sikkink 1998; Khagram, Riker, and Sikkink 2002; Knoke 1990; Risse, Ropp, and Sikkink 1999; Sabatier 1988; Sabatier and Jenkins-Smith 1993; Sangiovanni 2005) and 'epistemic communities' (Haas 1992).

Scholars have tried to explain the State–society aspect through 'a small, intimate dense network' of urban/upper-caste/upper-middle-class people from common social, educational, and professional backgrounds with political connections (Sharma 2015), or through Bourdieu's idea of 'symbolic capital', where 'eminent activists' use their 'relevant capital' collectively (Pande 2014). I find these explanations problematic, because the evidence examined points towards a continuity of ideas around openness, transparency, accountability, and access to information that emanated from the press, political and permanent executive, and the academia much before these processes started taking formal shape in the mid-1990s. In a sense, this epistemic network was an extension of the earlier ideas. Hence, the linkages were more ideational than the dense inter-personal networks. Moreover, the evidence points towards a process where actors from both the State and the societal realm were ideationally bound and working in tandem. Hence, it was not a one-way process in which eminent activists with 'symbolic capital' negotiated with the differently layered state.

Global–Local Linkages

The mainstream literature does not mention the role of global norms either. Most of the scholarly work that focuses on the evolution of the RTI Act stresses the endogenous 'bottom-up' nature of institutional change and marginalizes the global influence. Even if it is flagged, the elaboration is parsimonious (Baviskar 2007). Admittedly, some scholars acknowledge the significance of the global influence. One such scholar argues that information laws worldwide were often invoked during policy discussions for their instrumental and symbolic value in achieving the state's aspiration of being seen as an 'advanced democracy' (Sharma 2015). Yet another scholar analyses the role of international institutions (such as the World Bank [WB], Asian Development Bank [ADB], and the World Trade Organization [WTO]) and the new good governance agenda that these institutions propounded (Mathur 2015). Additionally, it is also argued that the institutional change was due to the adoption of the liberalization policy at the national level.

I will show that even though global norms influenced the emerging discourse around openness and access to information at the national level, its role has to be placed within endogenous processes.[9] The ideational churning at the national level had been occurring independent of global norms. Policy processes were not being forced to adopt the norm of openness due to global policy imperatives such as the new public management after liberalization; instead, global norms had a demonstrative and operative impact on the endogenous process in what we term as 'norm demonstration' and 'norm localisation' (Acharya 2004). I argue that global norms informed and influenced the ongoing discourse at the national level in the process of 'norm demonstration'. Also, drawing upon Acharya's (2004) argument of 'norm localisation', I show that global norms were drawn upon and adapted at the national level, and that the state did not adopt it as a 'passive learner'.

Book Structure

This book is organized around two phases; each phase is treated as a layer. It deals with two distinct, yet interrelated, layers of the ideational and policy moves within the State apparatus and related institutions. The processes within State and society, and the role of global norms, are part of these phases/layers. The first phase starts with Independence in 1947 and extends until 1989. The second

[9] I have made similar arguments elsewhere—see Jha (2019).

phase covers the period from 1989 until 2005, when the RTI Act was enacted. Tracing the processes through these phases demonstrates a multi-layered movement of ideas on openness; these emerge in the periphery and gradually take centre stage with regard to policy to displace the persisting norm of secrecy. I cover these time periods across five chapters. The chapters explain the why and how of institutional change in the context of the RTI Act. Each chapter examines the evidence and draws its own set of conclusions.

Chapter 1 covers phase I or what I term the first layer. The norm of secrecy was institutionalized in phase I; it took firm root within the State apparatus, and reinforced what North (1990) terms 'nested rules' at all the systemic levels. At the same time, ideas on openness emerged on the fringes within the State. Additionally, to a limited extent, rudimentary emerging ideas around openness were reinforced within segments of the state and embedded as norms. I find a significant role of opposition politics in the first layer.

Chapter 2 examines the emerging processes in phase II, which is treated as the second and final layer. It shows that the incremental effect of emerging ideas on the state's thinking resulted in tangible policy movements and led to institutional change. I show that in the final stage of layering the transition from opposition to mainstream politics was consequential in institutional change. Nascent ideas emanating from the opposition politics got embedded within the mainstream politics, resulting in political commitment and tangible policy actions.

Chapter 3 traces the trajectory of ideas that emanated from the judiciary. It interpreted Article 19 (1) (a) of the Constitution of India to mean that the freedom of expression and speech was a fundamental right. The ideational movement within the judiciary coincides with the first two phases discussed in Chapters 1 and 2. This chapter discusses judicial verdicts and places them in the broader context of the discourse around openness emerging within the State.

Chapter 4 examines the processes around State and society, traces the role of social forces outside the State realm, and conceptualizes these processes as the complementarity of State and society, where strong ideational linkages led to the formation of an 'epistemic network'. These processes played a significant role in the final phase of the enactment of the RTI Act. The period covered in this chapter coincides with the latter half of phase II, which starts in the mid-1990s.

Chapter 5 examines the role of global norms in institutional change. I trace the nature and extent of the impact of global norm diffusion on domestic discourse. The global–domestic linkages around global norms on transparency, accountability, and access to information are spread in the two phases.

In the Conclusion, I draw upon the evidence presented in the book and engage with some broad conceptual points that emerge.

Methodological Concerns

Before embarking on this study I faced three significant methodological questions:

1. What items of information need to be collected?
2. Where are they to be collected from (geographical, institutional, and temporal units)?
3. What methods can be deployed to collect this information and use them appropriately to make a coherent argument?

Collectively, these concerns defined the data that needed to be collected from the units using the chosen method. This study uses the case of RTI to verify the process of institutional change in the information regime in India. This enables the study to engage with 'micro-correlations' to explain a macro-level phenomenon, that is, the enactment of the RTI law in the country specifically and the process of institutional change at the macro level (Bennett and George 1997).

To examine the multi-level sociopolitical processes that led to institutional change in the information regime in India, a series of causal variables needed to be unravelled and examined. Institutional change was treated as the 'dependent variable' and contingent on 'independent variables' at the sociopolitical level. The independent variables were treated as part of the causal chain that leads to institutional change.

To evaluate the causal processes within a case, the 'process tracing' method was used. This method does not merely explain variations across the variables in a single case; it investigates and explains the 'stimuli' or 'decision-making' process that creates the conditions necessary for a specific outcome (George and McKeown 1985: 35). This method identifies and analyses the intervening causal processes within a causal chain between independent and dependent variables (George and Bennett 2005: 206). Instead of treating the ultimate outcome as the only dependent variable, new dependent variables can be added within a single case study. 'Each decision in a sequence, or each set of measurable perceptions by decision-makers of others' actions and intentions, becomes a new variable', and often ultimately leads to the individual level (King, Keohane, and Verba 1994: 227). Thus, the process tracing method of searching for evidence is 'consistent to the overall causal theory'. It is an in-depth examination of the decision-making process that produces the outcome. It is argued that process tracing examines 'sequential processes' within a case rather than data correlations across a number of cases (George and Bennett 2005: 13).

One can illustrate process tracing using the dominoes metaphor. Imagine that dominoes numbered from 1 to 50 with blinds in front of them and dots facing the same way are lined up on a table. Once we enter the room, we see the dominoes numbered 1 and 50 'co-varyingly' toppled in the same direction, and signifying the co-variation. Two scenarios emerge: they co-vary where other dominoes caused the fall, or someone toppled the dominoes numbered 1 and 50. It is necessary to lift the blinds and see the state of the other dominoes—that would explain how the dominoes fell (Bennett and George 1997). I too try to lift the blinds to reveal the processes that led to institutional change.

'Tracing potential processes through such inquiries helps narrow the list of potential causes'. This method entails interviewing actors and examining written records to establish the reasons for their action (King, Keohane, and Verba 1994). In addition, the research using process tracing may involve 'examining histories, archival documents, interview transcripts, and other sources' to verify 'whether the causal process [that] a theory hypothesises or implies in a case is in fact evident in the sequence and values of the intervening variables in that case' (George and Bennett 2005: 6).

I used several sources and methods of data collection during my fieldwork spread over little more than a year.

1. Open-ended discussions were held with the main stakeholders and forerunners of the RTI movement. I identify three categories of stakeholders. The first category constitutes the pioneers of the RTI movement who have been influential from 'outside' the State apparatus. The second category constitutes persuaded technocrats in the system (bureaucrats, members of parliament [MPs], the judiciary, and so on). The third category constitutes actors working from both 'within' and 'outside' the system (members of the National Advisory Council [NAC], bureaucrats, and others).
2. I studied internal government documents such as the minutes of committee discussions, cabinet papers, and internal notes of departments of the Ministry of Home Affairs (MHA); the Department of Personnel and Training (DoPT); and the Ministry of Personnel, Public Grievances and Pensions (MPPP; the latter two being the main nodal government agencies within which policy discussions around the RTI took place).[10]
3. Guided in-depth interviews were conducted with activists, bureaucrats, former and current MPs, and commissioners.
4. I used official documents such as official letters and communications, documents of RTI institutions and organizations, and official press statements at different levels of the government.
5. Official records such as the parliamentary debates, reports of parliamentary committees, and of various committees constituted by the GoI to examine the possibility of granting citizens' access to information.
6. Archival material related primarily to the internal papers of the MKSS and of the NCPRI. The MKSS archive is located at the Nehru Memorial Museum and Library, New Delhi. The NCPRI archive is located at their New Delhi office.

[10] The RTI was used to procure these documents. I received them through some contacts who had these documents in possession.

7. Newspaper archives, primarily the *Times of India* (ToI) database, accessed at ProQuest.[11] I used some other secondary sources to corroborate the facts emerging from interviews. I have relied on the primary documents for my arguments and discussions. Interviews served as a guide to these documents.

[11] Available at www.proquest.com (accessed 20 January 2020).

1 Nascent Ideas to Embedded Norms

Ideational Churning within the State

This chapter unravels the first layer in the process of institutional change. I explore the role of the State and the emerging ideas within its segments to illuminate the process of ideational churning. The friction between the nested norm of secrecy and the nascent ideas on openness sowed the seeds of an ideational churning within the State even when it moved to institutionalize and reinforce the legal framework towards secrecy. The process of ideational churning can be likened to an institutional cropping where the seeds of the norm of openness were in the process of being planted on the policy periphery. This process was set in motion right after Independence. I examine the twin processes of 'emergent ideas' and 'norm diffusion' to explain the logic and trajectory of institutional change. I also establish that there was a continuity of ideas on openness and transparency, which gradually emerged on the fringes and moved to the centre stage of policymaking. Since the norm of secrecy can be traced to the OSA, it serves as both the starting point and the point of departure.

The phase covered in this chapter starts primarily from Independence in 1947 till 1989. During this period, the norm of secrecy was in the process of being 'locked in' (Pierson 2000) at systemic levels. The legal framework provided by the OSA, and accompanied by other laws such as the Civil Services Conduct Rules, 1964, and the Indian Evidence Act, 1872 (Sections 1, 2, and 3), and the Manual of Office Procedures of the GoI intensified the locking in process.[1] However, even when the norm of secrecy was in the process of getting institutionalized within the State, a counter-narrative emerged around ideas of openness and transparency.

In this context, two significant points emerge in this phase. First, on the one hand, the State pushed for secrecy; on the other, segments of the State were sensitive to the idea of openness. Ideas on openness, though rudimentary, signify the beginning of the ideational churning within the State on issues of secrecy and transparency. Second, I show the role of opposition politics in demanding greater openness regarding the internal affairs of states. These demands from the opposition parties were complimented by similar ideas on openness asserted by the government committees. This demand attains acute proportions in later years.

In the first phase, the ideas emanated from two sources. First, the initial stream of ideas was articulated by the technocratic elements within the State, which was manifested in the reports of the government committees starting from Independence. Second, actors from the opposition parties demanded greater access to State information. This reflected in parliamentary debates and discussions. The initial demand for greater access to information from the opposition parties reached a threshold during the Janata Party government in 1977.

In the post-Janata phase, the ideational churning continued but became profound. The evidence shows that the push for greater openness intensified, and that technocratic elements and opposition politics played a more profound role. Unlike the previous phase, where the ideational churning was more along the lines of questioning the prevailing culture of secrecy and stressing that greater openness was desirable, the post–Janata Party government advanced ideas, the articulation of which had previously been only rudimentary. I trace three broader processes that took root in this period. First, the

[1] Pierson (2000) explains how institutional settings are locked in at systemic levels. Previous institutional arrangements (in this case, the OSA) are locked in a self-enforcing loop, where previous institutional choices result in the formation of elaborate social and political networks. This makes the adoption of alternatives highly cost-ineffective and, thereby, renders exiting previous institutional arrangements impossible.

nascent ideas that had been emerging on the fringes were now getting embedded within the State. Second, the idea of openness was beginning to be articulated as the 'right to know', and directly challenging the nested or locked-in norm of secrecy entrenched within the State. Third, the evidence shows the significance of opposition politics in this initial phase of ideational churning. The opposition parties' demand for access to information enters a new trajectory in this phase, evident in the introduction of a private member's bill, The Freedom of Information (FoI) Bill, 1983, and from discussions in the parliament.

In this light, I treat this phase as the first layer in the multi-layered process of institutional change, where opposition politics and sporadic ideas articulated by government committees were instrumental in setting the ideational churning within the State in motion.[2] This is the first stage of layering, where initial ideas on openness emerged on the fringes and challenged the nested institutional arrangement that perpetuated the institutional landscape of secrecy. I establish the causality of ideas and politics. I also demonstrate the limited role of technocratic elements within the State. They are significant links that help us understand how the incremental push of ideas lead to institutional change. The engagement of the technocracy with the nested norm of secrecy and with the desired norm of openness was manifested in the form of government committee reports. This was an early sign of the role of an 'epistemic community'[3] (Haas 1992) taking root in this ideational churning, which reached its peak later, when policy processes were initiated towards legislation on access to information.

[2] Layering is a process in which the old institutions are eventually layered out when new institutions are placed on top of old ones (Mahoney and Thelen 2010).

[3] In this case, I am treating technocrats or experts in the area as part of an epistemic community who are defined by Haas (1992) as 'a network of professionals with recognized expertise and competence in a particular domain and authoritative claim to policy relevant knowledge within that domain or issue area'.

Official Secrets Act, 1923: Institutionalization of the Norm of Secrecy

To understand the institutional change in the information regime in India, it is pertinent to trace the process of transition from a secrecy-oriented information regime governed by the OSA to a comparatively open and transparent regime under the RTI Act. Scholars view institutions to be path-dependent on history and, therefore, resistant to change (Boettke, Coyne, and Leeson 2008; Mukherji 2014a; North 1990; Pierson 2000; Page 2006). For instance, Acemoglu and Robinson (2012) argue that the variation in the wealth of nations is path-dependent on colonialism, which results in the formation and persistence of either 'inclusive' or 'extractive' institutions. Similarly, Mukherji (2013, 2014a) argues that the institutional change in the economic policy of India is path-dependent on the incremental causal effect of endogenous ideas that had taken root among technocrats and the political class and reached a tipping point in 1991.

The emergence of new norms or changes in the legal framework is path-dependent on historically nested norms. History matters, and institutions are path-dependent on specific historical developments. Therefore, institutions can be viewed as persistent features of the historical landscape. In this context, the institutional persistence of the OSA for at least the first 50 years of independent India resulted in a 'self-perpetuating loop of network externalities and learning' (North 1990: 94–100) and created 'nested rules' at all systemic levels and administrative hierarchies.

The OSA was path-dependent on (*a*) the laws taking shape in Great Britain and (*b*) on the norm of secrecy that emanated from the need to safeguard national interests, especially during wars.[4] The OSA resulted from World War I, and stronger constitutional amendments in 1967 resulted from the wars with China (1962) and Pakistan (1965).

[4] The OSA was a combination of earlier Acts such as the 1889 and 1911 Act of Britain and 1911 Act of India (Central Legislative Assembly Debate, 14 February 1923).

After Independence, the first amendment to the OSA was made in 1951 to remove all references to Great Britain (Singh 2009). The OSA was amended again in 1967 to an even stronger version after the Indo-China War (1962) and Indo-Pak War (1965) by adding espionage and sharing of information to outsiders as a legal offence (Maheshwari 2002: 338). The norm of secrecy was further intensified through the 1967 amendment of Sections 2, 3, 5, 6, 7, 8, 9, and 10 of the OSA. Executive powers (against the parliament) not to share information were amended to be stronger and further intensified under Section 5. With a stronger version of the OSA, governance could now be carried out in complete secrecy. For instance, Clause C of Section 3(1) was amended to classify all documents as secret or top secret. The amended bill treated all offences under the OSA as cognizable and non-bailable, and increased the prison term for violating any section. Further, Clause 6 of the amended OSA indicated that information of any government office is official information.

Secrecy was further reinforced through other laws, such as the Civil Services Conduct Rules, 1964, which prohibited the bureaucracy from sharing official information without proper authorization. Additionally, the Indian Evidence Act, 1872 (Sections 1, 2, and 3), prohibited government officials from providing evidence of unpublished official records without the authorization of the department head (Second Administrative Reforms Commission 2006: 4). As a result, the norm of secrecy took firm root, both formally and informally, within the State apparatus as the policy movement in the form of legislation took a categorical turn towards the adoption of the norm of secrecy. These Acts emerged from the logic that secrecy was important for security, which was now the norm.

I will now turn to discuss the processes that took shape during the phase covered in this chapter. I find that the State was puzzling over the two opposing norms of secrecy and openness resulting in a churning (Heclo 1974).

Counter-ideational Movement from within the State

The churning process was characterized by a narrative being pulled both ways, between secrecy and openness, signifying a polarity of ideas within the State. It points towards a process of movement and counter-movement around openness and secrecy running parallel to each other. This two-way movement in turn catalysed a vibrant discourse around secrecy and openness in India.

A press conference held on 23 October 1957 in New Delhi is symptomatic of the prevailing ideational polarity of the State. In this press conference, the first PM, Jawaharlal Nehru, warned that the government might have to take action against newspapers for publishing reports on excerpts of the Law Commission's interim report and the PM's fortnightly letter to the chief ministers (CM), both of which were considered confidential. The PM was reminded that the OSA had been enacted by the British and was asked whether there was any distinction between the secrets related to national security and those of State interests. What is the logic behind documents being 'labelled secret to suit the political convenience of the government'? Nehru opined that it was for the courts to judge on the matter. In the same press conference, his answer favoured more openness in government affairs, representing the other end of the narrative. On being asked whether the government should rethink the issue of indiscriminately marking all official papers confidential or secret, Nehru replied: 'Perhaps there is a tendency to make too many things "confidential" or "secret"' (*ToI* 1957). This is an early example of how the narrative was pulled both ways.

The views on secrecy and openness articulated in the reports of various government-constituted committees and in debates in the parliament during the first phase are indicative of a similar churning process. In this context, I examine and present the evidence provided primarily by: (*a*) reports of committees and government institutions; (*b*) debates held in the parliament; and (*c*) the formation of the Janata Party government in 1977.

Embryonic Ideas Favouring Openness and Challenging Secrecy: Reports of Government Committees and Institutions

During the earlier phase of the institutionalization of secrecy within the State apparatus, one can see a clear pattern of the counter-narrative of ideas emerging from technocratic elements within the State itself. This pattern points towards an emerging epistemic community (Haas 1992) within the State around the issues of secrecy and openness, evident in some of the early reports of the committees constituted by the government. For instance, the report of the Press Law Enquiry Committee published in 1948 deemed the operation of the OSA necessary to protect national interests and recommended that the government should decide the extent of secrecy and disclosure (*Report of the Press Laws Enquiry Committee* 1948; see Box 1.1).[5] However, dissent was expressed from within the committee itself when two

Box 1.1 Press Laws Enquiry Committee—OSA Deemed Necessary

The report stated,

> Most of the witnesses, who appeared before us, have conceded that an Official Secrets Act is necessary. It is a well recognised principle that matters, which must remain secret in the vital interests of the State, should not be allowed to be disclosed, and this limitation of the right of freedom of expression has been accepted in the United Nations Conference on Freedom of Information and the press. (Press Laws Enquiry Committee 1948: 30–1)

The report further declared:

> We are unable to accept the contentions that the application of this Act should be confined to a national emergency or war emergency, and that the scope of the definition of document, information, etc., in Section 5 should be narrowed down to documents and information likely to imperil public safety in times of emergency. We recognize that the necessity of guarding State secrets is not confined to an Emergency; nor is it practicable to define which confidential information could be published in the interest of the public and without prejudice to the interests of the State. We have no doubt that the government must be the sole judge in this matter, and we trust that popular democratic Governments in India would utilize the provisions of this Act only in case of genuine necessity and in the larger interests of the State and the public. (Press Laws Enquiry Committee 1948: 30)

[5] The committee was constituted in 1947 to examine the laws regulating the press, review the existing laws in the context of fundamental rights, and provide appropriate recommendations to the government.

members (S.A. Brelvi and K. Srinivasan) wrote a note that objected to the blanket application of the OSA, which would make most issues secret. Instead, they argued, '[The Act must remain] confined, as the recent Geneva Conference on Freedom of Information has recommended, only to matters which must remain secret in the interest of the national safety' (*Report of the Press Laws Enquiry Committee* 1948: 31).

Yet another important link can be seen in one of the first critical reviews of public administration in post-Independence India by Paul H. Appleby in 1953[6] (Maheshwari 1981: 61–3; *ToI* 1953; see also *The New York Times* 1953). Appleby's report, while providing recommendations on improving administrative efficiency, touched upon the lack of openness and the related issues of record-keeping in the Indian administration. Appleby observed, 'The new government has not yet got away from an *arbitrary secrecy* [my emphasis] unnecessarily depriving Indian university professors and citizens generally of desirable information' (Appleby 1953: 30).

Appleby's report made two broad recommendations to the government—one, was to set up a 'Methods and Organisation Branch' under the umbrella of the 'Public Administration Division' and second, to establish an 'Institute of Public Administration' (Appleby 1953: 64–5). Following these recommendations, the GoI established the Indian Institute of Public Administration (IIPA) under the Planning Commission, set up the Organisation and Methods Division (O&M Division), and appointed a full-time principal for the Indian Administrative Officers Training School (Subbaroyan 1953). The O&M Division was set up in 1954 within the Cabinet Secretariat (*ToI* 1954).[7] The ideas articulated by Appleby were later echoed by both the O&M Division and the IIPA.

During the same period, the first report of the Press Commission published in 1954 challenged the logic of secrecy dictated by the

[6] Paul H. Appleby, a well-known academic and administrator from the United States of America (USA), was invited by C.D. Deshmukh, the minister of finance in the GoI, and the Ford Foundation.

[7] S.B. Bapat, joint secretary in the MHA, was the division's first director.

OSA and other laws. The Press Commission Report stated, 'Merely because a circular is marked secret or confidential, it should not attract the provisions of the Act, if the publication thereof is in the interest of the public and no question of national Emergency and interest of the State as such arises' (1048).

In the 1960s, the Indian State pushed for greater secrecy through the Central Civil Services (Conduct Rules) of 1964 and the amendment of the OSA in 1967. Like earlier reports, the reports of government committees constituted during this period also articulated similar views on excessive secrecy and exigency of openness. For instance, in 1962, a committee was constituted under the chairmanship of an MP, K. Santhanam, to examine and suggest institutional mechanisms and processes to check corruption (1962–4). Notably, it was on the recommendation of Santhanam's report that the Central Vigilance Commission was instituted by the GoI in 1964. The committee made several recommendations. As secrecy facilitates corruption, it recommended that, to the maximum extent possible, the transaction of government business should be 'open', in line with procedures, and should avoid undue secrecy (Muhar 1965: 7; Santhanam Committee 1964: 71). In recommending greater openness, the Santhanam report observed:

> Another matter that was brought to our notice was that undue secrecy in transacting Government business leads to 'sale of information'. The extent to which secrecy should be observed is a question that could be answered only by each Ministry/Department. *We can only recommend that to the extent possible transaction of government business should be open* [my emphasis] and in accordance with declared principles and procedures and there should not be any undue secrecy. (Santhanam Committee 1964: 71)

In 1965, one of the publications from the IIPA, set up on the recommendation of Paul H. Appleby, demanded the liberalization of the government's policy towards access to official archival records. The report noted: 'The attitude of the Government of India in regard to access to records has throughout been extremely rigid' (Mukharji 1967: 16).

Similarly, in 1968, a study team on the machinery of the GoI and its procedures of work constituted by the GoI on administrative reforms (also known as the Deshmukh Study Team) recommended amendments to the OSA, Civil Services Conduct Rules, 1964, and to the Management of Office Procedures.[8] It recommended that the clause of secrecy should only be used whenever necessary and called for a more 'open information policy' (Shrivastava 2009: 114). The report said,

> Coming to supply of information at the instance of members of the public, fresh thinking need to be done in regard to secrecy in the government before a really worthwhile information policy for this area can be formulated ... there should be no hesitation in amending the India Official Secrets Act, 1923, the Conduct Rules and the Manual of Office procedure, if that should be found necessary. (Deva 1977: 355)

In 1971, the 43rd Report of the Law Commission of India dealt with laws related to national security and raised questions about the culture of secrecy within the government (Law Commission of India 1971; Second Administrative Reforms Commission 2006: 6–7). In the commission's view, some sections of the OSA had a wide scope, which could 'lead to some controversy' (Law Commission of India 1971: 50). Yet, like the Press Law Enquiry Committee report, the Law Commission report observed that the government is prudent enough to decide which information would be adverse to national security and thus should be kept secret, and which is trivial.

Views expressed by the government reports notwithstanding, the ongoing policy movement towards secrecy within the State led to its institutionalization (both formally and informally) at different levels

[8] One finds interconnection and continuity of ideas on openness. For example, C.D. Deshmukh, then minister of finance, and the Ford Foundation invited Paul H. Appleby, who questioned needless secrecy in the government administration and favoured greater openness in his report of 1953. The 'Report on the Machinery of Government of India and Its Procedures of Work' published in 1968 under the chairmanship of C.D. Deshmukh was consistent with Appleby's report. This report also challenged unwarranted secrecy and called for amendments in the existing institutional framework.

of the State apparatus, which intensified following the amendments in the existing Acts. Two processes—one of the institutionalization of the norm of secrecy and the second of the emergence of ideas around greater openness—pulled the narrative on the State's openness both ways. Jawaharlal Nehru's view on secrecy and openness is symbolic of this polarity. In another example of intensification of the norm of secrecy, an MP from the Praja Socialist Party, H.V. Kamath, alleged in 1963 that a cabinet secretary had violated the OSA by quoting from the draft of the president's speech (to be delivered at the parliament's joint session) at the meeting held at the IIPA (*ToI* 1963).

At the same time, a counter policy movement emerged from within the State as well. This is evident from the views expressed in the reports of the government committees and some policy initiatives. I argue that such a process of counter-movement of ideas on transparency and openness provides important links that, eventually, reached critical mass. This two-way movement of ideas catalysed a vibrant discourse around secrecy and openness in India. The counter-narrative created pulls and pressures within the State.

Policy Initiatives around Access to Information

It is revealing that as early as in the mid-1950s the discourse around secrecy and openness was not limited only to ideas expressed in the government reports. Some policy initiatives catalysed by the recommendations of the government reports were visible as well. For instance, the O&M Division took the initiative to open government reports to the public domain, although the bureaucracy, who restricted the circulation of the reports, thwarted it (Maheshwari 1981: 62). The prevailing thinking within the O&M Division on the issue of secrecy and openness within the government is evident in its first annual report published in 1955. Picking up from where Appleby had left, the report lamented that 'government departments and agencies have fallen into the habit of restricting the circulation of printed reports, pamphlets, compilations, etc., issued by them by marking them for "official use only"' (Maheshwari 1981: 61). It observed further that the lack of public circulation of government documents 'prevents the free availability of valuable information to the public'. As a result of the O&M Division report, initial steps were taken to ensure greater openness in administrative affairs. The O&M Division's annual report of 1954–5 declared:

> [The division has adopted measures] to ensure that the restrictive classification shall not be assigned to any printed reports, pamphlets, compilations, etc., issued by the ministries and departments of the Government of India and their attached or subordinate office unless the reports, etc., will ordinarily be made available to educational institutions, public bodies and members of the public generally. (Maheshwari 1981: 61; see also O&M Division 1955: 19)

Initial signs of policy initiative towards greater openness in government were visible at the sub-national level as well. An information centre was established in Madras in 1956 where citizens could get any information regarding government activities. While inaugurating it, the union minister for information, Dr B.V. Keskar, stressed that 'in a democracy where there was complete freedom of speech it was necessary that the people should be provided with correct and factual information about public activity' (*ToI* 1956).

Like the reports of the government committees, the opposition MPs expressed counter-ideas on openness in response to the prevailing secrecy in government affairs. In the following section, I will examine this emerging trend in the parliament.

Debates and Policy Moves in the Parliament: Challenging Secrecy

While the movement towards secrecy intensified within the State, the parliament became the hotbed of the counter-movement that demanded openness in the affairs of the State. In this light, it is pertinent to discuss the 1965 ruling of the speaker of the lower house of the parliament that extended to members the privilege of quoting from confidential documents. This policy move was important, since it was made immediately before the 1967 amendment to the OSA. Providing continuity to this counter-movement, dissent was expressed by opposition members during the introduction of the OSA (Amendment) Bill in the parliament in 1967.

1965 Ruling of the Speaker in Lok Sabha

In response to the prevailing secrecy in government affairs, counter-ideas on openness were expressed in the parliament. The question of which government reports should be kept secret and which could be discussed in the parliament came up in the lower house in 1965. The reports in question were those of the Central Bureau of Investigation (CBI) and a union subcommittee, both of which were rather damaging to two former CMs of Odisha, Biren Mitra and Biju Patnaik (Bhatia 1965).

In dealing with the question, a counter-trend of emerging ideas around openness emerged in 1965, when the speaker of the lower house, Hukam Singh, ruled that members could freely quote from 'secret'[9] official documents without being booked under the OSA (*ToI* 1965c). The thinking around such a ruling was triggered by an episode on 22 February 1965: While putting questions to the PM on the ongoing probe of corruption against two former CMs of Odisha, P.K. Deo, an MP from the Swatantra Party, wished to quote from the two reports. Another member of the house, H.V. Kamath, who was from the ruling party, had earlier brought this report into the house and quoted extensively from it.[10] However, when Deo started citing from these reports, several members of Congress (the ruling party and the party of the then minister of external affairs, Swaran Singh) objected to this and questioned the authenticity of the report (*ToI* 1965a, 1965c). Subsequently, when the PM made a statement on the cabinet subcommittee's findings, Deo, yet again,

[9] At that juncture, when the institutional setting under the OSA was dictated by the culture of secrecy, this move was important. All official documents were considered 'secret' and the executive branch had absolute authority over the disclosure of these state documents.

[10] This was the same Kamath who had publicly objected to the cabinet secretary quoting from the president's draft speech, as it was to be treated as 'secret'.

quoted from the reports in questioning the PM. The speaker of the Lok Sabha refused to grant Deo permission to quote from the report as it was confidential (*ToI* 1965b). Deo objected to this, pointing out that Kamath had been allowed to quote from the report just two hours earlier, and demanded to know why and under which rule he was not allowed to use the same report.

The speaker replied that he was not aware of what had transpired earlier, but that he held that the document was confidential, and that he presumed that the report was procured clandestinely and in an illegal fashion, which is 'either theft or robbery' (*ToI* 1965a). Several opposition members objected to the speaker's response and caused a furore in the house.[11]

The opposition demanded the right to quote official documents during the course of parliamentary debates and discussions because it would result in greater probity in public life (*ToI* 1965a: 9). The opposition argued that the bureaucracy often took refuge under the public interest clause to evade the public gaze, especially in cases that might invite the administration's criticism. Their stand was that the government could claim privilege over the public interest by refusing to divulge certain information and still have the right to discuss those facts in the parliament, except when such facts might compromise national security. Following this, the speaker put forth six related issues for consideration that dealt with the question of quoting from confidential documents, the authenticity of the document, prior circulation of the document among the members before quoting the content in the house, and the source of such a document (for details of this ruling see A1 in book-end Appendices).

The speaker upheld the MPs' right to speech but not their free licence to exercise it. In other words, they could quote government documents that were deemed secret or confidential in public interest

[11] Opposition members who expressed objection to the speaker's views on confidentiality of the report were Homi Daji (Communist Party of India [CPI]), S.M. Banerjee (independent), Madhu Limaye (Samyukta Socialist Party), Hirendranath Mukherjee (CPI), U.M. Trivedi (Bharatiya Jan Sangh), M.R. Masani (Swatantra Party), L.M. Singhvi (independent), and Renu Chakraborty (CPI).

in the house, but not if it would affect the national interest or security. An overriding clause was added that empowered the speaker to deny MPs the right to quote from an official document if it was pertinent to national interest or security. Interestingly, the speaker ruled that MPs could procure such documents by any means, 'either by leakage or stealth' (*ToI* 1965c).

This was one of the first instances of the opposition demanding greater openness and transparency in State processes and affairs. Interestingly, later, when the provisions of the RTI Bill on the extent of disclosure were being discussed, MPs' privilege of access to information was considered a norm for inclusion.

Oddly, on a similar issue, the chairman of the upper house refused to grant permission to a member to quote from a confidential government report. This represented the other end of the narrative, that is, secrecy (*ToI* 1965a, 1965c).

Significantly, a few months after this ruling, in May 1965, a note was circulated to all central ministries to protect official secrets from leaking out. The note also sought the ministries' opinion on the Cabinet Secretariat's proposal to amend the OSA to make the offence both cognizable and non-bailable (*ToI* 1965d). On 3 September 1965, the minister of state for home affairs, J.L. Hathi, announced in the upper house that the government was considering amending the OSA to make it more comprehensive (*ToI* 1965e). The Indo-Pak war of 1965 was the reason for both the note and the minister's announcement. In a sense, this was the State's move to intensify and institutionalize secrecy further within the State through the 1967 amendment of the OSA.

Parliamentary Debate: 1967 OSA (Amendment) Bill

The opposition members in both the upper and lower houses across party lines expressed dissent when Minister of State for Home Affairs V.C. Shukla moved the 1967 OSA (Amendment) Bill[12] in the upper

[12] Even when the OSA was being enacted in 1923, one could see a stream of dissenting voices emerging from within the legislative assembly. Members, such as H.S. Gour, K.B.L. Agnihotri, and K.C. Neogy, raised issues with the blanket application of the Act and the danger of the Act

house (the Rajya Sabha) on 24 July 1967 and in the lower house (the Lok Sabha) on 12 August 1967.[13]

M. Ruthnaswamy's intervention is significant in this particular parliamentary debate.[14] He questioned the efficacy of such a bill in a democratic government. He expressed his concern about the lack of clarity on the secrecy clause and advocated that only specific cases should be treated as a secret; 'Those acts that are prohibited must be strictly defined and delimited' (Rajya Sabha Debates 1967: 1457–8). Ruthnaswamy's intervention in the parliamentary debate is especially significant from the point of view of counter-ideas regarding openness in the government emerging from the opposition and within the State. He pointedly made reference to the 'right to know' and the 'right to be informed'. He said, 'After all, in a democracy one of

---

being misused to prosecute innocent citizens (Central Legislative Assembly Debates 1923: 2245–64; see also Maheshwari 1981 and Singh 2009).

[13] For instance, opposition members of the upper house, such as K. Chandrasekharan (Janatha Dal, Kerala), Bhupesh Gupta (CPI, West Bengal), M. Ruthnaswamy (Swatantra Party), and Raj Narain (Socialist Party, Uttar Pradesh), objected to the amendment bill (see Indian Official Secrets (Amendment) Bill, 1967, Rajya Sabha Debates 1967). S.M. Banerjee (independent member from Kanpur), K.A. Nambiar (CPI-M), M.L. Sondhi (Jan Sangh), and Srinibas Mishra (Praja Socialist Party) were the Lok Sabha members who opposed the amendment bill (see Indian Official Secrets [Amendment] Bill, 1967, Lok Sabha Debates 12 August 1967).

[14] Ruthnaswamy was associated with the Justice Party and later joined the Swatantra Party, which was founded by C. Gopalachari. Ruthnaswamy was one of the ablest spokespersons for the Swatantra Party in the Rajya Sabha. A professor of political science and the vice chancellor of Annamalai University, he had an active political career. After the disintegration of the Justice Party, he published a paper called *Democrat* and contemplated forming an opposition party as early as 1951. His ideas were contrary to the established principles of the Congress and of the left but converged with the principles of the newly established Swatantra Party. Perhaps Ruthnaswamy's ideas on openness are reflective of this contrarian/alternative ideology that the Swatantra party stood for (Erdman 1967: 132–3).

the *most important rights* is the *right to know*, the *right to be informed* [my emphasis] about the affairs of the State. Therefore, the first and the most important principle governing the framing of an Official Secrets Act is that *publicity should be the rule* and *secrecy should be the exception* [my emphasis]' (Rajya Sabha Debates 1967: 1457–8). It is important to flag here that the policy move of the speaker in the lower house in 1965 was triggered by the demand from P.K. Deo, another Lok Sabha MP from the Swatantra Party.

Ruthnaswamy and Deo's interventions in the parliament have to be seen in the context of my argument regarding opposition politics and non-ruling parties' demand for access to information. This is evident from the fact that both Ruthnaswamy and Deo were part of the Swatantra Party, which was founded to provide an alternative to the dominant socialist and hyper-statist ideologies of the Congress and the left parties (Erdman 1967). In this case, the ideas on openness expressed by the party members are reflective of the alternate ideology propagated by the Swatantra Party.

Another non-Congress member of the upper house, Raj Narain (Socialist Party, Uttar Pradesh), opposed the bill in no uncertain terms. Terming it a *kala vidhayak* or a 'black bill', he objected that the bill was against every democratic and parliamentary principle (Rajya Sabha Debates 1967: 1471–2). It is interesting to note that Raj Narain was part of the Janata Party government in 1977, which was formed right after the Emergency on the principles of anti-corruption, greater probity, and transparency of the State. Raj Narain defeated Indira Gandhi in the 1977 general elections on her home turf in Rae Bareli (Uttar Pradesh).

The policy moves in the parliament and opposition to the bill show early signs of an ideational counter-movement favouring openness from within the State, which intensified in later years. It is also important to point out that it emanated invariably from the opposition parties; this is evident in the profiles of the members in both the upper and the lower houses who opposed the 1967 amendment bill of the OSA. The privilege of exclusive access to official information belonging to the ruling party was at the root of such a demand by the opposition parties. I will discuss, in the following section, that the role of the opposition reached a threshold during the Emergency and the subsequent formation of the Janata Party government at the centre in 1977. This political dimension, I argue, catalysed the ideational push, which became unmistakably pronounced as the politics of the country at the centre moved from a centrist form of government to a more coalitional form.

Janata Government: Decisive Push for Transparency and Openness

This period is important from two perspectives. First, it is for the first time that a non-Congress government (in the form of an anti-Congress coalition of a number of parties) came to power at the centre. Second, this is the first instance when a government had formally expressed its political and policy intent for transparency and openness. In this sense, the Janata Party government proved to be a threshold in the ongoing ideational churning within the State; a continuity of this pattern can be seen unfolding in the post–Janata Party government.

It is in the context of two emergencies, an external emergency imposed after the 1971 Bangladesh war and the Emergency imposed on 25 June 1975, that political developments during this period are important. The period before and during the Emergency was characterized by the hyper-centralization of power. This was accompanied by a centrally controlled paramilitary and police force; the entire intelligence apparatus was under the direct control of the PM. State governments were also accountable to the PM. Centralizing tendencies were the highest at this point, and were accompanied by strife in public life, inflation, economic recession, and unemployment (Kohli 1991: 6; Kohli and Singh 2013: 4; Weiner 1978: 3).

Meanwhile, a series of political events convinced then PM Indira Gandhi to proclaim Emergency.[15] First, Raj Narain challenged

[15] However, it was as much a consequence of the 'leadership actions' as the prevailing sociopolitical conditions (Kohli 1991: 6), which emerged from Indira Gandhi's 'personalistic and populist' politics (Kohli and Singh 2013: 4).

the legality of Gandhi's 1971 election result in Rae Bareli in the Allahabad High Court. It was alleged that the PM had used her office to campaign for the elections (travels, organizing rallies, and so on) and charged the costs to the State and central governments. Justice Sinha presided over the case—while exonerating the PM on serious charges, he found her guilty of using the services of an on-duty officer, Yashpal Kapoor.[16] Additionally, the PM was also found guilty of using the official machinery to organize loudspeakers, power, and rostrums for her campaign. This meant that the PM was debarred from contesting elections for the next six years and could constitutionally remain in office only for the next six months. The PM and her aides challenged this ruling in the SC and procured a stay order, but Justice Krishna Iyer rejected it (Frankel 1978: 539–40). In fact, this judicial case is one of the first and most cited cases that interpreted the Constitution in terms of the 'right to know' (I will further discuss this case in Chapter 3).

At the same time, the PM's authority was eroding within her own Congress Party, while the widespread impact of Jayprakash Narayan's (JP) movement and clarion call for 'total revolution' was felt in the Gujarat assembly elections. The Congress was routed in the elections by a coalition formed under the leadership of Morarji Desai and based on the anti-corruption ideology of JP's popular movement. The Gujarat episode, JP's mass movement accompanied by the national railway strike, and his collective call for Gandhi-style complete civil disobedience brought about an 'impasse'; it convinced PM Gandhi to impose an Emergency on 25 June 1975 (Frankel 1978: 540–7). The Emergency devolved complete authority to the central government and suspended all constitutional rights. Subsequently, in the 1977 general elections, the Congress lost power to the new political formation under the Janata Party, which was essentially an anti-Congress coalition.

Against this background, the change of guard at the centre and the coming of the new Janata Party government to power in 1977 proves

[16] Yashpal Kapoor was still serving as an officer on special duty at the Prime Minister's Office (PMO) when he was involved in the election campaign of the PM.

to be an important juncture. For the first time, the incoming party committed formally to greater openness in government affairs in its election manifesto. In the aftermath of the Emergency, the Janata Party manifesto promised, among other things, 'an open government' that will not 'misuse' government authority and will have an open dialogue with citizens 'at all levels and on all issues' (quoted in Shakdher 1977: 44–5; see also Maheshwari 1981: 66).

To fulfil the promise made in the manifesto, Charan Singh, the home minister in the Janata Party government, constituted a working committee in 1977 to determine whether the existing OSA could be amended to allow greater dissemination of official information in the public domain.[17] Officials of the Cabinet Secretariat, the MHA, the Ministry of Finance, and the Ministry of Defence were the members of the newly constituted working committee. After due consideration, the committee concluded that the existing OSA should be retained without any amendment. On 4 June 1979, the government formally announced that the existing law of official secrets would not be amended but continued as it was (Noorani 1997: 115–16). Some of the reasons cited for this were that it was being done to protect the country against foreign agencies interested in procuring vital information; to preserve secrets regarding information pertinent to national security, defence, and nuclear energy; and to promote foreign relations. An exception was made with regard to news related to development work (Maheshwari 1981: 66–7; see also Noorani 1997: 115–16).

In fact, on 30 August 1978, Jyotirmoy Basu (Communist Party of India-Marxist [CPI-M]) raised this issue in the lower house in his question to the minister of state for home affairs. Basu asked if the government knew of the ongoing discussion in the United Kingdom (UK) on the enactment of a law on the RTI, and wondered why, even after Independence, India still followed the outdated OSA. He asked whether the government harboured any plans to guarantee

[17] I tried to procure the report of the government committee during my fieldwork, but it was hard to trace. I hope that in due course I will be able to trace this report either in the national archives or through the RTI.

all people the right to 'having access to all official documents' (Lok Sabha Debates 1978). Oddly, Dhanik Lal Mandal, the minister of state for home affairs, did not mention the working group constituted to amend the OSA in his reply, but reiterated that there was no need to amend it (Lok Sabha Debates 1978; Maheshwari 1981: 68–9; Noorani 1997: 116; Viswam 1983: 183).

The Janata Party government's commitment to an open government, as outlined in their manifesto, can also be seen in the enactment in 1977 of the Parliamentary Proceedings (Protection) Bill, which was passed to communicate parliamentary proceedings to citizens. The bill granted the media greater privilege and access of information to parliamentary proceedings (Limaye 1994: 296), and should be viewed in continuation to the 1965 ruling of the speaker of the Lok Sabha that granted parliamentarians the right to quote from confidential official documents in the parliament. The enactment of this bill was especially significant—now that the media had greater access to parliamentary proceedings, quotes from confidential official documents could indirectly find place in the public domain.

Three points emerge from the initiatives undertaken during the Janata Party regime.

First, the decision to continue with the original version of the OSA without any amendments notwithstanding, the constitution of a working committee to examine the possibility of amending the OSA in order to enable greater access of citizens to official information points towards the emerging thinking of the State on the issue of openness.

Second, the root cause of the need for openness and transparency in government affairs, felt by the political leadership at this point, is the experience of the Emergency, which entailed absolute censorship, absence of civil and political rights, and complete secrecy of official government affairs. This experience persuaded the new leadership to start thinking along the lines of participatory democracy, and government transparency and accountability. This intention is clearly outlined in the manifesto of the Janata Party, which contested the 1977 elections on the issue of corruption, and enhanced the probity of holders of public office. The promise of the manifesto was followed by the policy action of constituting the working group to amend the OSA. This intention to constitute a working committee to promote openness in government affairs by granting citizens greater access to official government information can be seen as part of a broader process that unfolded after the 1977 elections.

This is reflected in the number of policy steps taken by the Janata Party government on the lines of the commitments made in its election manifesto. The initiative of the working committee to amend the OSA needs to be located within a broader policy process. Several actions point towards it, such as the lifting of the Emergency Bill in 1978 to repeal the Objectionable Matter Act, 1951, adoption of Parliamentary Proceedings (Protection Bill), 1977, 43rd Constitution Amendment Bill, 1977, to repeal the archaic 42nd Constitution Amendment (Act), 1976, and the replacement of the Maintenance of Internal Security Act (MISA), 1971, with the Code of Criminal Procedure (Amendment) Bill, 1977 (Limaye 1994: 295–307).

Third, as discussed earlier, the push for openness from the new leadership emanated from the fact that the new coalition emerged from the conglomeration of opposition forces that had been at the receiving end of the Emergency. As the evidence demonstrates, the political opposition in the parliament was collectively against secrecy and demanded greater openness. On the other hand, the ruling party zealously deepened the norm of secrecy and protected information. The Emergency marked the acme of this tendency. The political forces that were part of the anti-Congress coalition then came together as the Janata Party. Hence, the push for openness and transparency was reflected both in political intent and policy steps towards such intent. I argue, therefore, that the role of opposition politics is a significant explanatory variable in understanding the institutional change from the norm of secrecy to openness. Institutional change was part of this churning characterized by the intensification of the norm of secrecy on the one hand and the emerging incipient ideas on openness on the other.

The Post–Janata Party Phase

After the term of the Janata Party government, the nascent ideas around openness gained much weight and momentum within State thinking. Indeed, the emerging ideational narrative around openness and transparency is relatively categorical and pointed after the Janata government. The dominant norm of secrecy, which was locked in at the systemic level, was challenged by initial ideas articulated by government reports, bills tabled in the parliament, public statements, and policies adopted at the sub-national level.

Reports from Government Institutions: Emerging Epistemic Ideas on Openness

The earlier trend—of technocratic elements from State institutions articulating ideas on openness and access to information—continued in this period, but was more direct.

For instance, an edited volume was brought out by the IIPA on *Secrecy in Government* in 1980. The volume brought together scholars and practitioners to critically examine the relevance of the OSA and provide recommendations for a more transparent and accountable government (Chaturvedi 1980). It gave the clear message that the norm of secrecy inherited historically was incompatible with the 'people's right to know how they are being governed' (Rowat 1980: 1). This was followed by yet another important academic intervention on the subject by the IIPA titled *Open Government in India* (Maheshwari 1981). This intervention pointed out the need for greater openness in the flow of information, arguing that it enhances 'citizens' sense of pride, stabilizes democracy and safeguards public interest' (Maheshwari 1981: 97).

A year after the IIPA's publication *Open Government*, the Press Council of India (PCI) and Indian Law Institute jointly published a tract called *Official Secrecy and the Press* to ascertain the impact of secrecy laws on the freedom of press (Aggarwal 1989; Jain 1982). The study recommended liberalizing the laws on secrecy (OSA and Contempt of Court Act and Parliamentary Privileges Act) to ensure the freedom of the press. The report observed, 'The two wings of the government namely, the legislature and the judiciary, function in the open. ... On the other hand, the Executive does its business in its strict chambers to which people have hardly any access' (Aggarwal 1989: 134).

Similarly, in the report it submitted in 1982, the second Press Commission recommended the repeal of Section 5 of the OSA and its replacement with provisions that would facilitate citizens' access to information regarding State affairs (Aggarwal 1989: 139). According to the commission, the OSA was 'one of the chief obstacles to the free flow of legitimate information to the people' (para 47) and 'has a chilling effect on the freedom of press' (Noorani 1997: 130). The commission suggested that Section 5 of the OSA be amended such that both 'national security and other vital interests of the State as well as the right of the people to know the affairs of the State affecting them' are protected (Report of the Second Press Commission 1982, para 52). 'The Press Commission suggested that the amended legislation should be *modeled after the British Freedom of Information Act* [my emphasis] and strike a judicious balance between the *people's right to know* [my emphasis] on one hand and vital interests and national security of the State on the other' (*ToI* 1982b). When the recommendation of the report was tabled in the parliament, on 17 July 1986, the government rejected it (*ToI* 1986a).

These reports mirrored the prevailing churning of ideas within the State. This emerged clearly during my interview with T.N. Chaturvedi, who was the editor of the IIPA volume (discussed earlier) and the director of the IIPA at that time.[18] He commented: 'There was a climate of opinion, the affairs of the State was a "mystique" as common people did not have access to information. This was questioned by many of us, as how can democracy be participative in a true sense without openness and transparency.'[19] Chaturvedi added, 'In a sense, the IIPA reports have to be placed within the prevailing mood of the bureaucracy,' and recalled: '[A] series of seminars [was] organised on anti-corruption, vigilance, etc. where we invited bureaucrats,

[18] Chaturvedi, also a former bureaucrat, later assumed the position of governor of the southern Indian state of Karnataka.

[19] Interview with T.N. Chaturvedi, 24 April 2015, Noida, India.

legislators, and the academicians'. The 'climate of opinion' that Chaturvedi mentioned during the interview was a product of the openness and transparency stressed upon by the Janata government: the 'Janata government certainly was supportive of these initiatives; the party had a liberal view regarding openness and transparency'.

The significance of the IIPA studies and the reports of the Press Commission can be viewed from the perspective of the shaping of ideas around openness and transparency. The interventions were instrumental in sharpening the emerging ideational discourse and, for the first time, in categorically negotiating discourse spaces within the State around the right to know or to information. The framing of the issue here is pointed and upfront, and challenges the dominant and rooted norm of secrecy.

Early Signs of Epistemic–State and State–Society Synergy

During this period one can also see the process of epistemic–State synergy taking shape, deepening the ideational churning further.

These publications were not mere academic exercises; these had deep inter-linkages with the broader discourse on openness emerging elsewhere within the State that pointed towards the epistemic–State synergy. For example, in the significant case of *S.P. Gupta* vs *President of India and Ors* (1981: para 66), the SC of India judgement recognized and upheld the constitutional RTI and right to know as part of the freedom of expression and speech under Article 19 (1) (a) of the Constitution (this case is discussed in Chapter 3). The verdict, delivered on 30 December 1981, quotes verbatim from pages 95 and 96 of the IIPA publication of 1981 on 'open government'.[20]

Similarly, in 1982, at a meeting held at New Delhi, the National Union of Journalists (NUJ) council demanded amendments to the OSA and the Indian Penal Code (IPC) to remove provisions that

[20] The verdict draws upon the IIPA publication stating, 'The need for an open Government where there is access to information in regard to the functioning of government has been emphasised and the [arguments] in support of it have been ably and succinctly summarised in the following passage from the book of Dr. S.R. Maheshwari on "Open Government in India" at pages 95 and 96.'

restricted the freedom of the press, and suggested that the government enact a law on the freedom of information that would obligate it to provide information to the press on demand (*ToI* 1982a). This issue was then raised in the upper house of the parliament on 1 March 1982 by Shiva Chandra Jha of BJP (Rajya Sabha Debates 1982: 190–1).[21] One can infer from this parliamentary discussion that there was an emerging cooperation between the press and opposition parties. The demand for openness and access to information emerged as a common link between the opposition and the press.

Policy Moves and Discussions in Parliament

As the ideational push towards openness gained momentum, a process of norm diffusion took root in the form of pointed policy demands from the opposition in the parliament. This process was evident in the introduction of a private member's bill on the freedom of information and in questions raised by members of both houses of the parliament. The demand for transparency and openness in government affairs by opposition parties in the parliament continued and intensified after the term of the Janata Party government.

Private Member's Bills on Freedom of Information, 1983 and 1984

Two significant initiatives were taken in the form of private members' bills[22] on the freedom of information in 1983 and 1984.[23] These

[21] Jha inquired if the NUJ had asked the government for the enactment of a FoI Act and what the response of the government was (Rajya Sabha Debates 1982: 190–1). Jha further asked whether the government was planning any specific steps to ensure freedom of information to the press and if not what the reason was.

[22] An MP who is not part of the cabinet is a private member. A bill moved by such a private member is a private member's bill. In the history of the Indian parliament, only fourteen private members' bills have been passed; three of these were passed in 1956.

[23] These are significant initiatives which find no mention and are conspicuous by their absence in the mainstream literature dealing with RTI.

bills were introduced by G.C. Bhattacharya, a Rajya Sabha MP from the Lok Dal Party,[24] in 1983 and Subramanian Swamy, member of the Janata Party in the Lok Sabha, in 1984. The significance of these bills lies in the fact that this was the first time that a formal bill on freedom of information was moved in the parliament. This was important not only from the perspective of a concrete policy move but also from the clear framing of the law as 'freedom of information' as opposed to the earlier focus on amending the OSA. The proposed bill represents the deepening of the discourse on openness and access to information.

In 1983, Bhattacharya moved a private member bill in the upper house (Bill No. XXVIII of 1983) to 'provide for certain agencies to ensure freedom of having access to and obtaining public information for the citizen and for matters connected therewith' (222–3).[25] The Statement of Objects and Reasons of the bill Stated that there was 'widespread' public discontent resulting in 'turmoil' and 'disturbances', especially against the government. This was due to the lack of 'adequate information available to the people leading to mistrust among them regarding the working and the pronouncements of the government'.

A few months after Bhattacharya's private member's bill was moved in the upper house, Subramanian Swamy of the Janata Party introduced a private member's bill on the freedom of information in the lower house on 3 May 1984 (Lok Sabha Debates 1984: 320; *ToI* 1984a, 1984b). This was the same bill that Bhattacharya had moved in the upper house.

[24] The Lok Dal was founded by Chaudhary Charan Singh, who was an integral part of the political coalition that opposed the Emergency in 1975. Singh was also part of the Janata Party government. Interestingly, as discussed in the first section, as the home minister in the Janata Party cabinet, Singh constituted a committee to examine the possibility of amending the OSA and explore legislative provisions to have more openness in government affairs.

[25] I am indebted to senior journalist Naresh Minocha for guiding me to this bill. The mention of this bill can be found on his website: http://nareshminocha.com/index.php/getting-started/120-polity/1620-madam-soniaji-please-check-facts-take-back-your-rti-brag (accessed 29 February 2020).

These bills, however, lapsed in the parliament due to the changing political environment and configurations in the country. By the time the bills came up for hearing again in the parliament, the policy processes to initiate such legislation had already begun within the State. Swamy, who introduced this bill in the parliament, pointed this out. During my interview with Swamy, he recalled,

> I introduced what is called in the Lok Sabha a private member's bill. It was titled 'freedom of information' because in America it was called the Freedom of Information Bill. The matter was listed for hearing in the winter of 1984 but Indira Gandhi was assassinated in October and Rajiv Gandhi advanced the elections, so the Bill lapsed. In 1984, we all lost the elections so we could not re-introduce it [the Bill]. By 1988, when I re-entered the parliament the government was already seriously considering the passage of such [a] Bill, so I did not pursue the Bill further. The time I introduced the Bill, the concept was shocking ... to say that the government secrets should be made available to the citizens.[26]

The ruling party had opposed this initiative. Swamy shared that 'Congress was hostile to the idea, and they did not want the Bill to come for discussion at all'. This account corroborates our argument that the demand for greater openness, transparency, and access to State affairs emanated primarily from opposition parties.

It is interesting to note that these private members' bills, at a very rudimentary level, bear an uncanny resemblance to the present RTI Act—the bills, such as the current Act, also provided for information commissions headed by a chief information commissioner. Although the bills lapsed, they provide an important link to the processes that eventually catalysed institutional change. The private members' bills tabled in the parliament should be viewed as a continuation and evolution of initial ideas and limited policy initiatives on openness by the Janata Party government in 1977. In this sense, the bills represented concrete policy articulation of these earlier ideas.

[26] Interview with Subramanian Swamy, 16 April 2014, New Delhi, India.

Swamy confirmed that the Emergency and the new political formation after the Emergency provided the backdrop for the introduction of these bills: 'Emergency was the background where we experienced absolute censorship, blocking of information ... so many contracts were signed by the government and we were not entitled to see the tender. So, the context was the need for transparency, about which we all felt very strongly during the Emergency.'[27]

Discussions in the Parliament

Ideational continuity can also be seen in the concrete policy demands from the opposition members in the parliament.

For example, Atal Bihari Vajpayee, Ashwani Kumar, and Pramod Mahajan of BJP jointly asked three questions in the Rajya Sabha on 14 August 1986. These pointed towards a political atmosphere where the norm of openness had taken root; MPs asked the minister of home affairs for the names of countries that had freedom of information and what steps had been taken in India to grant it. Additionally, they also wanted to know whether India had ratified the International Convention on Civil and Political Rights. The minister of state of parliamentary affairs, Ghulam Nabi Azad, however, was non-committal in providing answers by stating that information would be collected and laid on the table of the house (Rajya Sabha Debates 1986: 180).

Later, on 17 November 1987, in the upper house, Minister of State for Home Affairs P. Chidambaram indicated the government's willingness to amend the OSA. During the oral question and answer session on the topic of the 'Pak spy network', in his response to a question from an MP, Arun Kumar, Chidambaram said: 'Some amendments to the Official Secrets Act are under consideration. They are at a fairly advanced stage. I am not in a position to say when we will be able to introduce a Bill, but I hope it will be as soon as possible' (Rajya Sabha Debates 1987: 8).

[27] Interview with Subramanian Swamy, 16 April 2014, New Delhi, India.

Sub-national Policy Initiatives and Public Statements

The impact of the Janata Party's push towards openness and transparency could be seen at the State level as well. In 1988, when Karnataka was under the rule of the Ramakrishna Hegde-led Janata Party, Hegde introduced the Freedom of Press Bill, which granted journalists immunity from disclosing the source of their information and ensured their right to access official information, and instituted a penalty for harming journalists in the course of duty or for the intention to harm them. In the Statement of Objects and Reasons, R.L. Jalappa, then home minister of Karnataka, stated that open government is synonymous with free press (Kirpekar 1996a; *ToI* 1988a).[28]

The demand from opposition parties to enact legislation on the freedom of information was reflected in the public statements issued during this period. In March 1989, Ram Jethmalani, an eminent lawyer, and also a Rajya Sabha MP from BJP, declared that it was shameful that the country continued with the OSA.[29] Jethmalani said, 'Instead of having Freedom of Information we have Official Secrets Act;' for democracy to survive, people must have absolute access to information, which should be subjected to thorough scrutiny (*ToI* 1989a).[30]

Evidently, the ideas expressed by the press and the judiciary were converging with the ideas expressed by the opposition parties. For instance, on 19 March 1988, at a symposium organized by the Indian Federation of Small and Medium Newspapers (IFSMN) in New Delhi, Press Commission Chairman Justice A.N. Sen, reiterated the second Press Commission's view that the OSA curbed journalists' right to access official information, and that there is a need to relook at Section 5 of the OSA.

[28] Jalappa was also cabinet minister during V.P. Singh's regime at the centre.

[29] It may be noted that in 1998 Jethmalani, as union minister for urban development and employment, granted the public the right to access official documents.

[30] Ram Jethmalani was speaking at a seminar in Bombay organized on 'People's Manifesto for India's Progress' (*ToI* 1989a).

The prevailing political environment and mood affected the current thinking within the ruling party as well. For instance, while speaking on the Freedom of Information Day (8 May 1989), P.G. Gavai, leader of the state legislative council of Maharashtra, said that the OSA was outdated and that India, as a mature democracy, should repeal it and instead institute legal provisions to ensure freedom of information.[31] Similarly, in the IFSMN meeting, then union minister for water resources, Dinesh Singh, concurred with Justice Sen's view that Section 5 of the OSA was especially 'dangerous' and worked against the 'freedom of press' (*ToI* 1988b). Meanwhile, in 1989, the State government of Gujarat decided to remove the Sardar Sarovar Dam project from the ambit of the OSA in 1989. Therefore, it can be surmised that the ruling party had an undercurrent of progressive elements within it as well.

Counter-narrative Continues: State's Attempt to Deepen Secrecy

Yet, during this period itself, we see moves by the government to institutionalize secrecy. This can be seen in PM Rajiv Gandhi's move in 1986 to amend the Commission of Enquiry Act, 1952, to prevent the Thakkar Commission report from being tabled in the parliament. The Thakkar Commission was constituted to investigate the assassination of former PM Indira Gandhi—mother of Rajiv Gandhi (Hewitt 1994: 68). Among other things, the commission indicted Congress Party members and even individuals who were part of the PMO for lapses that contributed to the assassination. Under considerable political pressure, vehement protest from the opposition parties, and fulmination by jurists and the press, the government aborted the move.

In another instance, the culture of secrecy can be seen emerging in the parliament on the issue of a letter exchanged between the president and the PM (*ToI* 1987a). The contents of the letter showed

[31] P.G. Gavai spoke at a function organized by the Bombay Pradesh Congress Committee (*ToI* 1989c).

the government in a poor light as the president in his letter had refuted the PM's earlier claim in the parliament that he was briefed on all important matters. The opposition members of both houses demanded a discussion on the letter, but the speakers forbade them from discussing its content because it involved the highest constitutional offices and a nexus that lay at the heart of the cabinet system of governance (Chawla 1987; *ToI* 1987b).

As seen in the emerging patterns of opposing discourses discussed here, in this period, one can see the institution of secrecy stubbornly persisting on the one hand, and a clear pattern of norm diffusion around openness taking root on the other. Congress, the dominant ruling party at the centre, was non-committal towards promoting openness in government affairs. This is evident in their replies to opposition members' questions in the parliament. Meanwhile, the opposition parties continually expressed their demand for openness. This was accompanied by similar demands and recommendations from the progressive elements within the State.

***

In this chapter, I have discussed the first phase of institutional change, where the norm of secrecy was institutionalized and took firm root within the State apparatus. This resulted in what North (1990) terms 'nested rules' and in reinforcement at all systemic levels. At the same time, ideas on openness emerged on the fringes from within the State—albeit in a nascent form. This phase is the first layer in the process of *layering* that leads to institutional change. The first layer is characterized by the onset of an ideational churning within the State, where members of opposition parties, along with technocratic elements, articulated initial ideas on openness and demanded greater transparency from the State. The first stage of layering emerges clearly in this phase—secrecy as a norm got 'locked in' (Pierson 2000) within the State apparatus, and yet rudimentary ideas on openness were also expressed by elements within the State and emerged on the fringes of the persisting institution of secrecy.

In the post–Janata Party government period, nascent ideas gained momentum and transitioned from the periphery to a more strategic policy space. Ideas on openness were articulated as the 'right to know' and directly challenged the established norm of secrecy. The period was marked by continuity and progression of early ideas as concrete norms. This was evident in the continuation of ideas—expressed by the Janata Party government in 1977—to specific policy initiatives in the form of private member's bills in 1983 and 1984 and policy recommendations in government reports. The policy churning of norms was taking shape largely within the realm of the State. At the same time, this churning process got projected into the public domain by way of public statements, which resulted in the widening of the discourse beyond the realm of the State.

Opposition politics played a primary role in the first phase in deepening the process of ideational churning on openness and transparency within the State. This was evident in the debates and discussions in the parliament, the political and policy intent displayed by the Janata Party government around openness and transparency, and in private members' bills. On the other hand, the ruling party continually pushed towards deepening secrecy. In the process of *layering*, this first layer is important, as the friction between the ruling and opposition parties created pulls and pressures within which the ideational churning on access to information and transparency deepened within the State. I will show in Chapter 2 that this churning translated into concrete political and policy steps towards institutional change.

The emergence and expression of nascent ideas on openness, the articulation of these ideas as *norms*, and their being embedded in the State thinking add credence to the argument that the process of ideational churning is significant in explaining institutional change.

2 Changing State Thinking

Policy Movement towards Right to Information

This chapter examines the political and policy movement within the State—starting from the NF government in 1989 to the passage of the RTI Bill in 2005 under the UPA government. In the previous chapter, I discussed the first phase (treated as the first layer) in which opposition politics was a significant push factor, which resulted in the intensification of ideational change in the thinking within the State around openness as against the nested norm of secrecy. This chapter, starting from 1989, casts light on the emerging political and policy processes within the State which cumulatively reached a tipping point with the enactment of the RTI Act in 2005. This is the second phase, which is treated as the second or final layer of institutional change. In this layer, the norm of openness eventually replaced the persisting norm of secrecy. The weight and momentum of ideas incrementally rendered both the issue of openness and access to official information a sine qua non within the political and permanent executive.

Admittedly, it was also during this period that processes started to take shape outside the realm of the State. Indeed, State–society synergy was profoundly significant in the final stages of policy formation, especially during the UPA's term. Progressive elements from both realms worked in tandem to act as critical catalysts of institutional change. However, by the time State–society dynamics started to take shape, both the discourse and the policy trajectory from within the State were already in the process of displacing the norm of secrecy with openness and transparency (an aspect discussed at length in Chapter 4).

The evidence examined shows that the rudimentary ideas on the norm of openness matured and became embedded within State thinking. This is evident in the push for greater openness and legislation on access to information in both the political and policy intents expressed by the governments during this period.

As distinct from the previous phase, in which oppositional politics played a consequential role in initiating the ideational churning, in this phase the ideas became part of the 'mainstream politics' and deepened the churning process within the State. As a result, the cumulative push of ideas from within the State reached critical mass, eventually displacing the nested norm of secrecy in 2005.

I see a continuity of ideas from the previous phase. The political intent towards openness was expressed initially by the Janata Party, the first non-Congress government in the centre (in 1977). The era of coalition governments, starting with the NF government in 1989, was marked by a similar political willingness to have greater transparency and openness in State affairs. The process was evident in the declared political commitment and purposeful policy movement towards enacting legislation on the 'right or freedom of information'. Indeed, legislation on access to information was promised in election manifestos across party lines and expressed by all the PMs who came to power during this period.

The commitment towards the legislation was not limited only to political intent declared in election manifestos but was also reflected in the policy intent and processes that followed. The discourse moved beyond the intent and set in motion the policy processes within the executive. This resulted in a convergence of both political and policy intents with the policy processes within the executive.

Additionally, I also see a more structured engagement of the State with the 'epistemic' elements from within both the State and society. The State during this period was both 'powering and puzzling' (Heclo 1974) over the issue.

In light of these arguments, this chapter is organized around four themes. First, I examine the political will and policy intent articulated by various governments between 1989 and 2005 towards promulgating legislation to grant citizens the right to access information. Second, I discuss the policy processes initiated within the State following the political commitment. Third, I scan the seminars, conferences, and public statements that delved deeper into the discourse within the State. Lastly, I explore the emerging policy initiatives at the sub-national level that were complimenting the contemporaneous political and policy processes at the central level.

In the following section, I examine the political context and commitment towards legislation on access to information starting from the NF government.

Political Context: Articulation of Political Will and Policy Intent 1989–2004

This section discusses the ideational trajectory of various governments during this period articulated in election manifestos, speeches, and public statements. In this light, the political environment and context is discussed, as they will explain the origin of these ideas expressed by the governments. The politics, in this sense, explain the trajectory of ideas on openness within the State and vice versa.

National Front Government 1989–91

The formation of the NF government in 1989 provides us with evidence that points towards the politics–idea connection. The ideational push for freedom of or access to information received a fillip amidst the political developments leading to the ninth general elections in 1989. These were somewhat similar to the 1977 general elections when the Janata Party had formed the government at the centre. The political climate at this juncture was akin to 1977 on three counts. First, like the Janata Party's stress on corruption, the biggest rallying issue for the opposition was their allegation that

Congress leaders had received monetary kickbacks in an arms deal. It was alleged that PM Rajiv Gandhi had received kickbacks from a Swedish arms manufacturing company, Bofors, for their bid for the 155 mm Field Howitzer (a short gun to fire shells). The scandal was popularly known as the 'Bofors Gun Scandal'. V.P. Singh played the role of the whistle-blower in the scandal. This resulted in his fallout with the Congress apex leadership.

Second, similar to the coalition in 1977, a coalition of political forces came together to oppose the Congress, which was the majority party at the centre. V.P. Singh, who was the minister of finance in the Congress government, had initiated enquiries in the Bofors scandal, after which he was shifted to the Ministry of Defence. In protest, Singh resigned from the cabinet; subsequently, the PM and his close aides showed him the door. In response, V.P. Singh formed another party, named Jan Morcha, which subsequently forged a pre-poll alliance with a number of national and regional parties.[1] The alliance was known as the NF (or the third front).

Third, due to the foreign policy interventions in Sri Lanka on the Tamil issue, regional players—especially in Tamil Nadu—were dissatisfied with the central government's tackling of the issue. Additionally, Rajiv Gandhi's tendency towards centralization and intolerance, and, in the later years, towards increasing regionalization of politics brought regional and national forces together under the umbrella of the NF. The political climate was similar to the one in the mid-1970s (when the Janata Party coalition emerged), characterized by allegations of corruption, a tendency of over-centralization of power, and opposition political forces forging an alliance against the dominant party and coming together as a new political formation.

Even though Congress won 197 out of 529 seats in the elections, the NF formed the minority government at the centre with outside

[1] Janata Party, Lok Dal, and Congress (S), a breakaway socialist faction of the main Congress Party, formed a coalition under the banner of Janata Dal. Regional parties such as the Telugu Desam Party (TDP), Dravida Munnetra Kazhagam (DMK), and Asom Gana Parishad were part of this alliance as well.

support from the Bhartiya Janata Party (BJP) and the left party (CPI-M). This was the first time that a minority government was formed with outside support from other parties. The NF government was short-lived: the first, under V.P. Singh, lasted just about a year, and the second, under Chandra Shekhar, for seven months. These were the initial days of the coming together of various political forces to form a coalition. The trend of coalition politics came to dominate the Indian political scene starting with the NF, the minority Congress government under Narasimha Rao, the United Front (UF) government, the BJP-led NDA, and the Congress-led UPA.

Against this backdrop, the newly formed NF articulated its ideas on transparency, accountability, and greater openness in government affairs. Some of these ideas were expressed early on in the run-up to the 1989 general elections. For instance, while addressing a press conference on 1 July 1989, V.P. Singh listed the right to know as one of his priority areas and declared that the Janata Dal was committed to the people's right to know. This was to ensure transparency in government, as much of its corruption was made possible due to one fact: 'It hides information from the people behind the screen of secrecy' (*ToI* 1989d). These ideas took concrete shape in the NF manifesto of 1989, where it committed to 'open government' (similar to the Janata Party manifesto in 1977). It promised 'full freedom of the media, autonomous corporations for television and radio and elimination of practices that lead to direct and indirect arm-twisting of the press'. It further said, '*People's right to information shall be guaranteed through constitutional provisions* [my emphasis]' (Agrawal and Aggarwal 1990: 69).

The commitment made in the manifesto was elaborated further in PM V.P. Singh's first address to the nation on 3 December 1989. Singh said:

> Norms and values are the bedrock of democracy. Therefore, the sanctity of democratic institutions will be restored and the autonomy of judiciary, CAG [Comptroller and Auditor General of India] and the Parliament will be strengthened. We will establish a Lok Pal to ensure that moral values of public life are not violated. Even the Prime Minister will not be above such scrutiny. *For increasing people's control to curb corruption, government will have to increase access to information* [my

emphasis]. If the government functions in full public view, wrongdoing will be greatly minimized. The Official Secrets Act will be amended and will make the functioning of the government more transparent. Secrecy will be maintained only where the interests of national security and foreign relations warrant. Free flow of information is a prerequisite for democracy. The Right to Information will be enshrined in our Constitution. Doordarshan and AIR [All India Radio] will be given autonomy. (Agrawal and Aggarwal 1990: 202)

The idea of open and accessible government was also articulated in President R. Venkataraman's joint address to both houses of the parliament on 20 December 1989. On the occasion of the oath-taking of the NF government, the president outlined the commitment and policy agenda for the government by touching upon social, economic, democratic, and foreign policy imperatives. The president declared, '[The] government firmly believes that a participative democracy requires an enlightened and *informed* [my emphasis] electorate. It also believes that an open government functioning in full public view, will minimize the possibility of the wrongdoing' (Lok Sabha Debates 1989: 5). President Venkataraman then proceeded to outline the policy plan for the new government to amend the OSA suitably to facilitate and increase people's access to information. Autonomy was to be extended to Doordarshan and AIR to ensure free flow of information: 'A bill to this effect will be introduced in this session' (Lok Sabha Debates 1989: 5).

Subsequently, in the action plan announced by the PM on January 1990, the government declared that the Constitution would be amended to guarantee the RTI as a fundamental right, and that the bill would be introduced during the budget session (Agrawal and Aggarwal 1990). Cabinet ministers too were in line with this policy commitment; for instance, P. Upendra, the minister of information and broadcasting in the NF government, reiterated the government's commitment to enact legislation on the RTI in the 'forthcoming' session of the parliament.[2] The need for a legal

[2] P. Upendra, who made this Statement on 9 February 1990, was presiding over a symposium titled 'The Challenges before the Indian Press in

framework on the freedom of information was also manifested in the thinking of institutions such as the Planning Commission. A Planning Commission member, Rajni Kothari, emphasized on 2 March 1990 that a law on the freedom of information was a prerequisite for growth, development, and democracy.[3] Later, transparency as a prerequisite would find concrete expression in the 9th and 10th Five Year Plans.[4]

Darryl D'Monte, former resident editor of *ToI*, saw these commitments as a continuity of ideas, and wrote that the commitment of the NF government to democratic openness and access to information were 'the *brave new words* [my emphasis] of the fledgling regime—its precursor, the Janata Party reneged on a similar commitment a decade ago' (D'Monte 1989). The short-lived NF government did not get time to follow up on its commitment. Internal strife within the party[5]

---

the 1990s'. Noted journalists U.N. Kalkul, former chief editor of United News of India; Nikhil Chakravartty, former editor of *Mainstream*; Arun Shourie, former editor of the *Indian Express*; Kuldip Nayar; M.R. Malkani; and S. Sahay were present at the symposium and welcomed the government's announcement. On another occasion in Calcutta, on 2 September 1990, P. Upendra made a similar announcement regarding the enactment of the law on the RTI (*ToI* 1990a, 1990d).

[3] Rajni Kothari was a member of the Planning Commission from 26 December 1989 to 31 November 1990. Kothari was speaking at a seminar on 'The Future of Indian Democracy' organized by the Centre for the Study of Developing Societies (*ToI* 1990b).

[4] Significantly, Shekhar Singh, who was one of the prominent members of the NCPRI, was advisor to the Planning Commission during this period. This is an important aspect where linkages from both within and outside the State seem to be proving instrumental in the shaping of the policy trajectory later. The nature of these linkages will be explored further in Chapter 4.

[5] Devi Lal's political activities in Haryana and his decision to make his son CM of the state of Haryana resulted in the resignation of some members of his cabinet (see Kochanek and Hardgrave 2007: 326).

and the issues of Mandal[6] and *Mandir*[7] led to the withdrawal of BJP support.

The term of the NF government is an important juncture that clearly signifies the departure from the first layer of institutional change to the second layer. The political context and resultant political commitment of the NF government towards access to information is significant from the viewpoint that the ideational churning was now part of mainstream politics. This was markedly different from the previous phase, when this churning was still primarily part of opposition politics. The mainstreaming is evident in the political commitment towards the freedom of information expressed by all the governments following the NF regime.

Importantly, the earlier 'unconverted' elements now seem to be 'converted' about the idea of openness and access to information. For instance, in its 1998 election manifesto, the Congress, for the first time, changed its stance on the issue when it expressed its commitment towards legislation on freedom of information. Yet another example is as follows: In 1987, as the chairman of the upper house, R. Venkataraman, had disallowed opposition members from discussing the president's letter to the PM in the parliament in order to uphold the secrecy and confidentiality of official documents. Later, in 1989, when he assumed the office of the president during the NF regime, Venkataraman supported the government's intention in his joint address to both houses of the parliament on 20 December 1989: 'Government firmly believes that a participative democracy

[6] To tackle the internal turmoil within the party, V.P. Singh carried out the move of implementing the Mandal Commission, which ensured reservation of 27 per cent of all government jobs for other backward castes. This created mass protests against his government across the country where thousands of students immolated themselves in protest (Kochanek and Hardgrave 2007: 327).

[7] The BJP, unhappy with the Mandal issue as it was, withdrew its support when L.K. Advani, who was on his countrywide *yatra* (journey) on the issue of the Babri Masjid and Ram temple dispute, was arrested by one of the CMs of the Janata Dal, Lalu Prasad Yadav, in Bihar (Kochanek and Hardgrave 2007: 328).

requires an enlightened and *informed* [my emphasis] electorate. It also believes that an open government functioning in full public view, will minimize the possibility of the wrongdoing' (Lok Sabha Debates 1989: 5). Table 2.1 demonstrates how the idea of access to information was now part of mainstream politics.

Another significant process can be seen in the interconnections and linkages between ideas of openness becoming part of mainstream politics, the political commitment, and policy processes set in motion by various governments from 1989 onwards. Key coalition partners articulated ideas on openness before the NF

TABLE 2.1 Political Commitment by Various Governments, 1991–2004

Government	Political Commitment and Policy Intent
Congress	The Congress manifesto of 1991 declared that freedom of information is a precious right and that Congress would pass a law to that effect. This is for the first time that Congress articulates its commitment towards freedom of information.
United Front	The Common Minimum Programme (CMP) declared, 'Official Secrets Act will be reviewed and amended keeping in tune with the need for openness and transparency in governance … a bill on freedom of information would be introduced within six months to give the people access to information at all levels' (*UF Policy Statement* 1996).
National Democratic Alliance	BJP's election manifesto promised to 'enhance public access to information to the maximum extent feasible' (*BJP Election Manifesto* 1998).
United Progressive Alliance	The CMP promised that 'the Right to Information Act will be made more progressive, participatory and meaningful' (*The Hindu* 2004).

Souce: Author

government initiated the political commitment and policy processes. For instance, on 7 September 1988, speaking in Bombay, V.P. Singh stressed the need for freedom of the press and access to official information (*ToI* 1988c).

Similarly, on 23 April 1989, BJP leader L.K. Advani stressed the need to enact the bill on the RTI and repeal the OSA. Notably, the BJP supported the NF government from outside in 1989. Later, on 27 August 1990, at Raipur, Advani reiterated the idea of repealing the OSA and enacting the RTI Act.[8] Ideas expressed during the Janata Party term were antecedent to the current ideas. In 1979, as the minister of information and broadcasting in the Janata Party government, Advani had underlined the policy imperative to have an institutional mechanism to ensure the freedom of press.[9] In May 1992, as the leader of the opposition, L.K. Advani convened a series of meetings (three in total) to discuss the RTI with opposition members in the parliament and state legislatures. The context for these meetings was a Maharashtra government directive to the bureaucracy not to share information with opposition leaders. The PM and the speaker of the lower house were also invited for the last meeting in the series (*ToI* 1992a). These ideas had an incremental impact during the NDA regime (1998–2004), which initiated the policy processes to enact the FoI Act, 2002. Advani was part of the group of ministers (GoM) constituted by the NDA government to examine the passage of the FoI Bill. The positive orientation of Advani towards openness bears out in the proceedings of the GoM meeting, which categorically recommended an unrestrictive law with a list of mandatory information to be disclosed to citizens. The GoM also advised the MHA to repeal or review the 'outdated' OSA.

This linkage can be seen in the case of the UF government as well. In May 1993, H.D. Deve Gowda recommended that a

[8] Advani was speaking at a function to inaugurate a new printing unit for the BJP–RSS-oriented Hindi daily, *Swadesh* (*ToI* 1990c).

[9] Advani, then minister for information and broadcasting, was speaking at the inauguration of the seminar titled 'Pressure on the Press', organized by the Delhi Journalists Association (*ToI* 1979).

high-powered committee should be appointed by the Congress government to look into the amendments of some central Acts. He proposed that the government rethink the Prevention of Corruption Act, 1988; Trust Act, 1882; the OSA; and the Foreign Exchange Regulation Act, 1973, as these legislations shielded the corrupt. In his view, the opposition (BJP) should have taken the lead in moving amendments to these Acts (*ToI* 1993a). This thinking found concrete expression when Deve Gowda became the PM in the UF government.

Notwithstanding the initiatives taken by the various political regimes in power from 1989 onwards, no outcome could eventuate until 2005. But the salience of policy ideas within the State points towards a continuous churning within State thinking on the issue. Moreover, the narrative at this stage was attaining a homogenous and linear path, where all the quarters (across party lines) seemed to be in agreement regarding the notion of greater openness in government affairs. This change in State thinking is different from earlier debates and policy actions, where the narrative was being pulled both ways by different segments within the State. The push and demand for a legal framework for the RTI was turning out to be ineluctable from this point onwards. This is evident in the commitment of various political parties, which formed the government at the centre, to enact such a law in their election manifestos, and in the public speeches of various heads of State.

Politics and the Policy Trajectory: Policy Processes Set in Motion

As the ideational churning was instituted within the mainstream politics, the political leadership demonstrated the willingness to legislate the right or freedom to information. As a result, the policy movement towards that aim was initiated within the executive. The political commitment and the policy intent acted as push factors in kick-starting the processes within the State. This process can be seen unfolding during all the governments since 1989, starting from the NF government. This is evident in the formation of various government committees, and in processes set in motion within the permanent executive, to examine the feasibility and possibility of enacting legislation on the RTI and to review the persisting institution of secrecy. The emerging policy processes show the final stage of layering, where the ideas and norms on openness were placed on top of the existing norms of secrecy; eventually, the weight of these ideas replaced the norm of secrecy through the enactment of RTI Act in 2005. In the following section, I will examine the trajectory of these policy processes, starting from the NF government in 1989.

Policy Initiatives during National Front Government 1989–91

Following through on their commitments, the NF government constituted a cabinet committee on 8 December 1989 to study and examine different aspects of the possibility of granting legal RTI to the citizens (Rajya Sabha Debates 1991a). The high-level cabinet committee consisted of the foreign minister, the minister of information and broadcasting, the minister of surface transport, and the vice chairman of the Planning Commission. The committee, however, did not come out with a report and was subsequently dissolved on 27 August 1990 (*PUCL Bulletin* 1991).[10]

10

Near the beginning of its period in office, the government of V.P. Singh announced its commitment to promote freedom of information and appointed a cabinet committee, consisting of the Foreign Minister, the Minister of Information and Broadcasting, the Minister of Surface Transport, and the Vice Chairman of the Planning Commission to study means by which to accomplish this. To the great disappointment of advocates of freedom of information, the committee was dissolved on August 27 1990 without issuing a report or making any recommendations … On April 9 1990, the National Front government promised to amend the Official Secrets Act to facilitate greater access to information held by the government. At the beginning of September 1990 the Minister of Information, P. Upendra, repeated the pledge, but added that 'no action has been initiated towards this end. (*PUCL Bulletin* 1991)

Similarly, in 1991, the NF government constituted a twenty-five-member committee headed by MHA Joint Secretary B.S. Lali[11] to examine the possibility of amending the OSA and exploring the passage of an RTI Bill (Noorani 1997: 117; Zaidi 1991). The Lali Committee submitted its two-volume report to the government in 1991, recommending that apart from some sensitive areas, such as intelligence, defence, and finance-related matters, information related to all areas should be made accessible to citizens (Zaidi 1991).

Following up on the Lali Committee, the MHA set up an inter-ministerial task force in 1991 to examine the feasibility of enacting legislation on public access to government information. The task force visited the UK, Sweden, the USA, and Canada to study the functioning of freedom of information laws in those countries. The task force submitted its report to the MHA on 31 May 1991 (MPPP 2001).[12]

Congress Government 1991–6: A Hiatus, and Yet, Some Policy Initiatives

Despite the commitment to enact a law on RTI in its 1991 manifesto, one can sense a brief hiatus of activities around the RTI at the level of political executive during this phase of the Congress regime. In fact the government sustained the norm of secrecy and, in 1994, amended the Manual of Departmental Security Instructions issued in 1966 to instruct government departments to either classify or declassify documents—from 'top secret' to 'confidential' (Lok Sabha Starred Question No: 557; Nayak 2011). This shows that the longest ruling party in Indian politics was still resisting the idea of openness. One would have thought that the political regime at this point would

[11] *The Hindu* on 13 December 1991 reported that the Lali Committee had been set up around a year and a half before it submitted its report in 1991. It can thus be surmised that the committee was constituted during the NF regime. The Lali Committee Report is not a public report.

[12] Unfortunately, the report has been since lost, and only an incomplete copy of Volume I of the report was available with DoPT.

be more open to the idea of access to information, especially when the transformative institutional changes were being introduced in the economy through liberal economic reforms during this period.

However, two significant moves during the initial phase of the Congress government are pertinent and need to be flagged: a Constitution amendment bill to insert Article 19 (A) and a private member's bill on FoI. The bills introduced in the parliament need to be viewed in the broader context of similar initiatives within the legislature, which were discussed as part of the first phase, and demonstrate a continuity of ideas.

Constitution Amendment Bill for Insertion of Article 19 (A) Moved by Chitta Basu, 1991

On 13 September 1991, a Constitution amendment bill for the insertion of Article 19 (A) was moved in the lower house by Chitta Basu, MP, Lok Sabha, from Barasat constituency in West Bengal. Basu represented a left-wing party called All India Forward Bloc (AIFB).[13] The bill sought to include RTI as a fundamental right in the Constitution of India by citing examples of similar laws existing in Western countries such as Sweden and the USA and the government's own commitment to enact a law on RTI. In the statement of aims and purposes of the bill, Basu argued for citizens' entitlement to the information, pointing out that the government is the largest repository of information related to socio-economic policies. A bill to ensure citizens' RTI as a fundamental right would strengthen the democratic ethos of the country.

Basu had twice moved similar bills earlier—in 1983 and in 1989 respectively. The minister of state of home affairs and parliamentary affairs, M.M. Jacob, assured during the discussion on the bill that the government was considering its passage and was committed to extending such a right to citizens. He added that balance had to be

[13] The AIFB was a faction of the Indian National Congress that broke away from the Congress when Subhash Chandra Bose resigned from the presidency of the Indian National Congress in April 1939.

maintained between information that could be shared and sensitive information related to national security. Jacob pointed towards ongoing policy processes within the executive that were examining the passage of RTI such as the 'action plan of 1991 to modify OSA' and the constitution of an inter-ministerial study group that was in the process of examining the bill in consultation with various ministries. The bill received overwhelming support from all the members of the house who spoke on the bill. On receiving assurance from the minister of state for home affairs and upon his request, Basu withdrew the bill.

Private Member's Bill by Suresh Pachouri, 1992

Pushing the idea of transparency further, Suresh Pachouri introduced a private member's bill on the FoI in the upper house on 31 March 1992. Pachouri was a Rajya Sabha member representing the Congress Party, which was in power at the time this bill was moved. Interestingly, the content of the bill was an exact replica of the bill introduced by G.C. Bhattacharya in 1983. Just as in Bhattacharya's bill, the Statement of Objects and Reasons in Pachouri's bill started with Abraham Lincoln's dictum of government of the people. The Statement of Objects and Reasons further observed: 'People, being at the centre stage in a democracy, have every right to have the information as to what their representatives and government is doing for them at the national and international levels.' It argued that lack of information led to mistrust, resulting in widespread turmoil; therefore, it was necessary to grant citizens the right to access information. The bill also mentioned the global trend of granting similar rights elsewhere and urged to 'make a beginning by having a law providing for the freedom of information for the people' (FoI Bill 1992; Dutta 2014). It is important to note that Pachouri, who later assumed the role of minister of state for personnel, public grievances and pensions, introduced the draft RTI Bill, 2004, in the parliament.

The bill proposed by Pachouri yet again points towards the fact that the idea of a legislation on FoI was finding some sympathizers within the ruling party as well, since Pachouri was from the Congress Party.

The United Front Government 1996–8

During 1996–8, the UF government saw two PMs (Deve Gowda and I.K. Gujral) take the helm in quick succession. Both reaffirmed their commitment towards legislation on FoI. Indeed, true to these commitments, the wheels within the bureaucratic and political machinery started turning faster from this point onwards.

Committee on Right to Information and Transparency, 1997

The political commitment was manifested in the constitution of the Working Committee on Right to Information and Transparency, also known as the Shourie Committee. Its recommendations were significant as they formed the basis for further discussions on legal and policy provisions of the law within the State.

At this juncture, there was a consensus around the norm of openness within the State. This consensus, as an internal government document states, was on the 'need for a clean and responsive administration based on the principles of accountability, openness, decentralisation and citizen orientation' (MPPP 1997). In the backdrop of the 'national debate on effective and responsive administration',[14] the cabinet secretary approved the constitution of the nine-member Working Committee on Right to Information and Transparency, which was formally communicated through an official memorandum on 2 January 1997 (MPPP 1997). The committee was constituted with the objective of examining the feasibility, applicability, and operationalization of the 'full-fledged Right to Information Act or its introduction in a phased manner to meet the needs of open and responsive government'. H.D. Shourie, a well-known legal activist working on consumer rights, and Soli Sorabjee, an eminent jurist and the solicitor general of India from 1977 to 1980, were appointed as members of this government committee. Shourie was the chairman of the committee.

[14] This was stated in the office memorandum that constituted the committee.

Shourie was a retired civil servant and his experience in the government service, where he witnessed the plight of the common citizen at close quarters, motivated him to set up *Common Cause* in 1980 post-retirement (Rediff 1997). Sorabjee's contrarian views on 'secrecy' were all too known. These views were expressed unequivocally in an editorial in 1989:

> Obsession with secrecy is encountered with varying degrees in all governments, democratic and totalitarian. The bogey of national security is frequently invoked to withhold information in courts of countries that pride themselves on openness in government and adherence to the rule of law. (Sorabjee 1989)

Sorabjee touched upon similar issues in two of his earlier books on the laws of *Press Censorship in India* (1976) and *The Emergency, Censorship and the Press in India, 1975–77* (1977).

On 24 May 1997, the committee submitted its final report. It observed that transparency and openness in government functioning has a cleansing effect and said that 'sunlight is the best disinfectant'.[15] It held that 'the legislation should be enacted by the Parliament [to that effect] in order to ensure uniformity of its application throughout the country' (Working Group on Right to Information and Promotion of Open and Transparent Government 1997: 3–5). The report (*a*) recommended that the government enact the FoI bill based on the committee's 1997 draft of the bill; (*b*) proposed amendment of Section 5 of the OSA; Sections 123 and 124 of the Indian Evidence Act, 1872; the Code of Civil Procedure, 1908; and the Code of Criminal Procedure, 1973; and (*c*) recommended amendment to rule 11 of the Central Civil Services (Conduct) Rules, 1964 and 1965, and amendments to the Manual of Departmental Security Instructions dealing with classification of information (Internal Note for Committee of Secretaries 1997).

The policy discussions, however, were not limited to this committee. A working synergy was established within different segments

[15] This draws upon the famous and oft-cited quote of Justice Louis D. Brandeis of the US SC in 'What Publicity Can Do' (Brandeis 1913).

of the permanent executive. This was evident during the second meeting on 18 January 1997, when the working group discussed the categories of information excluded or included for disclosure (Proceedings of the Second Meeting of the Working Group 1997).[16] The basis of the discussion in this meeting was the PCI draft of the FoI Bill. Following the second meeting, the secretary of the MPPP circulated a letter to all the secretaries of the GoI seeking their opinion on the proposed bill, especially on the information that needed to be classified. The letter also sought a review of the existing legal and statutory provisions administered by the concerned department or ministry to ascertain the 'extent of legislative, statutory, or other amendments which may be required to be carried out' (Letter from DoPT, MPPP, to all the Secretaries of GoI 1997). In response, the secretary of the MHA raised some pertinent issues, such as the consideration of State–centre dichotomy; the inclusion of private entities; file notings; information related to budgets; scientific, economic, and technological matters; the personal responsibility of officers not to disclose information; and the provision of parliamentary privileges (see A2 in book-end Appendices). The process of endorsement of the 'idea on openness and access to information', which was done by taking on board the views of various departments/ministries and states, entrenched the idea further within different segments of the State.

[16] The second meeting held discussions on the draft bill prepared by H.D. Shourie on the basis of Justice Sawant's PCI draft bill, especially Clause 4, which provided a safeguard in certain cases of premature disclosures. It was decided that a subclause to Clause 4 would be added in the bill. Views were expressed in the meeting to safeguard premature disclosure of information and certain categories such as internal government communications, interdepartmental memoranda, and the budget (drawing on the precedent of the FoI Act of the USA and the code of practice regarding government information of the UK). It is in this context that it was decided to insert a subclause to Clause 4 to protect such categories of information. It was also decided that the FoI in the proposed bill would be subject to parliamentary privileges (Proceedings of the Second Meeting of the Working Group 1997).

Meeting of Committee of Secretaries, 1997

The FoI Bill proposed by the Shourie Committee was also discussed by the Committee of Secretaries (CoS), which met thrice in 1997—on 29 July, 21 August, and 23 September. The committee was principally not against the proposed bill and discussed the institutional mechanism of information identification and sharing. It was decided that the bill would be revised to incorporate strict parameters for classifying the document. This exercise would be carried out by top officials and only the appointed public information officer could deny the classified information. This would be accompanied by a well-worked-out mechanism to appeal at the level of authority that classified the information, and to make a second appeal to an even higher authority (Cabinet Secretariat Doc NO CD (CA.V) 97.1997).

Group of Ministers, 1997

Following the CoS meeting, the cabinet secretary constituted a committee to draft a revised bill and prepare a note for the cabinet. The personnel secretary chaired the committee. On 20 October 1997, the cabinet held a meeting to consider the draft note prepared by the committee (GoI Internal Note Ref: CD-740/97). After due consideration, the cabinet decided to refer the matter to the GoM.[17] The GoM held three meetings, on 18 October 1996, 17 December 1996, and 5 January 1997, to consider the draft bill and the proposed amendments to the OSA. In its first meeting, the GoM considered the issues raised by the departments and ministries. The home secretary and secretary-level representatives from the MHA, Legislative Department, Department of Administrative Reforms and Public Grievances, Cabinet Secretariat, Department

[17] The GoM comprised Indrajit Gupta, minister of home affairs; Janeshwar Mishra, minister of petroleum and natural gas; Murasoli Maran, minister of industry; and Ramakant D. Khalap, minister of state (independent charge) of Ministry of Law and Justice (Internal Government Paper on Legislative Proposal for Freedom of Information and Amendments to Related Acts and Rules 1997).

of Legal Affairs, and DoPT attended the meeting. The GoM recapitulated the commitment made in the CMP and proposed that the legislation should aim to provide citizens with as much information as possible within a strict time period. This should reflect in the draft bill. With regard to the exemptions and disclosures, the GoM made an important point: disclosure should follow the general principle that all information available to the parliament and state legislatures should also be made available to citizens under the law (Minutes of the Meeting of GoM 1997b). The GoM finalized the draft bill on 12 February 1998 and referred it to the law ministry, which concurred with the GoM's view (see Table 2.2 for the chronology of events during the UF government).

That by this time the idea on openness was taking root at the systemic level was evident in the *Approach Paper to the Ninth Five Year Plan (1997–2002)* of 16 January 1997. The paper laid emphasis on bringing 'institutional changes to bring in transparency in implementation and operation of programmes'. It added that: 'For this purpose, avoidable barriers to full flow of information must be removed' (Planning Commission 2002a: 123).

National Democratic Alliance and United Progressive Alliance Governments, 1998–2004: Final Passage of the Right to Information Act, 2005

Even though the policy movement to enact the legislation on FoI or RTI took root within the bureaucracy during the earlier governments, the Act could not fructify due to weak and short-lived coalitions at the centre. However, the weight of earlier ideas was perceptible during the continued policy processes within both the NDA and the UPA governments. Policy processes set in motion earlier continued with greater intensity and purpose during the two governments. The proposed bill was finally promulgated during the NDA as the FoI Act, 2002, and as the RTI Act, 2005, under the UPA. This was because these were the only two coalitions at the centre that lasted the full term. The proposed legislation on access to information by this time had become inevitable due to the cumulative ideational push.

Table 2.2 Chronology of Events during the UF Government

Date	Event
2 January 1997	Government constitutes the Working Group on Right to Information and Transparency under the chairmanship of H.D. Shourie, with Soli Sorabjee as one of the eight members.
10 January–25 April 1997	Working group holds six meetings.
16 January 1997	*Approach Paper to the Ninth Five Year Plan (1997–2002)* lays emphasis on bringing 'institutional changes to bring in transparency in implementation and operation of programmes. For this purpose, avoidable barriers to full flow of information must be removed' (Planning Commission 2002a: 123; see also Sharma 2015: 192).
21 May 1997	Working group submits its report to the government.
24 May 1997	Chief Ministers' Conference called Effective and Responsive Government comes to consensus that a legislation for RTI should be enacted by the GoI as early as possible. The report of the working group circulated in the conference.
3 June 1997	Copies of working group's report circulated to all the ministries/departments for their views and comments.
11 June 1997	Copies of working group's report circulated to all the state governments/union territories for their views and comments.
29 June 1997	CoS holds its first meeting to consider DoPT's note on FoI Bill.
30 June 1997	While answering supplementary to a starred question on 30 July 1997, PM makes a statement in the lower house that the 'Right to Information Bill' will be introduced in the winter session of 1997.

(*Cont'd*)

Table 2.2 (*Cont'd*)

Date	Event
15 August 1997	Announcement made by PM I.K. Gujral in course of speech on the 50th Independence Day that the FoI Bill will be introduced in the winter session.
21 August 1997	CoS holds its second meeting.
3–4 September 1997	Workshop titled National Workshop on Right to Information organized by National Institute of Research and Development.
23 September 1997	CoS holds its third meeting.
26 September 1997	Core group set up to finalize the draft FoI Bill.
6 October 1997	Core group holds its second meeting.
17 October 1997	Note for Cabinet sent to Cabinet Secretariat in order to obtain its approval to introduce FoI Bill in the parliament.
20 October 20, 1997	Meeting of the cabinet.
23 October 1997	Cabinet Secretariat constitutes the GoM.
28 October 1997	GoM holds its first meeting.
16 November 1997	Union Minister of Information and Broadcasting S. Jaipal Reddy reiterates the government's commitment to enact RTI Bill, stressing on the significance of free press in a joint seminar organized by PCI and Indian Institute of Mass Communication (*ToI* 1997b).
24 November 1997	Workshop on 'Right to Information' organized at Yashada by DoPT in collaboration with Lal Bahadur Shastri National Academy of Administration (LBSNAA).
17 December 1997	GoM holds its second meeting.
5 January 1998	GoM holds its third meeting.
12 February 1998	Draft bill as finalized by GoM referred to Law Ministry.
6 March 1998	Law Ministry concurs in FoI Bill.

Source: Author

This was evident in the policy processes during both the NDA and UPA governments. The policy trajectory for promulgating legislation on access to information was favourable and was evident in the formation of GoMs; referring of the draft bill to the cabinet; involvement of concerned departments and ministries such as the Legislative Department, MHA, and DoPT in drafting the law; and constitution of a department-related parliamentary standing committee (DRPSC) for the clause-wise examination of the proposed bill.

NDA I: 1998–9

The NDA, which formed the government after the UF, picked up the thread from the previous government. As soon as it assumed office, it sent a draft note on FoI to the PMO. On that basis, the PM constituted a GoM on 27 April 1998 to examine the proposed FoI and finalize its recommendations (Cabinet Secretariat 1998).[18] The GoM offered four recommendations.

1. Regarding restrictions on providing the type of information, the GoM held that the law should not give the impression on plain reading that it is too restrictive. The GoM found it worthwhile to revisit the Shourie Committee's cardinal principle that the RTI should be the rule and the denial of information should be the exception.
2. The GoM recommended that the legislation should be such that it clearly spells out the information available mandatorily to citizens rather than focusing on the list of restricted information. This will give the proposed legislation a positive outlook.
3. The GoM concluded that the OSA was an outdated law and urged the MHA to do away with meaningless, restrictive, and outdated

[18] Members of the GoM were L.K. Advani, minister of home affairs; George Fernandes, minister of defence; M. Thambi Durai, minister of law, justice and company affairs, and minister of surface transport; Sushma Swaraj, minister of information and broadcasting and minister of communications; Vasundhara Raje, minister of state in the Ministry of External Affairs (MEA); and R. Janarthanam, minister of state in the MPPP.

provisions, such as restrictions on photographing specific public areas.

4. The OSA should be retained as a separate statute, and 'official secrets' should be defined in consistency with the provisions of the proposed law on access to information.

Both the political and permanent executive were working together on the bill. For instance, on 25 June 1998, CoS held a meeting to discuss the matters raised by the GoM (Minutes of the Meeting of Committee of Secretaries 1998). CoS decided that two drafts of the bills would be prepared for the GoM's consideration, one which is original and the other which has incorporated the GoM's recommendations. An issue regarding the parliament's jurisdiction to legislate the proposed law came up during the meeting. This was referred to Soli Sorabjee, attorney general of India and former member of the Shourie Committee (Communication from Addl. Secretary, Department of Administrative Reforms and Public Grievances to Secretary, Department of Legal Affairs 1998). The CoS meeting was again followed up by the GoM in its second meeting held on 18 December 1998 (Minutes of the Meeting of GoM 1998b).

In 1998, while the passage of the bill was being worked out at the central level, independent policy initiatives on the issue of access to information were adopted by a cabinet minister. Through an Office Memorandum of 10 October 1998, Minister of Urban Affairs and Employment Ram Jethmalani granted citizens the right to inspect and copy any file of the Department of Urban Development under his ministry for a fee of INR 10 (except those with cabinet notes, budget, and vigilance-related papers). In many ways this was a radical departure from the norm in the ministry.

Independent thinking on the issue was evident from other quarters as well. For instance, in April 1999, the 55th Report of the Department-Related Parliamentary Standing Committee on Home Affairs (DRPSC-HA) categorically demanded for the amendment of the OSA and further action on RTI (DRPSC-HA 1999; Shrivastava 2009: 124).

NDA II: 1999–2004

The NDA I had to step down from the government only after one year of it being in power. After fresh elections, the NDA came back to power led by BJP with support from regional parties. This time, the NDA remained in government for the full five-year term from 10 October 1999 to 6 February 2004.

The new NDA government continued on its previous policy path and reconstituted the GoM in July 1999, which retained the old members from 1998 while including new ones (Cabinet Secretariat 1999).[19] The newly constituted GoM met on 22 November 1999 and took into consideration the note prepared by the DoPT (Minutes of the Meeting of GoM 1999). While upholding the previous decision on the positive list of disclosures, the GoM wanted the law to be re-examined in the light of the SC's judgement in *S.P. Gupta* vs *Union of India* (AIR 1982 SC 149). In this light, the GoM suggested that the clause dealing with exemptions and disclosure be redrafted and the Legislative Department was advised to have two lists listing the disclosure and exemptions separately.[20] The GoM referred the bill to the Legislative Department and the DoPT.

The DoPT along with the MHA prepared a clause-wise note (DoPT Internal Note for the GoM 1999) for the GoM addressing issues raised in the first meeting. In the second meeting of the GoM (held on 7 January 2000), the quorum unanimously agreed that the ambit and scope of the rights conferred under the proposed legislation

[19] Ram Jethmalani, minister of law, justice and company affairs; Arun Jaitley, minister for information and broadcasting; and Jaswant Singh, minister of external affairs, were included in the new GoM.

[20] The GoM wanted to redraft Clauses 8 and 9 of the draft bill (which dealt with the exemptions on disclosure) in line with Article 19 (1) and (2) of the Constitution in addition to Articles 74 and 78. The Legislative Department was directed to examine the draft bill and redraft it further. In view of the restrictive nature of Clauses 8 and 9, the GoM wanted Clause 4, which dealt with legal advice, recommendations, or minutes of deliberative nature. Instead, GoM suggested that Clause 8 should be divided in two parts, which would give a positive outlook to the bill.

would ultimately depend on governance being more effective. In this light, the GoM proposed to draft the bill in such a manner that it included the provision that the 'government would have the right to disclose more information than is provided for in the proposed Bill'. The Legislative Department redrafted the proposed bill taking into consideration the suggestions made by the GoM (Note of the Legislative Department for the GoM 2000).

In its third meeting (2 February 2000), the GoM considered the note prepared by the Legislative Department. Significantly, the GoM endorsed the formulation in Clause 26, which stated that the OSA and any other Act should cease to be operative in case it is inconsistent with the provisions of the proposed Act. In this light, the GoM urged the MHA to re-examine the OSA keeping in mind the changing scenario. This was an important decision by the GoM as, in this recommendation, the new norm of openness in the form of FoI would be subsequently layering out the nested norm of secrecy, which had been perpetuating since colonial times and was operationalized through the OSA. Finally, the GoM instructed the legislative department to draft the law so that it could be placed before the cabinet at the earliest.

Subsequently, the draft bill, along with a note from the cabinet, was jointly approved by the Ministry of Law, Justice and Company Affairs, Ministry of Finance, and the PMO. The bill was referred back to the cabinet for approval, which finally accepted it for introduction in the parliament on 13 May 2000. Subsequently, Vasundhara Raje introduced the FoI Bill, 2000, in the lower house on 25 July 2000.

Department-Related Parliamentary Standing Committee on Home Affairs

On 14 September 2000, the chairman of the upper house referred the bill to the DRPSC-HA with Pranab Mukherjee as the chairman of the committee (DRPSC-HA 2001). The committee considered the proposed bill in five sittings. Table 2.3 presents the chronology of the meetings held by the committee.

Table 2.3 Meetings of DRPSC-HA

23 October 2000	**First Meeting of the DRPSC-HA** Heard oral evidence of the secretary, MPPP
24 January 2001	**Second Meeting** Representations by: 1. Commonwealth Human Rights Initiative (CHRI) (Maja Daruwala, Abha S. Joshi, Bimal Arora, and Deepika Mogilshetty) 2. Madhav Godbole 3. A.G. Noorani 4. Consumer Education and Research Centre (CERC) (Manubhai Shah)
8 February 2001	**Third Meeting** Representations by: 1. MKSS (Kavita Srivastava, Nikhil Dey, Prabhash Joshi, Neelabh Mishra, Jharna Jhaveri, and Anuraj Singh) 2. PCI (Justice P.B. Sawant)
25 June 2001	**Fourth Meting: Clause-wise Discussions on the Bill** Representations by: 1. MPPP 2. Legislative Department 3. Department of Legal Affairs
10 July 2001	**Fifth Meeting** Considered the draft report and adopted the final version formally
25 July 2001	Report tabled in both the houses of the parliament

Source: Author

The proceedings of the DRPSC-HA (outlined earlier) throw light on a significant process (DRPSC-HA 2001). Depositions before the committee are not merely oral evidence but point towards a deeper multi-layered process of State–society synergy, which had begun to take root. In this case, progressive elements from both within and outside the State had come together on a single platform to deliberate on a common cause, that is, the RTI (or FoI). Indeed, the meetings of the DRPSCs were also an extension and formalization of the earlier process of taking on board different viewpoints and comments, to have a consensus on the issue. The process which found a formal space in the UPA created NAC later. It is important to flag this significant process here as it is an important dimension that unfolds in the DRPSC-HA meetings (subsequently discussed and explored in Chapter 4).

Finally, the FoI Bill, 2002, was moved in Lok Sabha on 3 December 2002 and was adopted as an Act by the house. The Rajya Sabha considered the bill and passed the Act on 16 December 2002. On 6 January 2003, the FoI Bill received presidential assent and was finally notified as the FoI Act, 2002, in the *Gazette of India* on 7 January 2003. However, eventually the bill did not come into force.

Meanwhile, State institutions such as the Planning Commission continued on their earlier stance to promulgate a legislation on RTI. The Tenth Five Year Plan Document (2002–7) advised:

> The Right to Information Act must be enacted expeditiously and implemented in letter and in spirit … and to a great extent, the task of the development administration would become easier if steps are taken to make available information, as a matter of right, to the citizens. The right to information has to be the starting point for much of the reforms proposed. The right to information is so important because very often people do not even know what programmes and schemes are available and what they are entitled to. Also, policy and procedural reforms can be effective only when people know that such changes have been made. (Planning Commission 2002b: 182)

The United Progressive Alliance Government, 2004–9: Right to Information Act, 2005, Enacted

After the NDA completed its five-year term, fresh elections saw a change of government at the centre with the UPA, led by Congress, assuming the office at the centre. The UPA, like its predecessors, was a coalition of more than thirteen parties led by Congress, which was supported by a left party and some major regional parties. Manmohan Singh was declared the PM and Sonia Gandhi became chairperson of the UPA. By this time the incremental push of ideas, which had started from the first layer, was so significant that the policy processes that had been set in motion within the State reached a tipping point.

Soon after assuming office, the UPA constituted the NAC to monitor the progress and implementation of the CMP, to provide policy inputs to the government, and to provide support to the legislative business of the government (631/2/1/2004-Cab). The PM, in consultation with the chairperson of the UPA, constituted the membership of the NAC, which consisted of representatives from civil society and academia, legislators, and bureaucrats (both former and serving).[21] Sonia Gandhi served as the chairperson of NAC.

At this juncture the constitution of the NAC was an important initiative. In a sense, the NAC represented 'State in society', a space where both State and non-State actors deliberated on an issue and the ideas that emerged from these deliberations were then relayed back to the executive—a process that worked out well in the initial phase of policy-making on social welfare during the UPA's term. The NAC played a pivotal role in the framing of the draft RTI Bill and in the passage of the final bill. This is the space where State–society synergy can be seen at work in all its practical policy imports (the NAC and the related dimension are examined at length in Chapter 4).

After the first three meetings on 17 July, 30 July, and 14 August 2004, the NAC finalized the draft bill on RTI by suggesting amendments in the FoI Act, 2002. The NAC suggested a number of amendments to the bill including four main changes that could be brought out in the draft RTI Bill: replacing 'freedom' with 'right', adding a penalty clause, including the principle of maximum disclosure, and inserting the provision for appellate mechanism. This draft RTI Bill

[21] Members of the newly constituted body were Aruna Roy, MKSS; C.H. Hanumantha Rao, Centre for Economic and Social Studies, Hyderabad; Jairam Ramesh, MP; Jean Dreze, Delhi School of Economics; JP, Loksatta; V. Krishnamurthy, UCAL Fuel Systems Ltd; Mirai Chatterjee, Self Employed Women's Association (SEWA); Madhav Chavan, Pratham; A.K. Shivakumar, United Nations Children's Fund (UNICEF); D. Swaminathan, Mahatma Gandhi National Institute of Research and Social Action; Sam Pitroda; and N.C. Saxena.

was forwarded to the concerned department in the government. Subsequently, the government declared that the bill would be introduced in the winter session of the parliament to seek amendments to the RTI Act, based on suggestions put forth by the NAC.

Consequently, the DoPT prepared a note (Internal Note of the Cabinet Secretariat to DoPT 2004) and sent it to the Cabinet on 13 December 2004 asking it to consider the proposal to repeal the FoI Act and enact the RTI Act. The Cabinet held a meeting on 15 December 2004 (Extracts from the Minutes of the Cabinet 2004) where it approved the proposal and directed the constitution of a GoM to consider the government's amendments to be incorporated in the bill.

The NAC recommendations, directions of the PM, and the cabinet approval of the proposed amendments triggered a chain of movements within the State apparatus that has been captured in the timeline given in Table 2.4.

Table 2.4 Timeline: Final Passage of the RTI Act

23 December 2004	RTI Bill, 2004, is introduced by Suresh Pachauri, minister of state for personnel, public grievances and pensions on the last day of the winter session of the parliament.
31 December 2004	RTI Bill, 2004, is referred to the DRPSC on Personnel, Public Grievances, Law and Justice. E.M.S. Natchiappan is appointed the chairman of the committee.
1 February 2005	First meeting of the DRPSC: oral evidence of the secretary of the MPPP is heard.
14 February 2005	Second Meeting of the DRPSC: oral evidence of civil society representatives and experts is heard. Committee also considered written statements. Depositions of the following people from the MKSS and the NCPRI were submitted: Aruna Roy (NAC member as well), Nikhil Dey, Prashant Bhushan, Jean Dreze (NAC member as well), Angela Rangad, Harsh Mander, Anna Hazare, Prakash Kardaley, Shekhar Singh, Shailesh Gandhi,

	Maja Daruwala (CHRI), Charmaine Rodrigues (CHRI), Venkatesh Nayak (CHRI), Jayaprakash Narayan (Loksatta), and Shanti Bhushan (eminent jurist).
16 February 2005	Third Meeting of the DRPSC: depositions are continued from 14 February 2005.
1 and 2 March 2005	Fourth and Fifth Meetings of the DRPSC: clause-wise discussion on the proposed bill is carried out.
16 March 2005	The final report is adopted.
21 March 2005	The report is tabled in both houses of the parliament.
5 January 2005	The GoM is constituted on the recommendation of the cabinet to consider the government amendment in the proposed bill (Internal Government Communique Notifying the Constitution of GOM 2005). The GoM consists of Pranab Mukherjee, minister of defence; Sharad Pawar, minister of agriculture, consumer affairs and food and public distribution; Shivraj V. Patil, minister of home affairs; S. Jaipal Reddy, minister of information and broadcasting, culture; P. Chidambaram, minister of finance; H.R. Bhardwaj, minister of law and justice, Dayanidhi Maran, minister of communications and information technology; Suresh Pachouri, minister of state for personnel, public grievances and pensions and parliamentary affairs.
26 April 2005	First Meeting of GoM: they considered the note sent by DoPT and examined the proposed RTI Bill, 2004.[22]

(Cont'd)

[22] The following recommendations were given by the GoM:

(*a*) The parliament should have the legislative capacity to enact the law; (*b*) there should be reasonable application fee to get information; (*c*) below poverty line (BPL) families should be provided information free of cost; (*d*) the NAC recommendations for the categories of information exempt from disclosures should be accepted; (*e*) a minister appointed by the PM

Table 2.4 (*Cont'd*)

30 April 2005	Second Meeting of GoM: they approved the draft bill. Recommendations came out from both these meetings.
3 May 2005	DoPT gives note for the cabinet (34012/1(S)2005-Estt. (B)) on proposal for repealing FoI Act and enacting RTI Act, 2004.
4 May 2005	Cabinet meeting takes place where they approve the proposal for RTI Act, 2004 (21/CM/2005).
5 May 2005	Suresh Pachouri, minister of state for personnel, public grievances and pensions, gives notice (34012/1(S)/2005-Estt. B) to the Lok Sabha secretary general for the intention to move the bill in Lok Sabha.
11 May 2005	RTI Bill, 2004, is moved in Lok Sabha. The PM speaks on the Bill: 'This Bill will see the dawn of a new era in our processes of governance, an era of performance and efficiency.' Discussions are held in the Lok Sabha on specific clauses from clauses 1–28. Bill is then passed in Lok Sabha.
12 May 2005	Rajya Sabha passes the Bill.
15 June 2005	The Act receives presidential assent.
12 October 2005	RTI Act comes into force.

Source: Author

---

should be the third member of the selection committee (PM and the leader of opposition of Lok Sabha being the other two members) of the Central Information Commission; (*f*) the penalty provision for public information officers in cases where supply of information is delayed should be approved; (*g*) there should be a fine of up to INR 25,000 for information officers giving wrong information; and (*h*) security and intelligence agencies should be exempted from the law.

Three points are discernible. First, politics impacted the policy processes within State, eventually resulting in institutional change. Since the idea of access to information was part of mainstream politics, it became part of the policy processes within the State as well.

Second, the process of endorsement of the idea on openness and access to information, by taking on board the views of various departments/ministries and the States, entrenched the idea further within different segments of the State.

Third, there was a congruence of ideas between different segments of the State. A working synergy was established between the political and the permanent executives. This was evident in the policy processes following the political commitments. Committees were constituted, internal processes were set in motion within the department and ministries, and the resultant draft legislations were referred to the GoM.

Political Will

The pronouncements and policy moves by various governments starting from the Janata Party government (in 1977) point towards a significant role of political will and the role of political leadership. Ideas on openness, which got embedded in the State thinking, shaped and influenced the political will. A favourable political will towards institutional change removed the uncertainties (at the level of bureaucracy or specific departments) of exiting from the status quo of a persisting norm of secrecy, convincing the political and executive leadership for institutional change. For example, in another case of institutional rearrangements in the telecom sector, the political will of the PMO was instrumental in removing uncertainties between the Department of Telecom and the new private telecom players (Mukherji 2009; see also Mukherji 2014a). In the case of the RTI Act as well, the political will and the transformed State thinking resulted in institutional change. This was reflected in the personal interest that various heads of different governments took in the passage of the bill starting from the NF government in 1989.

Political will was instrumental during the final passage of the bill. On the one hand, Sonia Gandhi, who was the chairperson of the UPA and headed the NAC, took initiative in pushing the bill at the level of the PMO. On the other hand, PM Manmohan Singh himself took personal interest in the bill. Then, was it the political will of the chairperson of the NAC and UPA along with the PM that was instrumental in the final passage of a more progressive bill in 2005? Indeed, internal government papers of the time show close involvement of both Sonia Gandhi and Manmohan Singh, with them often working as a team. A case in point is a letter dated 16 August 2004 from Sonia Gandhi, chairperson of the NAC, to the PM, which suggested a comprehensive list of amendments to the FoI Bill, 2002, on the lines of the commitment made in the CMP (see the letter in Figure 2.1). The PM promptly responded (18 August 2004) by giving assurance that the proposed amendments would be examined and processed by the government on a 'priority basis' (see the letter in Figure 2.2). The close involvement of the PM in the process of clause-wise amendment to the FoI Bill, 2002, was also clear from the internal government papers. Right after assuming office, the PM had instructed the DoPT to work on the RTI Bill on the lines of the commitments made in the CMP and produce a fortnightly report on the follow-up action. The PM directed the DoPT to prepare a note for the cabinet 'expeditiously', prepare a draft bill for the cabinet, put up a notification of the proposed rules on the DoPT website inviting suggestions from the public, and iron out differences regarding the rules with other departments such as the Legislative Department within a clear time frame (PMO Internal Note to DoPT 2004). Significantly, the PM was at that time in charge of the MPPP—the parent ministry of the DoPT. Clear directives were given to the concerned department to finalize the Bill on a priority basis in consultation with other relevant departments and ministries.[23] The PMO's response was on the basis of the NAC's suggestions.

Yet another example that points towards the salience of political will is the letter dated 14 January 2005 sent to the PM by Sonia Gandhi in her capacity as the chairperson of the NAC (Letter from Sonia Gandhi [Chairperson of NAC] Addressed to the PM given in A3 in book-end

[23] The content of the internal government papers and the file notings reflect the close involvement of the PMO in the clause-wise amendment of the FoI Bill, 2002 (Internal Government Document 2004).

FIGURE 2.1 Sonia Gandhi's Letter to the Prime Minister

SONIA GANDHI
CHAIRPERSON
NATIONAL ADVISORY COUNCIL

10, JANPATH
NEW DELHI - 110 011
PHONE - 23012686, 23014481
FAX - 23018651

16th August, 2004

Dear Prime Minister,

You would recall that the National Common Minimum Programme, inter-alia, indicates that "The Right to Information Act, will be made more progressive, participatory and meaningful."

2. In pursuance of the above commitment, the National Advisory Council has, after due deliberation, decided to forward to the Government of India a (draft) amendment to the Freedom of Information Act as inputs towards the fulfillment of this commitment.

3. It is suggested that the name of the un-notified Freedom of Information Act, 2002 is changed to Right to Information Act. The main object of the proposed amendments is to ensure:

1. Maximum disclosure and minimum exemptions consistent with Constitutional provisions.
2. Independent appeal mechanisms.
3. Penalties for failure to provide information as per the law.
4. Effective mechanisms for access to information, and disclosure by authorities.

Further, we see these amendments as an essential step (among others) towards fulfilling the CMP's opening pledge :

"The UPA makes a solemn pledge to the people of our country to provide a government that is corruption-free, transparent and accountable at all times, to provide an administration that is responsible and responsive at all times."

4. A copy of the draft amendment, a tabulation of the original Act and proposed amendments and a note on the proposed amendments are enclosed herewith for your kind attention and for the urgent consideration of the Government.

With regards,

Yours sincerely,

Encl.: as above

Dr. Manmohan Singh,
Prime Minister of India,
New Delhi.

Source: Author procured through use of RTI Act.

Appendices). In her letter, Gandhi raised some pertinent omissions in the draft RTI Bill with regard to the legal competence of the centre to legislate a bill applicable to the States as well, the penalty provisions in the bill, and the fees for procuring information from public authorities. A directive immediately followed from the PM through a letter

FIGURE 2.2 Prime Minister's Reply to Sonia Gandhi

प्रधान मंत्री

Prime Minister

New Delhi
August 18, 2004

Respected Shrimati Sonia Gandhi ji,

I have received your letter of 16th August, 2004 regarding the proposed amendments to the Freedom of Information Act.

I am asking the Department concerned to look into this matter on priority and bring a formal proposal in this regard to the Cabinet as soon as possible.

With regards,

Yours sincerely,

(Manmohan Singh)

Smt. Sonia Gandhi, MP
Chairperson
National Advisory Council
10, Janpath
New Delhi –110 011

Source: Author procured through use of RTI Act.

from the PMO on 27 January 2005 to the DoPT with instructions that the department should immediately examine the issues raised by the NAC and prepare a note (Note from PMO to the Secretary, DoPT 2005) to be submitted for the consideration of the GoM (see A4 of book-end Appendices). Veritably, social actors such as Aruna Roy were instrumental in raising these issues within the NAC[24] (see Chapter 4),

[24] Between Sonia Gandhi's letter to the PM and the PMO's directive, Aruna Roy raised similar issues in a letter (dated 18 January 2005) sent to Pulok Chatterjee, joint secretary with the NAC and the PMO which indicates the involvement of Aruna Roy. This is discussed in Chapter 4.

but the personal involvement and political leadership of Sonia Gandhi and the PM were equally instrumental, showing ample political will. This was corroborated by E.M.S. Natchiappan, who was the chairperson of the DRPSC on Personnel, Public Grievances, Law and Justice during the final passage of the RTI Bill.[25] Natchiappan acknowledged the leadership role played by Sonia Gandhi in ironing out the prevailing hesitancy regarding some specific provisions of the RTI Act.

Political will and leadership needs to be understood in the broader context of institutional change. I hold that both political will and the leadership are part of the State 'powering' (Blyth 2007; Heclo 1974) over an alternative policy choice. As the State thinking moves favourably towards a norm on account of 'puzzling', the State also powers to deepen and institutionalize that norm. In this case it was the norm of openness.

Creating an Epistemic Consensus

Haas (1992: 3) emphasizes the role of an epistemic community in removing uncertainty regarding a policy choice, describing it as 'a network of professionals with recognised expertise and competence in a particular domain and authoritative claim to policy relevant knowledge within that domain or issue area'. Along with the political and policy commitment, the State at this point had also started building the 'epistemic consensus' around the issue. The State was 'powering and puzzling' (Blyth 2007; Heclo 1974) over a policy choice. The powering of the State was through the political and policy commitment as well as through the initiation of policy processes within the executive. The State was also 'puzzling', on the other hand, through seminars and conferences, which were initiated both by the State and by external actors. Technocratic elements from both the State and society were involved in this consensus-building exercise. Seminars and conferences were symptomatic of the initial State–society synergy taking shape, which gained momentum from the late 1990's onwards (see Chapter 4). This section will examine the process of

25 Interview with E.M.S. Natchiappan, 7 April 2015, New Delhi, India.

epistemic consensus-building in forums such as seminars, conferences, and statements delivered in the public domain.

The Centre for Policy Research Workshop, 1990

On 21 and 22 March 1990, a workshop was organized by the Centre for Policy Research (CPR) at New Delhi called 'Freedom of Information and Official Secrets Act' under the aegis of the MHA (CPR 1990). The commitment made by the NF government under the leadership of the PM V.P. Singh provided the impetus and backdrop for this workshop. Government officials, legislators, academicians, journalists, Planning Commission members, PCI members, and senior civil servants from the ministries of home affairs, information and broadcasting, personnel, and external affairs participated in this workshop.

Discussions in the workshop were held around the possible scope of RTI and the contemporary relevance of the OSA. Definition of government information and changes in the contemporary information regime—especially related to the State with regard to social, political, and economic matters—were discussed during this workshop. Rajni Kothari, a member of the Planning Commission, participated in the CPR workshop. Kothari was sympathetic towards the idea of legislation on access to information, which is evident in his statement (2 March 1990) where he emphasized the need for a law on freedom of information as a prerequisite for growth, development, and democracy.[26] Similarly, T.N. Chaturvedi, who was instrumental in bringing out the IIPA volumes on open government in 1980–1 (see Chapter 1), was also part of this workshop.

NAMedia and Fredrich-Ebert-Stiftung International Seminar, 1992

Institutions external to the State organized seminars on the issue where State actors (former and serving) also participated. This is

[26] Rajni Kothari was a member of the Planning Commission from 26 December 1989 to 31 November 1990. Kothari was speaking in a seminar called 'The Future of Indian Democracy' organized by the Centre for the Study of Developing Societies (*ToI* 1990b).

evident in the international seminar jointly organized by NAMedia and Freidrich-Ebert-Stiftung in 1992 on RTI. Justice P.N. Bhagwati and Justice R.S. Sarkaria (then chairman of the PCI) participated in the seminar and stressed on the need for RTI in a democratic system, without which there cannot be people's participation in the decision-making process.[27]

Consumer Education and Research Centre Initiative, 1993

Similarly, in 1993, the CERC, a consumer rights group in Ahmedabad, took significant initiative. In the context of consumer rights, CERC produced a draft of access to information bill under which citizens were granted the right to access information from the government and government undertakings (Gandhi 1996; Girimaji 1994). The bill was an outcome of an international workshop organized by CERC in 1993 following an educational trip undertaken in 1991 by Manubhai Shah, managing trustee of CERC, and Preeti Shah, deputy manager of CERC, to the USA, Canada, and the UK to learn about the FoI laws in these countries. The trip produced a paper entitled 'A Study on the Access to Information: In US, Canada, and UK' published in the journal *Consumer Confrontation* in 1991–2 (Shah and Shah 1991–2). The draft bill of CERC was later used by the Shourie Committee in 1997.

Press Council of India's Committee, 1993

A similar trend can be seen in other institutional arms of the government such as the PCI. In 1996, on the initiative of its chairman, Justice P.B. Sawant, the PCI drafted a bill of freedom of information. Like the CERC bill, this bill also formed the basis for discussions within the Shourie Committee. The PCI RTI draft bill of 1996 needs to be placed in the broader context of initial ideas emerging from within the PCI. In 1993, the PCI constituted a six-member committee to look into the question of national security

[27] The seminar was attended by noted jurists and media representatives such as Dilip Padgaonkar; who was editor of *ToI* at that time (*ToI* 1992a).

and media.[28] While concluding that the concept of national security in India is both narrowly and broadly defined, the committee recommended that the OSA should be amended to ensure greater transparency and accountability in defence matters (*ToI* 1993b). The chairman of the PCI concurred with the committee's view. Speaking during the Journalism Congress, organized by the Department of Journalism, University of Calcutta, in 1993, Justice R.S. Sarkaria, chairman of the PCI, expressed that there was a need to repeal the outdated OSA and related legal provisions and then a new legal framework should be ushered in, in tune with the constitutional provisions such as Article 19 (1) (a).[29]

Annual General Meeting of Uttar Pradesh IAS Officers Association, 1995

The epistemic consensus was also emerging from within the permanent executive. This is evident from the annual general meeting (AGM) of the Uttar Pradesh IAS Officers Association held on 4 July 1995. Officers of the IAS gathered in the AGM unanimously concurred with the proposal that the OSA should either be amended or replaced by a law on RTI. That this was not mere rhetoric is evident from the fact that the proposal was incorporated formally in the secretary's report (Sharma 1995).

Conference of Chief Secretaries, 1996

It is evident that the ideational climate of the times was becoming conducive to the RTI and even the permanent executive was not overtly averse to the idea. This can be seen in the recommendations

[28] Members of the committee were Geeta Mukherjee, an MP; B.G. Verghese, winner of the Ramon Magsaysay award for exceptional journalism; Ramu Patel, editor of *Western Times* in Gujarat; Harihar Swaroop, Press Trust of India (PTI); R.C. Pandit, *Aaj* (a Hindi newspaper from Uttar Pradesh); and Umashankar Padhnis.

[29] Justice R.S. Sarkaria was delivering the keynote address during the Journalism Congress on 16 September 1993 in Calcutta (*ToI* 1993c).

of the Conference of Chief Secretaries held on 28 November 1996. The Conference of Chief Secretaries was significant as the conference concurred with the view of the PM during the UF government and stressed on the need for 'efficient, open, responsive, accountable, clean and dynamically adjusting administration at all levels'. The conference recommended, 'It is necessary to introduce greater transparency and openness in the functioning of government and public bodies. This would cover, for example, movement towards a Right to Information Act, transparent and well publicised procedures for approvals by the general public.'[30]

Chief Ministers' Conference, 1997

Similarly, the Chief Ministers' Conference was held on 24 May 1997 at the behest of PM I.K. Gujral during the UF government. The theme of the conference was 'Effective and Responsive Government'. In its resolution, the conference decided to work specifically towards three main themes: (*a*) accountable and citizen-friendly government; (*b*) transparency and RTI; and (*c*) improving the performance and integrity of public service. Among other things, the conference collectively recognized that the idea that lack of openness in administration results in corruption is in direct contradiction to the ethos of democracy and transparency. By way of concrete action, the conference resolved that the GoI would enact legislation on freedom of information by the end of 1997.

National Institute of Rural Development Seminar on Right to Information, 1997

Autonomous institutions located within the government complemented the consensus-building exercise. The National Institute of Rural Development organized a national-level seminar on 3 and 4 September 1997 on the RTI. A mix of eminent jurists, activists,

30 Secretary of MPPP's communication to the secretaries of various ministries. Letter dated 5 May 1997.

academicians, journalists, senior civil servants, and legislators attended this seminar. A draft bill was prepared in the seminar on the basis of the PCI's draft bill and the H.D. Shourie Committee's bill.

Shourie Committee, 1997: Epistemic Formation within the State

Moving beyond seminars, workshops, and conferences, epistemic elements were introduced consciously by the State within the government committees themselves. This was evident in the membership of the Shourie Committee. As in the case of the CPR workshop, the Shourie working group also points towards the epistemic formation within the policy processes of the State. The leadership of the working group, Shourie and Sorabjee, were experts in their own right, which is evident from their involvement prior to their formal engagement in the working group.

Haas (1992) argues that the epistemic community with its control of knowledge removes uncertainties within the State regarding a policy choice, which in turn impacts the policy thinking within the State. Similar process seems to have taken shape within the Shourie Committee. For instance, the working group was divided in its views, which is apparent from the minutes of the first meeting of the working group held on 10 January 1997 (Proceedings of the First Meeting of the Working Group 1997). While H.D. Shourie in his opening remarks stressed on the need for the right to access official information, a joint secretary in the MHA expressed the ministry's reservations regarding the implementation of Justice Sawant's PCI RTI Bill. A deputy secretary of the DoPT pointed to the resource constraints and the financial costs involved in making the information available to citizens. A representative from the Ministry of Railways raised an issue regarding the extent to which the internal workings of an organization should be opened up and pointed to the generation of fruitless work, which might result in frittering away the energies of officials. However, the joint secretary of the DoPT, the joint secretary of the Ministry of Information and Broadcasting, and the additional secretary unanimously concurred with Shourie's proposal to open up information related to administrative functioning for the general public. According to them, the difficulties and constraints expressed by others were a symptom of the existing mindset of the executive, which should change. It is pertinent to note that in the first meeting itself, Shourie framed the issue as being about 'freedom' of information rather than a 'right' to it, as calling it a 'right' would make the proposed legislation more susceptible to litigation and as freedom has a much broader and more positive connotation. The divided quorum of the first meeting was moving towards a unanimous concurrence by the time the second meeting of the working group took place on 18 January 1997. Soli Sorabjee laid out the principles, which should dictate the approach of the working group. These principles were mentioned in the final report discussed earlier. Sorabjee also stressed upon the strengthening and capacity building of institutions and procedures concurrently with the framing of law, drawing upon the experiences in the USA and Australia. With their expert knowledge in the field, both Shourie and Sorabjee were able to iron out the difference of opinions within the committee.

The discussions, resolutions, and recommendations of the seminars and conferences were significant from four standpoints. First, they complimented the ongoing internal processes within the State and epistemically deepened the State's thinking on a possible policy path. Second, they provided an opportunity to actors with similar ideas on FoI or RTI to come together and reach an 'epistemic consensus'. This resulted in the deepening of ideational churning, which cumulatively had the impact of affecting institutional change.

Third, these participants and discussions at the seminars and conferences point towards an early process of an 'epistemic community' emerging around the FoI or RTI. The role of the epistemic community became profound in the final passage of the bill with the involvement of the NCPRI (discussed in Chapter 4). These were early signs of the epistemic formation around the issue.

Fourth, an 'ideational confluence' seems to have emerged. This is evident from the fact that various actors, such as legislators, bureaucrats, jurists, and journalists were expressing similar sentiments around the idea of FoI or RTI. It is clear from the discussions presented that both political and permanent executives were in sync regarding the idea and were not necessarily against the issue of openness of the State.

Move towards Right to Information at the Sub-national Level

While the passage of the legislation was being worked out at the central level, the ideational narrative was finding expression in the form of concrete 'norms' taking root at the sub-national level (see Table 2.5).

For instance, Harsh Mander,[31] a 1980-batch IAS officer of the Madhya Pradesh cadre, took one of the earlier initiatives in 1996

Table 2.5 State RTI Laws and Ordinances

1997	Tamil Nadu was the first state to pass the RTI Act in 1997. The RTI law was passed by the legislative assembly completely with the government initiative, there was no civil society involvement in the law.
1997	Goa RTI Act, 1997, was enacted with the state government's initiative.
1997	In Karnataka, executive orders were passed to make information available to citizens. State law was passed in 2000.
2000	Uttar Pradesh adopted the 'Code of Practice on Access to Information'.
2000	The Maharashtra State Act was modelled after Tamil Nadu. It was later replaced by a more radical ordinance in 2002.
2001	A similar law was enacted in Delhi.
2002	Assam passed a similar law.
2003	Madhya Pradesh enacted a similar RTI Act.
2003	Jammu and Kashmir's RTI Act was passed into law.

Source: Author

[31] Harsh Mander was one of the core actors in the NCPRI as well. He extended his support to the MKSS and was the linking factor in the NCPRI, bringing together varied actors. Mander was instrumental in organizing the first NCPRI meeting at LBSNAA, Mussoorie, along with N.C. Saxena.

when he was the commissioner of the Bilaspur Division in Madhya Pradesh. Through a government order (2 September 1996), the people of Bilaspur were granted the RTI for the public distribution system (PDS) (Order No. 8344/Samanya/Sa.Vi.Pra./96). A penalty clause was applicable to the relevant levels within the hierarchy of the PDS system in case the information was not provided to the consumer within fifteen days. In the second phase, on 26 November 1996, the RTI in Bilaspur was extended to other departments such as transport, water resources, literacy, employment relating to any vacant posts of government/local bodies, and the Mid-Day Meal Scheme under the Department of Rural Development. Notably, Mander shared a note on the RTI with the secretary of the Department of Administrative Reforms and Public Grievances on 28 March 1997, when the Shourie Committee was constituted to examine the passage of the RTI Bill at the centre (153/14/Steno/97).

The Bilaspur experiment was followed by the Madhya Pradesh government drafting an RTI Bill in 1997 and passing it in August 1998. However, the president of India did not assent to the Act and so it could not come into force. Despite that, the state government continued on the policy path. In February 1998, through a government order, the RTI was extended to 50 departments that were listed in a compendium of the Department of General Administration entitled *Janane Ka Haq* (Right to Know) (Paul 2006). Later in 2002, the Madhya Pradesh government enacted another law titled Madhya Pradesh Jankari ki Swatantrata Adhiniyam, 2002 (FoI Act), which received the governor's assent on 24 January 2003 and was published in the *Madhya Pradesh Gazette* on 31 January 2003. The Act could not be operationalized. The Madhya Pradesh government under CM Digvijay Singh of the Indian National Congress took a number of similar initiatives, such as decentralization by establishing panchayati raj institutions, devolution of finances, and empowering of rural local bodies in order to implement rural development projects such as citizens' charter, right to recall, employment guarantee scheme, watershed programme development, and joint forest management in tribal areas (Shrivastava 2010). The idea was to have a participatory model of governance resulting in a responsive administration. The policy process on RTI in Madhya Pradesh has to be located within this broader process of an evolving institutional framework during Digvijay's government.[32]

Similar initiatives were seen in other states. On 5 April 1995, Rajasthan CM Bhairon Singh Shekhawat announced in the legislative assembly that a sarpanch (village head) or a panchayat (village government) could obtain photocopies of records relating to rural development work undertaken between 1990 and 1995 on payment. It is significant to keep in mind that the societal processes were also shaping up outside the State system at this point led by the MKSS. The process at this level of society was directly and inextricably linked to the movements occurring within the State, where the pressure on the State to deliver on its commitments was being built from outside (the MKSS and related processes in the societal realm will be discussed in Chapter 4). State–society dynamics played a significant role at the state level and later at the central level

The case of Rajasthan can be treated as the epicentre for such State–society movement. However, society triggering a policy movement within the State was visible earlier in some other cases as well. For instance, the Department of Urban Development of the Government of Maharashtra through a circular dated 11 September 1992 granted access to information specifically related to the development permissions granted by the urban development authorities. The circular (TPS/3692/1606/UD-11) directed the urban planning authorities to allow people to 'inspect development permissions granted by the planning authority including approved building plans and other related paper' on demand. It also clarified that this

[32] S.C. Behar, who was the chief secretary of the state during Digvijay Singh's tenure as the CM, concurred with this. Behar pointed towards a broader process of governance within which the initiatives around RTI emerged. Bureaucrats such as S.C. Behar had a role to play in this. He says:

> I was the one who gave him the idea, convincing him [Digvijay Singh] was not difficult. Before I became the chief secretary I gave him a long list of things to be implemented, which included ideas on transparency and accountability. It was not difficult to convince him about the idea of empowering citizens through RTI, like Gram Swaraj. (Interview with S.C. Behar, former Chief Secretary, 8 May 2014, Madhya Pradesh)

directive would 'not be applicable to cases where due to security reasons information cannot be revealed'. The circular was in response to the direction issued by the high court (HC) on the writ petition of an environmental action group called Bombay Environmental Action Group (BEAG). In yet another example, on 18 October 1993, the Gujarat government withdrew OSA from twelve villages, which were in the vicinity of the Narmada Dam project. The action was prompted by the HC order on the issue of the petition filed by the Narmada Bachao Andolan (*ToI* 1993d). These were initial signs of push from the societal realm playing the role of catalysts in these policy steps adopted by the state governments. The role of judicial pronouncement is an important link in the multi-dimensional processes contributing to the evolution of RTI (elaborated and discussed in Chapter 3).

In 1997, Tamil Nadu enacted the RTI Act. This initiative needs to be placed within the broader political context of the state. In the backdrop of the new government, the DMK led the front, taking the office in Tamil Nadu in 1996. The DMK under the leadership of M. Karunanidhi replaced Anna Dravida Munnetra Kazhagam (ADMK) amidst widespread allegations of corruption and high-handedness against the ADMK chief Jayalalitha. DMK's manifesto promised investigation into these allegations along with the promise of establishing an 'ombudsman like institution and provide an open, transparent, and corruption-free administration' (*ToI* 1997a). On assuming office, the CM made an announcement during the budget speech of 1997–8 that the government would enact the legislation on RTI. Subsequently, the Right to Tamil Nadu Information Act was passed on 5 May 1997 followed by the notification, the Tamil Nadu Right to Information Rules, 1997, published in the *Tamil Nadu Government Gazette* of 6 May 1998 (From Public and Rehabilitation Department, Government of Tamil Nadu, to DoPT 2000). An incumbent government assuming power in the backdrop of corruption and mismanagement allegations against the previous government is a significant process within which the push for openness and transparency has to be placed. This can be seen at the central level as well, in the case of the Janata government of 1977 and the NF government of 1989. Similar to Digvijay Singh's state of Madhya

Pradesh, Karunanidhi's Tamil Nadu also saw a number of initiatives being adopted by the DMK government, such as the establishment of the State Human Rights Commission; the removal of the single tender system, which was the source of massive corruption in the previous government; and the setting up of a high-level committee under Justice Ramanujam to study sources of corruption, to name a few (*ToI* 1997a). The Tamil Nadu RTI Act needs to be placed in this broader context of initiatives adopted by the new DMK government. The law, which was enacted, was rather weak in the view of legal experts.

Similarly, in 1997, the Karnataka state government issued executive orders to display and make available records related to all development projects in urban and rural local bodies (UDD 443 MLR 97). The orders were expanded as the Karnataka Right to Information Ordinance on 25 August 2000, granting citizens the right to access information, which was to be given by the public authorities (DPAL 29 Shasana 2000). During the same period Goa passed the RTI Act in 1997.

The movement around the RTI at the sub-national level points towards three crucial processes.

First, state laws and ordinances provide continuity to policy movement at the centre. The state legislations and initiatives provided an ideational base for the future course of the policy formulation, which was evident from the fact that all the subsequent DRPSCs, GoMs, and government task forces constituted at the central level referred to the state Acts as a starting point.

Second, the specific policy formulation around the RTI was part of the broader process of governance, which was taking shape in these states.

Finally, these initiatives emerged right after the Chief Ministers' Conference in 1997, which, along with the RTI, adopted an action plan on initiating reforms to create an accountable and citizen-friendly government. Citizen's charter, decentralization, grievance redressal mechanisms, and systems of independent monitoring are some initiatives that constituted the action plan. It is noteworthy that on 2 July 1997, N.C. Saxena, secretary of the Department of Rural Development, communicated to all the state governments to grant citizens access to information at the panchayat level. Referring to the forthcoming Chief Ministers' Conference, the letter directed the state governments to pass orders to the rural local bodies to display all the vital information related to allocation and expenditure of funds in the development projects, to open all records for inspection, and grant the citizens access to information by allowing them to get photocopies of the documents on demand. This points towards the broader process of governance within which the RTI processes were shaping up at the state level.[33]

***

In this phase, we see ideas becoming embedded in the State thinking, which is evident in the articulations by various governments in both commitment and policy intent. Moreover, starting from the NF government in 1989, the policy processes within the State to enact a law on the freedom of information show that the norm of openness was in the process of layering out the nested norm of secrecy, and eventually displaced it in 2005. Institutional change was a two-layered process.

In the first layer (discussed in Chapter 1), one can see nascent ideas on openness were appearing on the fringes even while the norm of secrecy was becoming further embedded in the State's administrative framework through the 1967 amendment of the OSA. In this phase, the ideas were emerging in a very rudimentary form. At the same time, the norm of secrecy was becoming institutionalized, and was pulling the narrative in two directions. Additionally, opposition politics was deepening ideas of openness, which were in the process of becoming nuanced after the Janata Party government assumed power in 1977. This found expression in various pronouncements, public statements, election manifestos, studies, and moves from within the legislature (such as private members' bills).

[33] Saxena was also part of the NCPRI, and along with Mander was instrumental in organizing a meeting at LBSNAA, Mussoorie, where initial ideas about the NCPRI and its agenda were discussed. This linkage is explored further in Chapter 4.

This chapter shows the second stage of layering. In this stage, the ideational churning transitioned from being part of opposition politics to becoming part of mainstream politics. The norm of openness became embedded within the State thinking which, in turn, played a consequential role in initiating policy processes within the executive. The norm of openness was accumulating on top of the established norm of secrecy. This resulted in State initiatives to channelize the embedded ideas to form a concrete policy, making institutional change inevitable, a sine qua non. This is similar to the process of institutional change discussed by Mahoney and Thelen (2010). In their account of incremental, slow-moving institutional change, they present a model of political processes in which institutional change occurs due to layering of new structures on top of old ones (Mahoney and Thelen 2010: 13).

The evidence examined points towards the role and extent of the State as well. In this sense, the State needs to be brought 'back in' (Skocpol 1985) to explain institutional change. This is distinct from the linear view of societal interests playing an instrumental role in influencing the State's policy thinking and affecting institutional change. The evidence examined shows how the cumulative push of emerging ideas played a consequential role in shaping concrete norms and policies, eventually leading to the tipping point of institutional change. Emerging ideas eventually became embedded in the State thinking and led to change in the State's policy choices and preferences. The long-drawn churning process from within the State provided an ideational base for future change in the norm and the final push towards institutional change. In a sense, the institutional change marked by the occurrence of the RTI Act in 2005 was path-dependent on the emerging ideational narrative that I have traced in the evidence presented previously. It was the weight and momentum of earlier ideas on openness that reached critical mass in 2005. The ideational move around openness and transparency gradually and cumulatively shaped the interests of both political and permanent executive in favour of access to information or RTI.

3 Constitutional Interpretation by the Judiciary

Right to Know Inherent in Article 19 (1) (a)

This chapter provides continuity to the arguments I have established in the Chapters 1 and 2. In this light it is pertinent to examine the judiciary in depth, as it is a significant arm of the State. This chapter examines the trajectory of ideas emanating from the judiciary. In some significant cases, the SC has interpreted Article 19 (1) (a) of the Constitution of India, which grants citizens the freedom of expression and speech, as a fundamental right. This interpretation provides the link to the long-drawn process of emerging ideas on openness emanating from within the State and specifically from the judiciary. Here, I trace the emergence of ideas from the judiciary by discussing judicial verdicts, and by examining them in the broader context of the emerging discourse around openness in government affairs, which eventually led to the legislation on RTI.

The judicial interpretation of Article 19 (1) (a) of the Constitution in different phases is important for understanding the process of norm formation. This interpretation found expression in numerous verdicts of the SC and the HCs. In these cases, the articulation of the judiciary demonstrates how it often checked the State's overzealous quest for secrecy. To understand this role of the judiciary, one has to keep in mind the distinction between what Baxi (2010) calls the 'political State', which is represented and maintained by the permanent and political executive, and the 'constitutional State', whose custodians are the judges or the court. The judicial verdicts provided constitutional basis to the ideas of free speech, rights, transparency, openness, and the RTI; deepened the ideational churning process ongoing within the State; and resulted in the convergence of both ideas and policies between different arms of the State. This adds credence to the argument that the incremental and cumulative role of ideas was instrumental in institutional change.

The process unfolded in two phases. In the first phase, starting from the early 1950s until 1975 (and ending just before the national emergency was imposed), the initial ideas on openness from the judiciary emerged, albeit in a nascent form, and contributed to the process of norm formation at the macro level (largely in relation to the press). The judicial interpretation of Article 19 (1) (a) of the Indian Constitution that deals with freedom of expression and speech formed the basis of these initial ideas. These verdicts are significant insofar as they establish the linkage between the freedom of press and the importance of information flow and dissemination in a democracy.

The second phase covers the period from 1975 until the early 2000s. This phase is marked by the moving of the judiciary beyond the specifics of freedom of press and examining the question of openness in government affairs, challenging the locked-in norm of secrecy. The emerging judicial challenge to the norm of secrecy was framed especially with regard to the State's tendency to treat government papers as confidential or secret. Significantly, the latter part of this phase coincided with the emerging trend of public interest litigations (PILs) in the courts on various public issues. In this phase, the judicial stance was categorical in interpreting the Constitution in such a manner as to recognize the right to know as a fundamental right, an integral part of the freedom of expression and speech, and provisioned for in Article 19 (1) (a). This interpretation was not only challenging the norm of secrecy but was, in some senses, also displacing the persisting norm. Significantly, the Constitution of India served as an ideational base for the judicial verdicts. Finally, I will examine the judicial precedent on openness and transparency, which formed a major part of the policy discussions on RTI.

Admittedly, the pattern of judicial verdicts in India has been ambiguous and contradictory on many occasions. Judicial verdicts at times can go against constitutional provisions. This often emanates from the constitutional interpretation. Take, for example, Article 19 (1) (a), which grants the right to freedom of speech and expression, and sub-Article 19 (2), which places (reasonable) restrictions on it. Seervai argues that:

> Laws which fall under sub-Art. 19 (2) are expressly permitted by our Constitution and the problem in India is to determine whether an impugned law falls within Art. 19 (2), and *that is essentially a problem of construction*. No doubt Art. 19 (2) must *prima facie* be presumed to be constitutionally valid and due weight must be given to the legislative judgment on the question of reasonableness, *though that judgment is subject to judicial review* [my emphases]. (Seervai 1983: 490)

Hence, I am not claiming that the path of judicial verdicts around Article 19 (1) (a) is linear. The multi-linear path of judicial verdicts is not the focus of this chapter; instead, it discusses cases that are relevant from the perspective of casting light on the role of the judiciary in the norm formation around openness, transparency, and access to information.

Phase I (1950–75)

In this phase, I will examine some significant judicial verdicts starting from the early 1950s till 1975. The judicial cases examined in this section will demonstrate two points. First, that the initial ideas on rights related to freedom of expression and speech or free speech were important in shaping the early discourse on openness. This was primarily related to cases that came up for hearing before the SC in relation to freedom of press.

Second, this phase indicates a polarity of ideas, where the State is curtailing free speech and expression while the judiciary through its constitutional interpretation is upholding it. This is consistent with my argument about polarity of ideas discussed in Chapter 1. At this stage the issue of access to information did not directly emerge in the verdicts, which primarily focused on freedom of expression and speech.

It is pertinent to point out that the judicial verdicts upholding free speech during this phase played an important role in sustaining democracy in a newly independent State. In the absence of free speech, democracy itself could have been in jeopardy. In this sense, the churning represented by this polarity was part of the evolving democracy in India. The verdicts during this phase underline the norm of openness through the notion of free speech and expression.

Judiciary and Freedom of Press

Judicial precedent on Article 19 (1) (a), in terms of interpreting and ensuring the rights of the citizens enshrined as the fundamental rights in the Indian Constitution and going beyond the mere legal interpretation, can be seen in a series of judicial verdicts starting right after Independence.[1] Cases such as *Brij Bhushan* vs *the State of Delhi* (1950), *Express Newspapers (Private)* vs *The Union of India* (1959), *Romesh Thappar* vs *the Union of Madras* (1950), *State of Madras* vs *V.G. Row Union of India and State* (1952), *Dwarkadas Shrinivas of Bombay* vs *The Sholapur Spinning & Weaving* (1953), and *Virendra* vs *The State of Punjab* (1959) were crucial from the judicial standpoint on Article 19 (1) (a) of the Indian Constitution.

Significantly, in these judicial pronouncements the court stressed on the importance of granting and ensuring rights to the citizens. In these judgements the courts took a broader view of the Constitution as opposed to the 'narrow' and 'pedantic' interpretation. As the judiciary put it in the *Sakal Papers (P) Ltd and Ors* vs *The Union of India* case in 1961, while considering the 'nature and content of those [fundamental] rights the Court must not be too astute to interpret the language of the Constitution in so literal a sense as to whittle them down'. Further, the judiciary opined,

[1] The judicial precedent of these cases has been cited in the judgement on *Sakal Papers (P) Ltd and Ors* vs *The Union of India* on 25 September 1961. The author has taken the reference for these cases from this judgement.

> The Court must interpret the Constitution in a manner which would enable the citizen to enjoy the rights guaranteed by it in the fullest measure subject, of course, to permissible restrictions. Bearing this principle in mind it would be clear that the right to freedom of speech and expression carries with it the right to publish and circulate one's ideas, opinions and views with complete freedom and by resorting to any available means of publication subject.

Continuing with this stance, in *Romesh Thappar* vs *the Union of Madras* (1950), the court observed that it (the court) is the 'the protector and guarantor of fundamental rights' and that 'there can be no doubt that freedom of speech and expression includes freedom of propagation of ideas, and that freedom is ensured by the freedom of circulation'. In the following section I will examine this significant case.

The Romesh Thappar and Brij Bhushan Cases (1950)

The Romesh Thappar case came before the SC in the context of the Madras government declaring the communist party illegal and banning a left-oriented magazine *Crossroads* as it was critical of PM Jawaharlal Nehru's policies. This was followed by another petition that came for hearing before the SC in the context of the chief commissioner of Delhi's pre-censorship order against the right-wing magazine *Organizer* (patronized by the Rashtriya Swayamsevak Sangh [RSS]) to submit the pre-published content of communal matters for scrutiny before the Delhi government. The order was challenged as a direct attack on petitioners' right to freedom of expression and speech under Article 19 (1) (a) of the Indian Constitution.[2]

2 The editor of the magazine, M.M. Malkani, and printer and publisher, Brij Bhushan, challenged the order. The order was served to the magazine under Section 7 of the East Punjab Public Safety Act, 1949, which required the editor and the publisher to submit all communal news items, views, photographs, and cartoons regarding Pakistan other than those procured from official sources or supplied by news agencies.

The court upheld the petitioners' right to freedom of expression and speech viewing pre-censorship of a journal as restrictive to the freedom of press. The court delivered a judgement interpreting Article 19 (2) of the Constitution, which, while allowing the provisions of Article 19 (1) (a), dealt with the conditional restrictions of freedom of expression and speech, such as interest of sovereignty and integrity of India, security of India, friendly relations with foreign States, public order, incitement, and defamation. In both the Romesh Thappar case and the Brij Bhushan case (regarding *Organizer* magazine), the SC found the government orders in excess of the scope provided under Article 19 (2) and found that the government action was more extreme than it had been in cases of serious seditious offences on security of the State. The court was of the view that since the restrictive provisions under Article 19 (2) were wide in scope they should be done away with as they were in direct conflict with the provisions of Article 19 (1) (a) (Mirchandani 1977: 16; Rai 2011: 73). Interestingly, the judicial verdicts emanated from both the far left and far right of democratic politics in India—the Romesh Thappar case representing the left and the Brij Bhushan case representing the right.

Polarity of Ideas: Openness vs Secrecy—the First Amendment to the Constitution

It is in the broader context of these earlier judicial verdicts upholding freedom of expression and speech in relation to the press and the court's placing a check on the restrictions imposed under the constitutional provisions of Article 19 (2) that PM Jawaharlal Nehru sought to introduce the first amendment to the Indian Constitution (in response to the judicial verdicts in the Romesh Thappar and Brij Bhushan cases).[3]

[3] The Statement of Objects and Reasons to the proposed Constitution (First Amendment) Act, 1951, clearly outlines PM Nehru's perceived anxiety and angst regarding the ramifications of the 'recent' (Romesh Thappar and Brij Bhushan cases) judicial verdicts. It states that,

The first amendment proposed to curtail the freedom of press and strengthen the government's control over the restrictions by adding a subclause to Article 19 that sought to empower the State to legislate on matters relating to public order, incitement to an offence, and the affecting of friendly relations with foreign States (*ToI* 1951b). Indeed, the original draft of the Constitution included the terms 'sedition' and 'public order' aiming to partially inhibit the freedom of speech. However, in the final draft both these terms were eliminated from the Constitution. The first amendment sought to alter the existing constitutional framework dealing with strings attached to the freedom of expression and speech by inserting terms such as 'public order' and 'relations with friendly States' in Article 19 (2) and strategically placing the word 'reasonable' before 'restrictions'. This meant that Article 19 (2) provided the State with enough safeguard against the use of the restrictive provisions of Article 19 (2).[4]

During the last fifteen months of the working of the Constitution, certain difficulties have been brought to light by judicial decisions and pronouncements specially with regard to the chapter on fundamental rights. The citizen's right to freedom of speech and expression guaranteed by Article 19 (1) (a) has been held by some courts to be so comprehensive as not to render a person culpable even if he advocates murder and other crimes of violence. In other countries with written constitutions, freedom of speech and of the press is not regarded as debarring the State from punishing or preventing abuse of this freedom. The citizen's right to practise any profession or to carry on any occupation, trade or business conferred by Article 19 (1) (g) is subject to reasonable restrictions which the laws of the State may impose 'in the interests of general public'. While the words cited are comprehensive enough to cover any scheme of nationalization which the State may undertake, it is desirable to place the matter beyond doubt by a clarificatory addition to Article 19(6). (18 June 1951)

[4] The amendment proposed: Amendment of Article 19 and validation of certain laws. (1) In Article 19 of the Constitution, (a) for clause (2), the following clause shall be substituted, and the said clause shall be deemed always to have been enacted in the following form, namely: '(2) Nothing in sub-clause (a) of clause (1) shall affect the operation of any existing law, or prevent the State from making any law, in so far as such law imposes *reasonable* [my emphasis] restrictions on the exercise of the right conferred

The move to amend the Constitution was opposed by the press, parliamentarians, and the courts alike.[5] Discussions in the parliament were marked by fierce opposition spearheaded by Syama Prasad Mukherjee (*ToI* 1951c).[6] The legislative move towards the first amendment indicates the emerging narrative around transparency being pulled both ways (the first phase discussed previously is also characterized by this tendency of a two-sided narrative). The judicial interpretation of upholding freedom of expression and speech represented openness while the move towards the first amendment to the Constitution illustrated the other end of the narrative, that is, secrecy.

Judiciary Strikes Balance between Freedom of Expression and Speech, and Restrictions Imposed on This Freedom

The judiciary, however, has interpreted the Constitution in such a manner as to strike a balance between the freedom of expression

---

by the said sub-clause in the interests of the security of the State, *friendly relations with foreign States, public order*, [my emphasis] decency or morality, or in relation to contempt of court, defamation or incitement to an offence.'

[5] Organizations such as the Supreme Court Bar Association and All India Newspaper Editors Conference (AINEC) opposed this move. Deshbandhu Gupta, president of AINEC described the amendment as a 'sorry episode' and a 'tragedy'. The Supreme Court Bar Association regarded the step as being taken in 'indecent haste' and immoral (*ToI* 1951a, 1951d).

[6] Parliamentary proceedings during this debate were reported to have reached 'lowest level of parliamentary dignity' according to a report in the *ToI*. Syama Prasad Mukherjee charged that the amendment sought to curtail freedom and liberty merely sixteen months after it was consciously granted to the citizens. Mukherjee added that the logic given by the government is 'riddled with inconsistencies' and the bill was liable to be misused for repression. Jawaharlal Nehru in his reply angrily charged Mukherjee of 'scandalous speeches', 'falsehoods', and 'lies'. Nehru further added, 'We have put up with much from a few members who dared to oppose us.' Mukherjee thought this statement to be of a 'dictator' (*ToI* 1951c).

and speech and restrictions imposed on this fundamental right under Article 19 (2). In the significant case of *Kedar Nath Singh* vs *State of Bihar* (1962) related to sedition, the court inferred from the Constitution and judicial precedent that the ambit of Article 19 (2) and laws that place restrictions on fundamental right to free speech and expression need to be applied in a narrow legal sense so that they are not ultra vires of Article 19 (1) (a).

Significantly, in this case the judiciary upheld the constitutionality of the law of sedition as distinct from the citizens right to freedom of expression and speech under Article 19 (1) (a). In this case the petitioner, Kedar Nath Singh, belonged to the Forward Communist Party in the state of Bihar and had delivered a speech attacking the Congress Party on corruption and black marketing as well as Vinoba Bhave's attempts of land reform (calling him an agent of the Congress Party), and calling for revolution by overthrowing the nexus between the Congress Party, capitalists, and the zamindars (feudal landlords) (see also Narrain 2010).[7] The trial court convicted Kedar Nath Singh

[7] Vinoba Bhave was a well-known social and political reformer who started the *bhoodan* (land gift) movement in 1951 to ameliorate the inequity in land distribution. On 26 May 1953, Kedar Nath Singh delivered a speech that led the government to initiate sedition charges against him,

> Today the dogs of the C.I.D. are loitering around Barauni. Many official dogs are sitting even in this meeting. The people of India drove out the Britishers from this country and elected these Congress goondas to the gaddi and seated them on it. To-day these Congress goondas are sitting on the gaddi due to mistake of the people. When we drove out the Britishers, we shall strike and turn out these Congress goondas as well. These official dogs will also be liquidated along with these Congress goondas … The blood of our brothers—mazdoors and Kisans—is being sucked. The capitalists and the zamindars of this country help these Congress goondas. These zamindars and capitalists will also have to be brought before the peoples court along with these Congress goondas … The Forward Communist Party does not believe in the doctrine of vote itself. The party had always been believing in revolution and does so even at present. We believe in that revolution, which will come and in the flames of which the capitalists, zamindars and the Congress leaders of India, who have made it their profession to loot the country, will be reduced to ashes and on their ashes will be established a Government of

under Section 124A[8] and 505B of the IPC sentencing him to rigorous imprisonment for one year. Singh appealed the conviction in the HC of Patna, which upheld the conviction and rejected the appeal. The appeal found its way to the division bench of the SC in 1959, where the appeal was made against the conviction on the grounds of Section 124A and 505B being in direct contradiction with the fundamental rights (freedom of expression and speech) provided under Article 19 (1) (a) of the Constitution.

Since the appeal was concerned with constitutional provisions, it was eventually referred to the constitutional bench of the SC in 1961, which, in its judgement, made a clear distinction between the concept of State as 'government established by law' and the bureaucracy as 'person's for the time being engaged in carrying on the administration'. The court opined that a distinction needs to be made between the two, where, 'disloyalty to Government established by law is not the same thing as commenting in strong terms upon the measures or Acts of Government, or its agencies, so as to ameliorate the condition of the people or to secure the cancellation or alteration of those Acts or measures by lawful means'.

In this case, the judiciary cautioned the necessary delineation between laws on sedition and ensuring freedom of expression and speech by striking a balance between the needs to enforce legislations

---

> the poor and the downtrodden people of India. It will be a mistake to expect anything from the Congress rulers. They (Congress rulers) have set up V. Bhave in the midst of the people by causing him wear a langoti in order to divert the people's attention from their mistakes. To-day Vinova is playing a drama on the stage of Indian politics.'

8 Section 124A of the IPC deals with sedition. The law on sedition state,

> Whoever, by words, either spoken or written, or by signs, or by visible representation, or otherwise, brings or attempts to bring into hatred or contempt, or excites or attempts to excite disaffection towards, the Government established by law in [India], shall be punished with [imprisonment for life], to which fine may be added, or with imprisonment which may extend to three years, to which fine may be added, or with fine.

related to sedition and 'to protect and guarantee the freedom of speech and expression, which is the *sine quo non* of a democratic form of Government that [our] Constitution has established'.

The judiciary in this significant case constitutionally reiterated the citizens' right to free speech and expression with regard to the government's actions or policies as long as the citizen's expression does not incite the people to overthrow the 'government established by law' with the 'intention of creating public disorder'. The case provides an important judicial interpretation of the Constitution where the legislative restrictions placed on the right to freedom of expression and speech is constitutionally upheld but within the ambit of the existing law, making clear distinction between intent to harm the State and criticism directed against the administration. The judiciary held that a wider application of Article 19 (2) that is beyond its defined scope would render it unconstitutional: 'The explanations appended to the main body of the section make it clear that criticism of public measures or comment on Government action, however strongly worded, would be within reasonable limits and would be consistent with the fundamental right of freedom of speech and expression.'

The verdict established a judicial precedent, where the government's attempt to place restrictions on freedom of expression and speech (through the first amendment) was 'constitutionally' subverted by, first, limiting the scope and application of such legal restrictions as outlined in Article 19 (2); and second, by making a clear distinction between the speech and expression with the intention of overthrowing the State, creating public disorder, and directing criticism against the government's policies and administrative behaviour. This was in continuation with the earlier judicial stance taken on fundamental right of freedom of expression and speech in cases such as *Romesh Thappar* vs *The State of Madras* and *Brij Bhushan* vs *The State of Delhi* where the court declared the restrictions imposed by the State on freedom of expression and speech as unconstitutional and void.

Similar constitutional questions were dealt with by the constitutional benches of the SC in earlier cases of *Ramji Lal Modi* vs *The*

State of UP (1957)[9] and *Virendra* vs *The State of Punjab* (1957). In the former verdict, the court declared that Article 259A is well within the ambit of restrictions outlined in Article 19 (2). In *Virendra* vs *The State of Punjab* (1957), the court upheld Article 19 (1) (a) categorically expressing, 'There is and can be no dispute that the right to freedom of speech and expression carries with it the right to propagate and circulate one's views and opinions subject to reasonable restrictions'.

In yet another important judicial verdict, the SC delineated the relationship between Article 19 (1) (a) and other existing statues by clarifying that the freedom of expression and speech are 'fundamental rights'. This question came up before the SC in *Jamuna Prasad Mukhariya and Ors* vs *Lacchi Ram and Ors* (1954). An election tribunal of Gwalior ruled the election of the top two candidates as void and declared that two other candidates in the list be declared elected instead. The election tribunal's ruling was challenged in a petition. The allegation that was placed before the election tribunal was that the elected candidates used unfair election practices such as distributing pamphlets that contained unfair statements about the personal character and conduct of other candidates. This was seen as a major corrupt election practice violating Section 123 (5) of the Representation of People's Act, 1951. Another violation was making systemic appeals to a specific low-caste community (Chamar caste) to vote in their favour—considered a minor corrupt practice under Section 124 (5) of the Act. Both these provisions were challenged in the SC as ultra vires of Article 19 (1) (a) of the Constitution. The SC rejected this contention, being of the view that the laws invoked did not prohibit the freedom of speech. The SC stated:

> These laws do not stop a man from speaking. They merely prescribe conditions, which must be observed if he wants to enter Parliament. The right to stand as a candidate and contest an election is not a

[9] In this case, Ramji Lal Modi an editor, publisher, and printer of a magazine, *Gaurakshak*, was prosecuted under Section 295A of the IPC for publishing an article in the magazine. This was challenged under Article 32 as ultra vires of Article 19 (1) (a).

common law right. It is a special right created by the statute and can only be exercised on the conditions laid down by the statute. The Fundamental Rights Chapter has no bearing on a right like this created by statute (see also Election Commission of India 1954–5).[10]

Judiciary Upholds Article 19 (1) (a)

One can see an emerging pattern of judicial verdicts upholding Article 19 (1) (a) of the Indian Constitution, vis-à-vis the press in a series of judicial pronouncements. I will now examine some noteworthy cases in detail.

Sakal Papers (P) Ltd and Ors *vs* The Union of India *(1961)*

The Sakal Papers (P) Ltd case, which came for hearing before the SC bench in 1961 provides one such link. The writ petition (filed by *Sakal*, a Marathi daily published from Poona) under Article 32[11] of the Constitution challenged the Provisions of Newspaper (Price and Page) Act, 1956, and the Daily Newspaper (Price and Page) Order of 1960. Additionally, two readers of *Sakal* filed petitions in the same case. The Act and the order sought to regulate the number of pages according to the price of the newspaper and number of supplements published by the paper, and regulated the size and area of the advertisements carried in the newspaper in relation to the other subject matters. Both the Act and the related order, according to the petitioners, presented a predicament: if the newspaper continued to publish the same number of pages it published then they would have to increase its selling price, which would adversely affect its circulation. On the other hand, if the daily reduced the number of pages in order to conform to the Act and the order, that would directly interfere with their right to disseminate news and views. Thus, the Act and the order curtailed freedom of press, directly violating Article 19 (1) (a) of the Constitution. The Union of India representing the Ministry

[10] *Jamuna Prasad Mukhariya and Ors* vs *Lacchi Ram and Ors*, 1954.

[11] Under Article 32 of the Indian Constitution, an Indian citizen can seek judicial redressal for the violation of their fundamental rights.

of Information and Broadcasting argued that the Act and the order sought to regulate the prices charged by newspapers in relation to the number of pages and also keep in check the monopolistic tendencies of bigger media conglomerates and prevent unfair competition. The SC bench headed by J.R. Mudholkar declared the Act to be ultra vires of the Indian Constitution as it infringed on the fundamental right of freedom of expression and speech under Article 19 (1) (a): 'Since circulation of a newspaper is a part of the right of freedom of speech the Act must be regarded as one directed against the freedom of speech.'

The intention of the judiciary to uphold the freedom of expression and speech under Article 19 (1) (a) is outlined in the judgement itself, where it cautioned the judiciary to be 'ever vigilant in guarding perhaps the most precious of all the freedoms guaranteed by our Constitution. The reason for this is obvious. The freedom of speech and expression of opinion is of paramount importance under a democratic Constitution which envisages changes in the composition of legislatures and governments and must be preserved'.

Bennett Coleman & Co. and Ors *vs* Union of India and Ors (1972)

Similarly, in an important judicial case of 1972, the newspaper conglomerate Bennett Coleman & Co. challenged the Newsprint Policy of 1972–3 as violation of Article 19 (1) (a) and Article 14 (grants civil rights and equality before law in the Indian Constitution). The Newsprint Policy of 1972–3, in effect, placed prohibitions on the import on papers for news printing and rationed the number of pages to ten on the basis of the circulation of the newspapers (based on the years 1971–2). The rationed quota was non-transferrable to other newspapers of the same ownership (Rai 2011: 137). The suspension of US aid in 1972–3 resulted in the shortage of 11,000 tonnes of imported paper and hence the restrictions were imposed through the Newsprint Policy. The policy was especially detrimental to big newspapers. The writ petition argued that since the policy hindered the quantum of circulation, size, and growth of the newspaper, it was a direct infringement of Article 19 (1) (a) of the Indian Constitution (exercised through the editors and the publication of newspapers).

The petition came up for hearing before the SC bench comprising Justices S.M. Sikri, A.N. Ray, P. Jaganmohan Reddy, K.K. Mathew, and Hameedullah M. Beg. The entire SC bench with the exception of Justice Mathew unanimously held that the Newsprint Policy of 1972–3 violated Article 19 (1) (a) and Article 14 and judged in favour of the petitioners Bennett Coleman & Co.

Interestingly, Justice Mathew provided a note of dissent contrary to the majority verdict by upholding the policy. Later, in a significant verdict of *State of UP* vs *Raj Narain and Ors*, one can see a transformed posture of Justice Mathew, upholding Article 19 (1) (a) (I will examine this case in detail in the section titled '*State of UP* vs *Raj Narain and Ors* (1975)'). Delivering the verdict, Justice Ray observed, 'Although Article 19 (1) (a) does not mention the freedom of the press, it is the settled view of this Court that freedom of speech and expression includes freedom of the press and circulation.' Justice Ray further added, 'In the garb of distribution of newsprint the government has tended to control the growth and circulation of newspapers. Freedom of the press is both qualitative and quantitative. Freedom lies both in circulation and in content.' Judgement opined that '*freedom of the press is indispensable to proper working of popular Government* [my emphasis]', adding further:

> The faith of a citizen is that political wisdom and virtue will sustain themselves in the free market of ideas *so long as the channels of communication are left open* [my emphasis]. The faith in the popular government rests on the old dictum 'let the people have the truth and the freedom to discuss it and all will go well'. The liberty of the press remains an 'Art of the Covenant' in every democracy. Steel will yield products of steel. Newsprint will manifest whatever is thought of by man. The newspapers give ideas. *The newspapers give the people the freedom to find out what ideas are correct* [my emphasis]. Therefore, the freedom of the press is to be enriched by removing the restrictions on page limit and allowing them to have new editions or new papers.

Incidentally, the RTI is upheld in this verdict to be part of the freedom of expression and speech enshrined in the Constitution.

The initial movement of ideas around openness within the judiciary is significant on three counts. First, the judicial interpretation of Article 19 (1) (a) has to be seen in the light of interconnection between the legality of upholding the fundamental right to freedom of expression and speech and the judicial view that information and ideas needs to be articulated in the public domain. It is in this context that the court treats press as an important source of vital information. This is reflected in the judicial verdicts discussed earlier.

Second, as articulated in the judicial verdicts, the court emphasized on citizens having the 'rights' (as part of the fundamental rights) of freedom of expression and speech. This is significant as it is the start of the process of legal interpretation of the Constitution within the rights framework, which became more pronounced in later verdicts.

Third, the judicial verdicts established linkages between the freedom of press and the need for information dissemination in a democracy. I argue that this interconnection between free press and information dissemination can be inferred as initial ideas being expressed by the judiciary around openness and the right to know. Similar to the trends discussed in the previous section, in this phase nascent ideas on openness and transparency emanate from the judiciary through the constitutional interpretation of Article 19 (1) (a).

Phase II (1975–2004): Judicial Verdicts on Transparency and Openness—Ideas Adopted as Norms

In this phase, starting from the National Emergency imposed in 1975 till the early 2000s (immediately prior to the promulgation of the RTI Act), the judiciary adopted an unequivocal stance on openness in government affairs. Primarily dealing with the question of disclosure of government documents (which have a tendency to be treated as confidential by the State), the judiciary directly challenged the nested norm of secrecy and advocated the right to know as a constitutional right. This framing by the judiciary added to the emerging discourse on openness within other realms of the State, where one can see a process of initial ideas being adopted and interpreted as norms of openness and transparency (examined in Chapter 2). The judicial interpretation of the Constitution in these cases are important as they provide the basis for the policy discussions in the executive (both permanent and political) on the legislation of RTI. This period starts with the political environment that led to the National Emergency imposed in 1975 as its backdrop. In this context, I will now examine the famous and oft-cited, *State of UP* vs *Raj Narain* case.

State of UP *vs* Raj Narain and Ors *(1975)*

As discussed, the National Emergency imposed by Indira Gandhi in 1975 provided the context for new political formations, which eventually led to the establishment of the Janata government in 1977. The new party at the centre formally committed to bringing greater transparency and probity in public life and took policy steps to amend the OSA. It is in this political context that the case of *State of UP* vs *Raj Narain and Ors* (1975) provides a significant link in the chain of emerging judicial interpretations on the idea of transparency. Raj Narain, a socialist leader from Uttar Pradesh, contested the 1971 general elections from Rae Bareli, the home constituency of then PM Indira Gandhi. Raj Narain lost the elections to Indira Gandhi (to his surprise, as he was so confident of his victory that he went to the extent of organizing a victory rally prior to the election results). Subsequently, Raj Narain moved an election petition against the PM in the HC of Allahabad alleging election malpractices, challenging the election of the PM. The petition filed by Raj Narain alleged that Indira Gandhi used the wherewithal that came with her office to fuel her election campaign—by bribing the voters, using the services of a gazetted bureaucrat (serving on-duty officer Yashpal Kapoor) during the election campaign, and exceeding the prescribed limit for campaign expenditure (Frankel 2005: 539–40).

On 12 June 1975, Justice J.L. Sinha eventually ruled on the four-year-long litigation. The judiciary found the PM guilty of election malpractices under Section 123(7) of the Representation of People

Act, 1951, while exonerating her on most of the charges—rejecting fifty of the fifty-two charges in the petition (Drieberg and Jagmohan 1975: 14–15). The 1971 election of the PM was declared void and she was disqualified from membership in the legislative assembly and the Lok Sabha for six years (Drieberg 1975; *ToI* 1975). The PM and her legal advisers challenged the verdict in the SC by filing a petition for a stay order on the HC verdict. This petition was rejected by Justice Krishna Iyer.

Significantly, it was during the course of this four-year litigation that the SC interpreted 'right to know' as inherent in the Constitution of India under Article 19 (1) (a). This verdict was in the context of access to an official document that the State claimed was confidential and secret. The petition when filed in the Allahabad HC in April 1971 was initially heard by the HC bench headed by Justice W.G. Broome. The case was shifted to Justice K.N. Shrivastava in March 1974 after the retirement of Justice Broome. Over the course of litigation both Raj Narain and the State approached the SC twice. On the first occasion, Raj Narain appealed against Justice Broome's rejection of Narain's plea that the PM should be deposed and interrogated before the court. On the second occasion, the State government filed an appeal in the SC against Justice Shrivastava's rejection of the State's claim for privilege (of disclosure) with regard to the 'blue book', which relates to instructions on the security arrangements of the PM and details of the PM's movements (*ToI* 1975).

It is in the latter case with regard to the question of disclosure of an official document (the blue book) that the SC's judgement attains significance in relation to the judicial interpretation of the Constitution of 'right to know' as inherent within the constitutional provisions contained in Article 19 (1) (a).

The judgement commented, 'To cover with veil of secrecy the common routine business, is not in the interest of the public. Such secrecy can seldom be legitimately desired.' Raj Narain claimed that the disclosure of details in the blue book would reveal the corrupt election practices of the PM. The legal team of the State on the other hand claimed privilege to the document under Sections 1, 2, and 3 of the Indian Evidence Act, 1872, which prevented unpublished official documents from being submitted as evidence in court without the appropriate permission of the higher government officials.[12]

The SC bench was headed by Justice A.N. Ray and included other members of the bench, namely Justice K.K. Mathew, Justice A. Alagiriswamy, Justice R.S. Sarkaria, and Justice N.L. Untwalia. The judgement delivered by Justice A.N. Ray with a separate note from Justice K.K. Mathew held that it is permissible to submit an official document as evidence in a court of law if the disclosure of the document is in the interest of the larger public and if public interest warrants disclosure as against secrecy of the document. The judgement stated,

> It is that injury to public interest is the reason for the exclusion from disclosure of documents whose contents if disclosed would injure public and national interest. Public interest which demands that evidence be withheld is to be weighed against the public interest in the administration of justice that courts should have the fullest possible access to all relevant materials.

The judgement further granted the right to the court to decide upon the disclosure of an official documents by declaring,

> If the learned Judge will feel inclined in spite of the affidavits to inspect the documents to satisfy himself about the real nature of the documents, the learned Judge will be pleased to inspect the same and pass appropriate orders thereafter. If the Court will find on inspection that any part of a document is innocuous in the sense that it does not relate to affairs of State the Court could order disclosure of the innocuous part provided that would not give a distorted or misleading impression.

[12] Sections 1, 2, and 3 of the Indian Evidence Act states that no one shall be permitted to give any evidence derived from unpublished official records relating to any affairs of State except with the permission of the officer at the head of the department concerned, who shall give or withhold such permission as he thinks fit.

As part of the same judgement, Justice K.K. Mathew in a separate note delivered a judicial interpretation of the Constitution in terms of 'openness' vis-à-vis 'secrecy'. Justice Mathew declared,

> In a government of responsibility like ours, where all the agents of the public must be responsible for their conduct, there can be but few secrets. *The people of this country have a right to know* [my emphasis] every public act, everything, that is done in a public way, by their public functionaries. They are entitled to know the particulars of every public transaction in all its bearing. *The right to know, which is derived from the concept of freedom of speech* [my emphasis], though not absolute, is a factor which should make one wary, when secrecy is claimed for transactions which can, at any rate, have no repercussion on public security.

Supreme Court During Emergency: Case of Additional District Magistrate, Jabalpur *vs* S.S. Shuka etc. *(1976)*

The proactive verdicts upholding freedom of expression and speech and right to know did not always follow a linear path. It must be pointed out that a 'darker shade' of judicial verdicts striking down the fundamental rights emerged during the emergency. The same judges departed from their earlier stance on freedom of expression and speech. This manifested in *Additional District Magistrate, Jabalpur* vs *S.S. Shuka etc.* (1976; also known as the habeas corpus case). The question that came up before the SC was that whether a writ habeas corpus challenging the ground for detention of a citizen can be considered by the HCs.

The five-member bench of the SC, namely, Chief Justice of India A.N. Ray,[13] Justice H.R. Khanna, Justice H.M. Beg, Justice Y.V. Chandrachud, and Justice P.N. Bhagwati decided the case. The bench supported the presidential order to deny the right of any citizen to move courts for the enforcement of rights conferred in the Indian

[13] Justice A.N. Ray was close to Indira Gandhi who had appointed him as chief justice superseding three judges above him. This shows that the higher judiciary was not always immune from politicization.

Constitution under Articles 14 (right to equality), 21 (right to life and liberty), and 22 (prevention against detention in certain cases)[14] while the Emergency was in force. The verdict favoured the government in power by stating,

> In view of the Presidential Order dated 27th June 1975 no person has any locus to move any writ petition under Art. 226 before a High Court for habeas corpus or any other writ or order or direction to challenge the legality of an order of detention on the ground that the order is not under or in compliance with the Act or is illegal or is vitiated by mala fides factual or legal or is based on extraneous considerations. (*Additional District Magistrate, Jabalpur* vs *S.S. Shukla*, 1976)

This ruling was directly against the constitutionally granted fundamental rights of the citizens. Except for one instance of dissent from Justice Khanna, the rest upheld the Emergency powers of the government against the fundamental rights. Surprisingly, Justice P.N. Bhagwati, who later upheld the citizens' right to know in *S.P. Gupta* vs *Union of India and Ors* case of 1982 and was actively part of the campaign on demanding the right to know from both within and outside the State, supported the Emergency powers of the government and the suspension of fundamental rights. It was also during Justice Bhagwati's tenure as chief justice of India that there was an increase in the number of PILs entertained by the SC. In 2012, during a video interview, Justice Bhagwati in hindsight conceded that his judgement in this case was 'an act of weakness' and that 'political ideology are bound to colour the judgements' (MyLaw.net 2012).[15]

[14] This move was allegedly initiated by Indira Gandhi to thwart the social and political mobilization of the JP movement. Indeed, most of the prominent opposition leaders were put under detention taking advantage of the suspension of these articles.

[15] Contrary to his activist stance both in and outside courts, Justice Bhagwati was at times seen close to the axis of power. This is evident in his 'adulatory' letter to Indira Gandhi congratulating her on the election victory in 1980 following the fall of Janata government in 1979. In a letter dated 15 January 1980, he wrote, 'May I offer you my heartiest congratulations on your resounding victory in the elections and your triumphant return as

Maneka Gandhi *vs* Union of India *(1978)*

The case of *Maneka Gandhi* vs *Union of India* (1978)[16] has to be discussed within the broader context of the National Emergency imposed in 1975 and the emergence of new political formations leading to the 1977 Janata Party government in the centre. Significantly, in this case, the judicial stance on Article 21 departs from its earlier stance during the Emergency period.

This case is important insofar as the constitutional interpretation of Article 21, granting right to life and liberty to the citizens, is concerned. Additionally, in the judgement, the judiciary also expressed its views on the prevailing tendency of secrecy and the need for greater openness in the affairs of the State. This was the first time that the court widened the scope of 'right to life' beyond the literal meaning to include related social and economic rights within its purview (Ghosh 2012: 67) initiating a process of infusing the idea of 'social justice' within the constitutional provisions.[17] These ideas emanating from the judiciary at a later stage resulted in the actualization of a spate of economic and social rights such as the right to education, right to work, and RTI, which were viewed as part of the right to life as well.

In this case, Maneka Gandhi was asked to surrender her passport in the safety of 'public interest' under Section 10 (3) (C) of the Indian Passport Act. Maneka Gandhi sought an explanation and reason for this order from the MEA (represented by regional passport officer). The ministry, however, refused to provide any reasons in the 'public interest'. The MEA order to surrender the passport was

---

prime minister of India. It is a most remarkable achievement of which you, your friends and well-wishers can be justly proud. It is a great honour to be the prime minister of a country like India.' See India Today 1980.

[16] It is important to point out that Maneka Gandhi was wife of Sanjay Gandhi and daughter-in-law of Indira Gandhi.

[17] Circle of Rights: Justiciability of ESC Rights—an Indian experience. Available at: http://www1.umn.edu/humanrts/edumat/IHRIP/circle/justiciability.htm (accessed 27 March 2020).

challenged in the SC under Article 32 as infringing upon Maneka Gandhi's fundamental rights guaranteed under Article 21 of the Constitution. In this light, the court widened the scope of 'personal liberty' reversing the earlier judicial stance of the concept of personal liberty in accordance with the 'procedure established by law' (*A.K. Gopalan* vs *The State of Madras*, 1950). The court stated, 'The expression "personal liberty" in Art. 21 is of the *widest amplitude and covers a variety of rights* [my emphasis] which go to constitute the personal liberty of man and some of them have been raised to the status of distinct fundamental rights and given additional protection under Art. 19 (1). Thus *Articles 19(1) and 21 are not mutually exclusive* [my emphasis].'

The judicial verdict was significant for another reason—it clearly established the link between Article 14 (equality), Article 19 (fundamental rights), and Article 21 (right to life) by propounding,

> The law must therefore be now taken to be well-settled that *Article 21 does not exclude Article 19* [my emphasis] and that even if there is a law prescribing procedure for depriving a person of personal liberty and there is consequently no infringement of the fundamental right conferred by Art. 21, *such law will so far as it abridges or takes away any fundamental right under Article 19 would have to meet the challenge of that Article* [my emphasis]. Equally such law *would be liable to be tested with reference to Art. 14* [my emphasis] and the procedure prescribed by it would have to answer the requirement of that Article.

It is pertinent to note that the judiciary in this judgement touched upon the issue of secrecy, which in its view was completely outdated and 'Sphinx-like', while advocating greater openness in government affairs. The court noted, 'A government which *revels in secrecy* [my emphasis] in the field of people's liberty not only acts against democratic decency but busies itself with its own burial. … *Public power must rarely hide its heart in an open society and system* [my emphasis].' On the issue of providing a vague reason of 'public interest' for the MEA to order the surrender of Maneka Gandhi's passport, the court commented that 'the reason for the action being strangely veiled from the victim and the right to voice an answer being suspiciously withheld from her, the surprising secrecy being labelled, "public interest" … the catchall expression "public interest" is sometimes the easy temptation to cover up from the public which *they have a right to know* [my emphasis]'. The judiciary viewed the tendency of secrecy in the government affairs as 'paper curtains wear ill on good governments' and felt that 'to side one's grounds under colour of statute, is too sphinx-like an art for an *open society and popular regime* [my emphasis]' (Justice Krishna Iyer in *Maneka Gandhi* vs *Union of India*, 1978).

S.P. Gupta *vs* Union of India and Ors *(1982)*

The *S.P. Gupta* vs *Union of India and Ors* case of 1982, also known as the 'judges transfer case', represents yet another significant landmark judgement where the judiciary interpreted the Constitution in terms of right to know. The SC verdict in this case for the first time recognized explicitly in unequivocal terms the need for granting constitutional RTI. In a series of writ petitions filed by lawyers in the Bombay, Delhi, Allahabad, Madras, and Patna HCs, the constitutional validity of the transfer of judges and the short-term appointment of additional judges was challenged.[18] The petitions grouped together came for hearing before a seven-member SC bench headed by Justice P.N. Bhagwati.[19] As part of the legal process, the petitioners challenged the

[18] Lily Thomas, an SC advocate, challenged the transfer of Justice M.M. Ismail, chief justice of Madras HC, to Kerala, and the transfer of Justice K.B.N. Singh, chief justice of Patna, to Madras; a group of practising lawyers of the Bombay HC challenged the law minister's circular to CMs about seeking consent from additional judges of the HC regarding their transfers; V.M. Tarkunde, an SC advocate, challenged the short-term extension of additional judges of the Delhi HC; S.P. Gupta, an advocate in the Allahabad HC, challenged the law ministers circular and short-term extension of additional judges (*ToI* 1981).

[19] The seven-member bench headed by Justice P.N. Bhagwati included Justice A.C. Gupta, Justice S. Murtaza Fazal Ali, Justice V.D. Tulzapurkar, Justice D.A. Desai, Justice R.S. Pathak, and Justice E.S. Venkataramiah (*S.P. Gupta* vs *President of India and Ors*, 1981; *ToI* 1981).

claim of privilege under Article 74 (2) of the Constitution and Sections 1, 2, and 3 of the Indian Evidence Act by the government with regard to disclosure of official documents, which was related to the case. The privilege of non-disclosure was claimed for documents such as the correspondence between then law minister, P. Shiv Shanker, the chief justices of certain HCs, and the chief justice of India (which contained relevant notes exchanged between them regarding the transfers and the appointment of judges). Additionally, the government also claimed privilege with regard to the circular issued by the central law minister to the CMs of the states. This claim of privilege to disclose was challenged, demanding disclosure of the documents. The circular related to the short-term appointment of the additional judges, giving them an extension of two to four months on completion of their prescribed two-year term. Candidates would require consent from 100 additional judges to be appointed as permanent judge outside their states. The petitioners interpreted this as a grave attack on the independence of the judiciary.

Following judicial precedent (*State of UP* vs *Raj Narain*, 1975) and changing democratic imperatives (openness vs secrecy), the SC rejected the claim for privilege to disclose these official documents by the State commenting that the disclosure of official information should be the rule rather than the exception.[20] Subsequently, the SC directed the government to disclose the official documents. The correspondence exchanged between the law minister, the chief justice of Delhi, and the chief justice of India on the appointment of the judges was deemed relevant for this case. However, the government claimed privilege for the non-disclosure of these documents as they were protected under Article 74 (clause 2) of the Indian Constitution and sections 1, 2, and 3 of the Indian Evidence Act, 1872. 'In the context of the *open society* [my emphasis] which we are trying to evolve *as part of the democratic structure* [my emphasis]', the court rejected the contention of the government.

[20] In the same case, on an earlier occasion, the SC directed the government to disclose the correspondence related to the transfer of Justice K.B.N. Singh of Patna HC to Madras (*ToI* 1981).

> It caused great concern to us for it involved a clash between two competing aspects of public interest, but ultimately after inspecting these documents for ourselves and giving our most anxious thought to this highly debatable question, we decided to reject the claim for protection against disclosure and directed that these documents be disclosed by the Union of India.

It is pertinent to note that the verdict is expressing 'open society' as part of the evolving democratic framework as the logic for rejecting the privilege for disclosure of official documents—it was 'the new democratic culture of an open society towards which every liberal democracy is moving and our country should be no exception'. Significantly, the verdict touched upon the tendency of secrecy in government affairs owing to the executive having prerogative to crucial policy data. The verdict can be placed within the broader context of the nested norm of secrecy in government affairs and the emergent idea of openness. The court's view in this case was that secrecy led to unaccountable government, which was antithetical to the democratic spirit, whereas, openness could be a 'powerful safeguard against political and administrative aberration and inefficiency'. In this important verdict, the court opined,

> Sometimes governmental action is influenced by political and other motivations and pressures arid at tunes, there are also instances of misuse or abuse of authority on the part of the executive. Now, if *secrecy* [my emphasis] were to be observed in the functioning of government and the processes of government were to be kept hidden from public scrutiny, it would tend to promote and encourage oppression, corruption and misuse or abuse of authority, for it would all be shrouded in the veil of secrecy without any public accountability.

On the other hand, it said, 'If there is an *open government* [my emphasis] with means, of information available to the public there would be greater exposure of the functioning of government and it would help to assure the people a better and more efficient administration.'

The judgement in this case stressed on the need for greater openness especially when the State as a primary policymaker formulates its agenda, which directly affects the lives of citizens. The court added,

> It may sometimes happen that the data made available to the policy-makers is of a selective nature, and even the policymakers and their advisers *may deliberately suppress certain view points and favour others. Such bureaucratic habits get encouragement in an environment of secrecy; and openness in governmental work is possibly the only effective corrective to it* [my emphasis], also raising, in the process, the quality of decision making.

The verdict drew upon the earlier SC judgement on *State of Uttar Pradesh* vs *Raj Narain* (1975) especially Justice K.K. Mathew's verdict and significantly pointed towards the argument on access to information made in the IIPA publication of 1981 on *Open Government in India* (discussed in Chapter 2). In this context of prevailing secrecy and the need for greater openness in government affairs, the verdict recognized the right to know as inherent in the freedom of expression and speech outlined in Article 19 (1) (a) of the Indian Constitution:

> The *concept of an open government is the direct emanation from the right to know* [my emphasis] which seems to be *implicit in the right of free speech and expression guaranteed under Article 19(1)(a)* [my emphasis]. Therefore, disclosure of information in regard to the functioning of government must be the rule and secrecy an exception justified only where the strictest requirement of public interest so demands.

The verdict emphasized on the need for accountability emanating from the disclosure of information regarding government affairs in the public domain—'where a society has chosen to accept democracy as its creedal faith, it is elementary that the citizens ought to know what their government is doing', thus making democracy more participatory. The court declared,

> The citizens have a right to decide by whom and by what rules they shall be governed and they are entitled to call on those who govern

on their behalf to account for their conduct. No democratic government can survive without *accountability* [my emphasis] and the basic postulate of accountability is that the *people should have information about the functioning* [my emphasis] of the government. It is only if people know how government is functioning that they can fulfil the role which democracy assigns to them and make democracy a really effective participatory democracy.

Judiciary Examining Environmental Issues: Right to Know Expressed by Both the Supreme Court and the High Court

In the context of emerging discourse on openness with regard to State affairs, the judicial verdicts regarding environmental issues are pertinent. On the one hand, the cases are important from the vantage point of ideas emerging around openness from within the judiciary. On the other, the involvement of social actors can be seen as playing the crucial role of a catalyst in inducing a significant arm of the State—the judiciary—to stress on the need for greater openness in the affairs of the State and citizens' RTI of official documents.

For example, an important PIL came up for hearing before the SC bench headed by Justice P.N. Bhagwati in 1985, when M.C. Mehta, an advocate, filed a writ petition in the SC seeking the relocation of the caustic chlorine and sulfuric plants of Shriram Food and Fertilizers, as they were located in a densely populated area of Delhi (*M.C. Mehta and Anr.* vs *Union of India and Ors*, 1986; Singh 2003: 10). By the time the case came up for hearing in the SC, hazardous leaks of oleum gas from the plant complex occurred twice, first on 14 December 1985 and second on 6 December 1985, affecting the general public, including some deaths that were reported to have resulted from the gas leaks (Ahuja 1997: 537). The SC took up the case promptly and ordered immediate medical care to the victims of the leak and appointed two expert committees (Agarwal Committee and Nilay Choudhary Committee) to oversee safety in the industry. It was during the trial that the court discovered that a committee was already constituted by the Government of Delhi to examine the safety aspects of the plant complex.[21] The report of this committee was neither shared with Shriram Food and Fertilizers, nor made public. Consequently, Justice Bhagwati expressed during the hearing that the issues of RTI should be taken up promptly. This remark during the trial led to the filing of another PIL by an environmental group called Kalpavriksha seeking RTI as a fundamental right (Singh 2003: 10–11). Environmental issues provided yet another trigger point for the judiciary to get into the question of RTI as inherently provided as part of Article 19 (1) (a) of the Constitution.[22]

Similarly, in 1986, the Bombay HC bench of Justice C.S. Dharmadhikari and Justice T.D. Sugla upheld the right to obtain confidential information regarding development infrastructure projects. The writ petition filed by an environmental group BEAG sought information regarding the building plans in Poona Cantonment area. According to BEAG, some buildings were illegally constructed, neglecting the building bylaws, and hence they requested inspection of documents related to the building plans. Significantly, the HC

[21] Delhi administration constituted an expert committee consisting of Shri Manmohan Singh; Chief Manager, IPCL, Baroda, and three other persons as members to check the existence of safety and pollution control measures covering all aspects such as storage, manufacture, and handling of chlorine in Shriram and to suggest measures necessary for strengthening safety and pollution control arrangements with a view to eliminate community risk (*M.C. Mehta and Anr.* vs *Union of India and Ors*, 1986).

[22] A similar point was highlighted in an interview with Shekhar Singh (9 January 2014, New Delhi, India). Singh commented that the cases on environmental issues were perhaps the first trigger, which elicited a response from the judiciary around RTI. The Shriram Food and Fertilizers Pvt. Ltd case was the first of its kind in a series of cases related to environmental issues. Singh himself was involved in the petition filed by Kalpavriksha. He later assumed the role of convener of the NCPRI and was one of the pivotal actors working for the cause of RTI. This is discussed at length in the Chapter 4.

bench in its order of 7 October 1986 permitted BEAG the inspection of the documents. The court held that if

> *Article 19 (1) (a) takes in its import the disclosure of information* [my emphasis] in regard to the functioning of the government and the right to know about it, which is *implicit in the right of free speech and expression guaranteed under Article 19 (1) (a) of the Constitution* [my emphasis], then the right of inspection as claimed by the petitioners in this writ petition must flow from the same fundamental right. (*ToI* 1986b)

Further, the HC bench of Justice Dharmadhikari and Justice Sugla connected this to the issue of 'democratic deepening' by stressing on the need for bottom-up democracy. Raising the question of 'who will watch the watchmen', the court commented that 'real democracy cannot be worked by men sitting at the top. It has to be worked from below by the people of every village and town. That sovereignty resides in and flows from the people' (*ToI* 1986b). Subsequently, *Special Petition for Bombay Action Environmental Group* vs *Pune Cantonment Board* came up for consideration before the SC in October 1986, where the scope of access to information laid down by the Bombay HC was widened further to extend the right to inspect documents to citizens' groups and public interest bodies. The SC directed that

> any person residing within the area of a local authority or any social action group or interest group or pressure group shall be entitled to take inspection of any sanction, granted or plan approved by such local authority in construction of buildings along with the related papers and documents. If such individual or social action group or interest group or pressure group wishes to take such inspection, except of course in cases where in the interest of security, such inspection cannot be permitted. (quoted in Singh 2003: 12)

The judicial verdict in this case triggered a policy response from the State in 1992, evident in the official order of the Department of Urban Development, Government of Maharashtra directing the concerned departments to allow citizens, environmental action groups, and social groups to inspect documents related to building plans (Circular No. TPS.5692/1606/UD-11). Additionally, the case was consequential in influencing the Ministry of Environment and Forests, GoI, which in its publication of 1993 advocated the citizens' right to know (CUTS Briefing Paper 1995: 2). This shows yet another point of intersection between different segments of the State, the emerging wave of ideas on openness and the interests emerging from the societal realm. I will establish this intersection in a detailed manner in Chapter 4. An overarching argument, however, is that this case demonstrates the emerging ideas from the judiciary getting synced with the ideas emerging from the other segment of the State, that is, the executive.

Representing another variant of the 'intersection', the HC order to the Gujarat government in the case of the Narmada Dam project demonstrated that the policies of the State around openness were at loggerheads with each other. On the one hand the HC order to the State government to withdraw the OSA represented a move towards openness and on the other the Gujarat government's move in 1988 to impose the OSA on twelve villages surrounding the disputed site for Narmada Dam epitomizes the tendency of secrecy regarding government affairs. A petition was filed in the Gujarat HC by a citizen's campaign called Narmada Bachao Andolan seeking the withdrawal of the OSA from the dam site as it violated Article 19 (1) (a) of the Constitution. In this light, the HC directed the State government to withdraw the OSA from the twelve villages around the dam site, which was subsequently lifted by the state government on 3 January 1989 and was formally informed again to the HC on 14 October 1993 (*ToI* 1993d; Khagram 2005: 115–16).

Judiciary Constitutionally Grants Citizens' Right to Know

Citizens' right to know under Article 19 (1) (a) and right to life provisioned in Article 21 of the Constitution were upheld in yet another case, *Sheela Barse* vs *State of Maharashtra* (1987). Sheela Barse, a journalist, sought permission to interview female prisoners of a Bombay jail, which was granted by the inspector general of the jail. During the recording of interviews, the permission was withdrawn by the jail authorities. This was challenged in the court as ultra vires of Article 19 (1) (a) and Article 21 of the Indian Constitution. Citing the position held by the SC in *S.P. Gupta and Ors* vs *Union of India* (1982), the court upheld the citizens' right to know under Article 19 (1) (a), declaring that it does 'endorse these observations [made in the S.P. Gupta case] as a correct statement of the position'. Additionally, the court also interpreted the right to 'life' under Article 21 specifically with regard to the rights of the prisoners detained in jail as including the living conditions of the prisoners and thus declared that information regarding life of prisoners should be allowed to be put in the public domain. Hence, the court declared, 'The pressmen as friends of the society and public spirited citizens should have access to information about, and interviews with, the prisoners. But such access has to be controlled and regulated.'

In a similar vein, dealing with the question of right versus duty, Rajasthan HC in *L.K. Koolwal* vs *State of Rajasthan* (1986) pointedly alluded to citizens' right to know, when a writ petition was filed in the HC by M.K. Koolwal regarding the sanitation conditions in the city of Jaipur. The HC, while dealing with the issue, commented,

> *Citizen has a right to know about the activities of the State* [my emphasis], the instrumentalities, the departments and the agencies of the State. The privilege of secrecy, which existed in the old times that the State is not bound to disclose the facts to the citizens or the State cannot be compelled by the citizens to disclose the facts, does not survive now to a great extent. *Under Article 19(a) of the Constitution there exists the right of freedom of speech. Freedom of speech is based on the foundation of the freedom of right to know* [my emphasis]. (*L.K. Koolwal* vs *State of Rajasthan* 1986)

The Court further added, '*Citizen has a right to know how the State is functioning* [my emphasis] and why the State is withholding such information in such matters'(*L.K. Koolwal* vs *State of Rajasthan* 1986).

In *M.C. Mehta* vs *Union of India* (1991), the court was petitioned with a request to intervene and give direction to cinema theatres and exhibition halls to mandatorily give an environmental message in the beginning of a programme.[23] In delivering the judgement in favour of such environmental messaging, the court insisted on the citizens' RTI and the State's obligation to disseminate information. The court expressed, 'We are in a democratic polity where dissemination of information is the foundation of the system. *Keeping the citizens informed is an obligation of the Government* [my emphasis]' (see also CUTS Briefing Paper 1995: 2).

Displacing the Persisting Norm of Secrecy: Right to Know as a Fundamental Right

From 1997 onwards, the judiciary responded to the growing concern and demand for greater probity and transparency of political and public offices. These verdicts were consequential in the formulation of the judicial stance on right to know as a fundamental right provided in the Constitution. The nested norm of secrecy was being directly challenged and displaced by declaring right to know or information as a fundamental right. This phase is also characterized by a proactive judiciary giving directions to the government to enact a law on access to information within a stipulated time period.

Dinesh Trivedi, MP, and Ors *vs* Union of India and Ors (*1997*)

The judiciary approached the issue of right to know by interpreting Article 19 (1) (a) of the Indian Constitution in a series of cases related to probity in public life from the late 1990s onwards. It is in the backdrop of increased criminalization in society having active linkages with almost all sections including political and government class that *Dinesh Trivedi, MP and Ors* vs *Union of India and Ors*

23 The case came up for hearing before the SC bench of Justice Rangnath Mishra.

(1997) is significant. The case related to constitutional interpretation of the right to know. This was in context of the demand to access the background reports, which formed the basis for the report of a high-level committee constituted by the government, headed by former Home Secretary, N.N. Vohra.[24] The committee was constituted under the growing concern within the government regarding the increasing criminal nexus.

The Vohra Committee based its final report on smaller background reports by other departments such as Customs, Research Analysis Wing, CBI, the Intelligence Bureau (IB), and the Department of Revenue. The Vohra Committee submitted its final report to the government on 5 October 1993 reaffirming that criminal networks have entrenched themselves within the political, bureaucratic, non-governmental, and media circles, and recommended an establishment of a nodal cell within the government to monitor these trends. Meanwhile, in 1995 the famous murder case of Naina Sahini, a young political activist, and the involvement of a high-profile politician in the murder resulted in intense debate in the public sphere, putting considerable pressure on the government to make the report public. In this light, different quarters from both within and outside the State demanded that the Vohra Committee Report should be put in the public domain as the government was reluctant to share it with a larger audience.[25]

[24] The Vohra Committee was constituted on 9 July 1993 through a government order (no. S/7937/SS(ISP)/93). The Committee was chaired by the home secretary and secretary (revenue), and the director of the IB, the director of the CBI, the joint secretary, MHA, the special secretary (Internal Security and Police) were other members of the committee.

[25] Unfortunately, the government has till date not released the Vohra Committee Report in the public domain. This is perhaps because of the sensitive information contained in the report about the deep nexus between the criminals, government functionaries, and politicians. An RTI query was filed in 2017 to the MHA to seek information about the Report and its contents. The MHA in its reply to the query stated that the records cannot be provided as they are secret/confidential and cannot be disclosed under section 8 (1) (h) of the RTI Act. See, Mishra 2016; 2017.

The Vohra Committee Report was subsequently tabled in the parliament on 1 August 1995, which was followed by intense debate. Dinesh Trivedi, an MP in the upper house (Rajya Sabha) who was representing Janata Dal (at that time),[26] actively participated during the parliamentary debates and demanded that the background reports on the basis of which the Vohra Committee Report was prepared should be made public as well. Trivedi, formally, in his official capacity as MP approached the Home Ministry but to no avail.

Finally, along with two NGOs, Public Interest Legal Support and Research Centre, and the CERC,[27] Dinesh Trivedi filed a PIL in the SC demanding the disclosure of the reports.[28] The petitioners argued that they had freedom of information as citizens of India and that Section 5 of the OSA was too broad. In this light, they demanded that since the Vohra Committee Report revealed such alarming trends, all annexures, memorials, and written evidence should also be made public along with the background reports. Subsequently, the division bench of the SC on 13 October 1996 directed the Union of India to place before the court an authenticated version of the report and also appraise the court of action taken on the recommendations of the report. Dealing with the

[26] Dinesh Trivedi was in Congress till 1990 before joining the Janata Dal. In 1998, he switched parties to join Trinamool Congress. This was also the period when policy movement around the RTI was initiated by the V.P. Singh government at the centre. The Dinesh Trivedi case coincides with this unambiguous policy drift within the State towards a legislation on the right to know.

[27] As discussed in Chapter 2, CERC was active on the cause of right to know from the mid-90s, involved in a number of studies, and also drafted a bill on RTI in 1995. The CERC's studies and the draft bill were referred to by the Shourie Committee in 1997.

[28] It is interesting to note that Ram Jethmalani was the counsel for the petitioners and, as the union minister for urban development, had initiated the right to know in his ministry in 1998. Jethmalani had been continuously advocating ideas on openness in the government affairs including the repeal of the OSA.

question of the disclosure of these reports and the related right to know of the citizens, the SC upheld the citizen's right to know and advocated 'openness' as a prerequisite for democracy and free society. The court in this case stated, '*In modern constitutional democracies, it is axiomatic that citizens have a right to know* [my emphasis] about the affairs of the government which, having been elected by them, seeks to formulate sound policies of governance aimed at their welfare.' Drawing upon the judicial precedent and contemporaneous Shourie Committee Report,[29] the SC quoted from the report that 'since sunlight is the best disinfectant',[30] it is imperative that the citizens must be 'kept informed of the vital decisions taken by the Government', which will ensure 'participation of the people in the democratic process'.

Union of India *vs* Association for Democratic Reforms and Ors *(2002)*

The issue of probity in public life came before the SC in *Union of India* vs *Association for Democratic Reforms and Ors* (2002). The SC in this case upheld the citizen's right to know as a fundamental part of freedom of expression and speech under Article 19 (1) (a). Responding to the issue of disclosure of vital information about criminal antecedents of electoral candidates, the SC recognized the RTI as a 'natural right flowing from the concept of democracy'. Connecting the issue of right to know with the information related to the election candidates, the verdict stated, 'The people of the country have a *right to know every public act*, everything that is done in a public way by the public functionaries. MPs or MLAs are undoubtedly public functionaries.'

[29] As discussed in Chapter 2, in 1997, the GoI constituted a nine-member Working Committee on Right to Information and Transparency headed by H.D. Shourie. The committee submitted its report in 1997 and recommended a legislation on freedom of information.

[30] The quote reflects that the judiciary draws upon the Shourie Committee Report, May 1997.

People's Union for Civil Liberties and Ors *vs* Union of India and Ors (2003)

In continuation of its 2002 judgement, the SC in *People's Union for Civil Liberties and Ors* vs *Union of India and Ors* (2003) examined the question of whether voters have a fundamental right to know relevant information such as educational qualifications, income, and assets of electoral candidates. Reiterating the earlier judgement of 2002, the court affirmed the citizen's right to know as a fundamental right, constitutionally provided under Article 19 (1) (a). A year later in *People's Union for Civil Liberties* vs *Union of India* (2004), RTI was again upheld and elevated to the status of a 'human right'. The petition in this case demanded the disclosure of information regarding safety violation and defects in nuclear installations in nuclear power plants across the country and specifically at Trombay and Tarapur.[31] The Court declared RTI as a fundamental right: '[It is] a facet of "speech and expression" as contained in Article 19(1)(a) of the Constitution of India. Right of information, thus, indisputably is a fundamental right.' Additionally, the court elucidated on the restrictions placed under Article 19 (2) and declared that no fundamental right can be absolute.

Ideational Convergence between Judiciary and Other Arms of the State

As the judiciary articulated the ideas on openness, one can see a process of ideational convergence between various segments of the State. For instance, an interconnection and continuity of ideas is established between the judiciary articulating on freedom of press

[31] It is interesting to note that the petitioner's counsel in this case was Prashant Bhushan, an eminent lawyer who was one of the main stakeholders in the NCPRI. On the other hand, Soli Sorabjee, who was part of the Shourie Committee, appeared on behalf of the Union of India in his official capacity as an attorney general. Soli Sorabjee took a counter-stance regarding openness in this case where he advocated the non-disclosure of sensitive information.

and need for openness and State institutions such as PCI expressing the need for openness. The judges of the SC, such as Justice J.R. Mudholkar, Justice N. Rajagopala Ayyangar, Justice A.N. Sen, and Justice P.B. Sawant, articulated the ideas on openness and transparency in their judgements, and later on they all assumed the position of chairman of the PCI.

Similarly, the Second Press Commission under the chairmanship of Justice K.K. Mathew called for the repealing of Section 5 of the OSA and underlined the need for legal provisions to facilitate citizens' right to know. Importantly, Justice K.K. Mathew expressed his ideas on openness earlier while delivering the judgement on *State of UP* vs *Raj Narain and Ors* (1975). As I have discussed in Chapter 2, the judicial verdict in *State of UP* vs *Raj Narain and Ors* was one of the primary triggers for the imposition of the Emergency in 1975. The Janata Party government, which came to power in 1977 after the Emergency, expressed the willingness to have 'openness and transparency' in government affairs in its party manifesto and constituted a committee to examine the possible amendment to the OSA.

This explains the congruity as well as continuity between the ideas emerging from the judiciary, PCI, and the government itself within which one can clearly ascertain a continuous expression of ideas around openness generally and specifically in relation to the press. Judicial precedent on Article 19 (1) as RTI inherently contained in freedom of expression and speech was often the basis of policy discussions around the RTI at various junctures within the policy domain of the State.

To start with, the judicial stance on the freedom of press and the need for information dissemination in the early phase starting from right after Independence contributed significantly to the churning process of ideas within the State on openness. The polarity of ideas represented by the first amendment to limit the freedom of press in response to the judicial verdicts in the Romesh Thappar and Brij Bhushan cases needs to be placed within the broader context of this churning process. Convergence of ideas can be seen with reference to judicial precedent often cited in the policy discussions within the State. For example, the judicial verdict of *S.P. Gupta* vs *President of India and Ors* (1982) has been often cited and formed the basis of discussions within various government committees constituted to examine the passage of RTI legislation. The Shourie Committee constituted in January 1997 to examine the RTI alludes to a series of judicial verdicts that interpreted right to know as part of the fundamental right to freedom and speech under Article 19 (1) of the Constitution. In this context, the Shourie Committee makes references to *S.P. Gupta* vs *President of India and Ors* (1982) (MPPP, 1997: 4). Significantly, the committee also consulted Justice P.B. Sawant, former chief justice of SC of India, and chairman of PCI. Justice Sawant's views on the right to know were all too well known and articulated in *S.P. Gupta* vs *President of India and Ors* (1982). Later, in 1996, Justice Sawant drafted an RTI bill that formed the basis for the bill drafted by the Shourie Committee. Similarly, the GoM that was constituted in 1999 to examine different aspects of the proposed legislation on RTI examined the exemption of disclosure clause of the proposed bill on the basis of the stance taken by the court around Article 19 (1) and (2) in *S.P. Gupta* vs *President of India and Ors* (1982) (Minutes of the Meeting of GoM 1999). The S.P. Gupta case (1982) is cited as precedent yet again at the final stage of the passage of the RTI Act in the report of the DRPSC (2005) constituted to examine the draft RTI Bill, 2004. The report (DRPSC 2005), while citing the excerpts from the judicial verdict, noted that 'the Supreme Court of India from time to time, interpreted Article 19 which upholds the right to freedom of speech and expression, to implicitly include the right to receive and impart information' (DRPSC 2005: 2). The flow of ideas from the judiciary, however, has not been entirely one way. The judiciary, in shaping up its ideational stance around openness, borrowed from similar assertions elsewhere. In the frequently cited *S.P. Gupta* vs *President of India and Ors* (1982), the judgement drew upon the notion of openness from a publication, *Open Government in India* authored by S.R. Maheshwari from IIPA (1981).[32] The convergence of ideas resulted in two processes that were instrumental in providing direction to the policy trajectory. The first process resulted in the diffusion of the

32 In his judgement, Justice Sawant draws upon arguments made in S.R. Maheshwari's book on openness in government affairs.

norm on openness horizontally between different segments of the State, that is, the legislature, the executive, and the judiciary. The second process demonstrated both congruity and continuity of ideas on openness emerging from within the State.

***

Four significant processes are discernible from the spate of judicial verdicts examined here.

First, the ideas around openness evolved gradually as the constitutional interpretation of Article 19 (1) (a) moved categorically towards citizens' (fundamental) rights and towards recognizing the right to know and to information as integral to the freedom of expression and speech. This gradual process demonstrates that institutional change in the information regime in India is a slow-moving process of the churning of ideas within the State that is endogenous and incremental in nature. Judicial verdicts contributed towards the gradual process of norm diffusion, which complemented the process in which ideas on openness became embedded as norms in the State thinking. Significantly, in the case of the judiciary, the Constitution of India provided the ideational base for the norm trajectory to take a specific direction regarding the freedom of expression and speech under Article 19 (1) (a), which was the judicial interpretation that the right to know is inherently part of this fundamental right. The emerging ideas on openness from within the judiciary has to be seen in the light of the expansion and widening of the scope of Article 32 to include PILs, what Upendra Baxi (1985) terms 'social action litigation' (1985: 118). The widening of the scope of Article 32 was evident in the early 1980s, when citizens would write to the court demanding redressal of a social or political issue, and the judiciary would convert it into a writ petition. This became an integral part of the judicial process within the higher judiciary during (Justice) P.N. Bhagwati's term as the chief justice of the SC of India (who was also the chairperson for the National Committee for the Implementation of Legal Aid at that time). Moving beyond the habeas corpus petitions of the court, this evolving trend of social interest litigations or PILs resulted in what Baxi terms as 'epistolary jurisdiction' (1985: 118).

Second, the analysis of judicial verdicts points towards a significant emerging pattern of the constitutional interpretation of Article 19 (1) (a) from various vantage points, such as the press, national and sub-national politics, environmental issues, criminalization of politics, and probity in public life. These issues acted as ideational catalysts by evoking a response from the judiciary. For instance, in the earlier verdicts in the Romesh Thappar, Brij Bhushan, and Bennett Coleman & Co. cases, the press acted as a catalyst. In the Raj Narain case it was the electoral politics and in the S.P. Gupta case it was the judiciary itself that prompted a constitutional interpretation around Article 19 (1) (a) and acted as an 'idea catalyst'. Similarly, in the cases related to environmental issues, the catalysts from outside the State realm moved the judiciary and brought about a policy response from the State (as in *BAEG* vs *Pune Cantonment* [1986]). A pertinent argument emanating from a study of this pattern is that actors from both within and outside the State have used the judiciary as a medium to ensure their fundamental rights are granted by the Constitution. At this juncture, even though the 'State–society' synergy has not yet been established directly, the judiciary as a significant arm of the State is being treated as an intermediary platform. This resulted in 'norm diffusion and judicial interpretation' from within the State where actors from both State and society acted as idea catalysts (see Table 3.1).

Third, the cases establish the role played by the judiciary in thwarting the executive's quest for secrecy. The norm of secrecy, locked in since colonial times at the systemic level within the State, resulted in an executive that perpetuated secrecy in its policies and actions. By directly challenging and often thwarting this tendency, the judiciary precipitated the convergence of both ideas and policies between different arms of the State. This was evident in the Poona Cantonment case in 1986.

Fourth, the movement of ideas within the judiciary in different time periods coincides with the process of *layering*, which I have examined in relation to other segments of the State. Layering is a process where new norms are placed on top of established norms, where eventually the nested norms are replaced by new ones (Jha 2018b). As discussed in the previous chapters, two distinct layers can be identified in the case of the judiciary as well. In the first layer, the

Table 3.1 Trajectory of Judicial Interpretations

Idea Catalyst	Judicial Cases	Emerging Norm
Press	*Brij Bhushan* vs *The State of Delhi* (1950), *Romesh Thappar* vs *The Union of Madras* (1950), *State of Madras* vs *V.G. Row, Union of India & State* (1952), *Dwarkadas Shrinivas of Bombay* vs *The Sholapur Spinning & Weaving* (1953), *Virendra* vs *The State of Punjab* (1959), *Express Newspapers (Private)* vs *The Union of India* (1959), *Sakal Papers (P) Ltd and Ors* vs *The Union of India* (1961), *Bennett Coleman & Co. and Ors* vs *Union* (1972), and *Sheela Barse* vs *State of Maharashtra* (1987)	• Freedom of expression and speech under Article 19 (1) (a) of the Constitution • Citizens' right to expression and speech • Press as an important medium to disseminate information linked to the citizens' right to know
Opposition politics; demand for transparency; and probity in public life	*State of UP* vs *Raj Narain and Ors* (1975), *Maneka Gandhi* vs *Union of India* (1978), *S.P. Gupta* vs *President of India and Ors* (1981), *Dinesh Trivedi and Ors* vs *Union of India and Ors* (1997), *Union of India* vs *Association for Democratic Reforms and Ors* (2002), *People's Union for Civil Liberties and Ors* vs *Union of India and Ors* (2003), and *People's Union for Civil Liberties* vs *Union of India* (2004)	• Openness in government affairs challenging the established norm of secrecy • Disclosure of official documents in the public domain (treated as 'secret' by the State) • Constitutionally provided citizens' right; rights-based framing of the Constitution • Right to know inherently contained in Article 19 (1) (a)

		• Establishing connection between right to know and access to information
Environmental issues	*M.C. Mehta and Anr* vs *Union of India and Ors* (1986), *Bombay Action Environmental Group* vs *Pune Cantonment Board* (1986), and *Narmada Bachao Andolan* vs *The State of Gujarat* (1986)	• Granting the citizens' right to know • Striking down the established norm of secrecy, that is, the OSA • Movement of ideas on openness at the sub-national level in the HCs

Source: Author.

ideas emerged in a rudimentary form on the fringes, mainly related to the judicial interpretation of Article 19 (1) (a), which upholds the freedom of expression and speech. This interpretation was primarily related to the necessity of a free press in a democracy as a medium to disseminate information, which is directly related to the right to know. This coincides with the first layer identified in the previous chapter, which demonstrated the polarity of ideas within the State in terms of openness vs secrecy. Judicial cases within the first layer have to be seen in this context, where the State's policy trajectory was directed towards curbing the freedom of the press, representing the norm of secrecy, and the judiciary in response was promoting openness, by upholding the freedom of expression and speech, free speech, and the necessity to have a free flow of information in a democracy.

In the second layer, the judiciary interpreted openness in government affairs as 'norms' mainly in relation to the disclosure of official documents (marked secret under 'locked-in' laws such as the OSA). As in the case of the second layer identified in the previous chapter, where the process of the norms on openness became embedded within the State apparatus and challenged the established norm of secrecy, the second layer in the case of the judiciary directly challenged the norm of secrecy and categorically upheld the citizen's right to know. Additionally, starting from the early 1990s, judicial responses were congruent with the emerging policy preference of the State around the RTI that took root in State thinking. In the case of the judiciary as well, this phase was marked by directly providing the constitutional interpretation of Article 19 (1) (a) as inherently containing the RTI. In the third layer, the judiciary treated the RTI as a fundamental right, and established a connection between the RTI and the right to life. This layer is characterized by the moving of the judiciary beyond the specifics of the case to its adopting a stance on the RTI.

The movement of ideas within the judiciary and the constitutional interpretation of Article 19 (1) (a) inherently containing the right to know complemented the ongoing ideational churning and policy movement within the political and permanent executive. In the next chapter, I examine yet another dimension of the complementarity of the State and society driven by epistemic elements from both the realms.

4 Social and Political Processes of State and Society

Progressive Ideas and the Emergence of Epistemic Community

In the previous chapters, I established the role of transformative ideas within different segments of the State, and illustrated how these played a pivotal role in the institutional change in the transparency regime in India. Progressive elements around openness and transparency from both within the permanent and the political executive, along with the judiciary, continually expressed ideas on openness and the RTI, which proved to be transformative in influencing State thinking. The evidence presented in Chapter 1 establishes that the churning of ideas started immediately after Independence when nascent ideas of openness emerged from within the State even as the norm of secrecy was further locked in at systemic levels. Gradually, these ideas started to move from the policy periphery to the policy centre stage, eventually displacing the norm of secrecy. Powerful ideas within the State evolved cumulatively and incrementally, and reached a threshold in 2005. Institutional change in this case was a two-layered process of the initial articulation of rudimentary ideas on openness, albeit on the fringes of the discourse on transparency, and of their becoming embedded as norms and, finally, of these norms becoming internalized in the policy machinery and eventually *layering* out the persisting norm of secrecy. Could it be that elements within the State exclusively played the transformative role, as the mainstream discourse on the RTI Act suggests? Or was it a broader process of intermingling of progressive elements within and outside the State that was consequential for institutional change?

This chapter examines the sociopolitical processes that emerged in the mid-1990s from both within the State and society. These processes coincide with the latter half of the second phase, or layer, discussed in Chapter 2. Emerging in the mid-1990s, actors from both within the State and society played a significant role in the final process of layering where epistemic actors forged ideational linkages. These linkages were consequential in deepening the churning of ideas and policy processes ongoing within the State. By the mid-1990s, ideas on openness and access to information were beginning to be viewed as a possible 'right' of citizens, to be granted in the form of legislation. By the mid-1990s, this view had moved from the periphery of politics to the mainstream. In this chapter, I establish that mainstream politics converged with the emerging sociopolitical processes led by the actors within the social movement, judiciary, the press, bureaucracy, and the academia. This convergence needs to be viewed as one of State–society synergy, where the collective 'epistemic push' of actors from both within the State and society 'tips over' the institution from 'secrecy' to 'openness'. The momentum and incremental weight of earlier ideas traced in previous chapters manifested themselves during this period within the State as well as in epistemic linkages.

In this light, the current chapter examines the social and political processes that emerged at the sub-national level in Rajasthan in the early 1990s, spearheaded by the MKSS, and at the national level, by the NCPRI. Both these cases represent similar dynamics and are interrelated at multiple levels.

Nuancing the Existing Explanations

The present chapter examines the role of social forces outside the State realm in a new light, and moves beyond 'the existing societal-interest based explanations of institutional change in terms of social or people's movement' (Baviskar 2007; Mander and Joshi 1998;

Mishra 2003; Pande 2014; Roy and Dey 2001; Shrivastava 2009; Singh 2010); the role of elite networks and broad-based civil society coalitions or alliances (Baviskar 2007; Sharma 2015; 2015); the 'small, intimate dense network' of the urban/upper-caste/upper-middle class (Sharma 2015: 150; 2015); and Bourdieu's 'symbolic capital' of 'eminent activists' who use their 'relevant capitals' from engagement in multi-scaled activism to negotiate with a differently layered State (Pande 2014: 146).

There is a need to problematize these arguments in explaining the institutional change. In this light, the chapter presents a nuanced understanding of the process by examining the State–society interactions. Two arguments are presented.

The first line of argument is placed within the larger body of literature which views State and society as complementing each other in a mutually enforcing power relationship (Migdal 1988; 2001; Migdal, Kohli, and Shue 1994). In this chapter, I show that from the mid-1990s onwards, there was a similar process of State and society being in a mutually empowering relationship, around a common norm of openness. I demonstrate that progressive elements from both within the State and society complemented each other and removed the locked-in political and policy uncertainty, which finally resulted in the 'tipping point' of institutional change.

The evidence points towards the processes around State and society taking root from the mid-1990s. As I have demonstrated in the previous chapters, the ideational churning around access to information and transparency was deeply entrenched within the State by the mid-1990s, prior to the interactions that emerged between the State and society. In this light, the State is still a significant explanatory variable for us, however not exclusively autonomous but embedded in society (Evans 1995).

The second argument necessitates a deeper engagement with literature dealing with 'networks' (Elke 2005; Gould 1993; Jenkins-Smith and Sabatier 1994; Keck and Sikkink 1998; Khagram, Riker, and Sikkink 2002; Knoke 1990; Risse, Ropp, and Sikkink 1999; Sabatier 1998; Sabatier and Jenkins-Smith 1993; Sangiovanni 2005; Tarrow 2005) and 'epistemic communities' (Haas 1992) by establishing interconnections from both within and outside the

State realm to further stimulate the policy movement around the RTI.

The evidence points towards an intertwining of 'epistemic community' and a 'network' of actors from varied backgrounds. Hence, I propose a nuanced argument of 'epistemic network' in the case of the RTI. My argument draws upon Haas's (1992) discussion on the role of an epistemic community with control over knowledge and information enabling norm diffusion (at the international level), which results in policy coordination, and reducing uncertainty within the system about a particular policy choice. Epistemic communities are defined as 'a network of professionals with recognised expertise and competence in a particular domain and authoritative claim to policy relevant knowledge within that domain or issue area' (Haas 1992: 3). Even though discussed in the context of international policy arena, Haas's notion of epistemic community explains the sociopolitical processes taking shape around the RTI Act. In this chapter, I show that actors from both State and society came together to pursue a 'common goal' with their own set of epistemic characteristics pointing towards an 'epistemic network'. This network played a consequential role in the final stages of institutional change.

Let us now examine the processes, which in many senses laid the foundations for this network, starting with the MKSS in Rajasthan.

Grassroots Processes in Rajasthan: Formation of Mazdoor Kisan Shakti Sangathan

Social and political processes started to cohesively take shape around the same time when the policy trajectory around the RTI was augmented by the coalition governments at the centre from 1989 onwards. In a sense, the sociopolitical formations external to the State coincided with the final layer of institutional change outlined in the previous chapters. This section provides the context and background for the formation of the MKSS, which focuses on the issues of livelihood, right to work, minimum wage, and land rights of the poor in rural Rajasthan. Through its work, the MKSS played a pivotal role in the development of emerging social and political formations around the RTI.[1] The grassroots movement around accountability and transparency spearheaded by the MKSS in Rajasthan has been viewed as the starting point of social mobilization articulating the demand for RTI in India.

The MKSS was initiated by three individuals in 1987 when Aruna Roy, a former IAS officer, a local resident, Shankar Singh, and a student activist, Nikhil Dey, set up base in the village Devdungri to work for the rural poor. In a way, the initial base of the MKSS is representative of a social formation, which was instrumental in social mobilization and articulated the demands of the 'subalterns'. Three distinct patterns explain their ideational make-up.

First, the idea of greater openness of the State emanated from Roy's experience with the IAS. Hence, the idea that the secrecy of the State hinders grassroots governance and promotes corruption provided the context even in the nascent stages of the social formation in rural Rajasthan.

Second, the three were bound together by a common idea of staring an 'alternate' political process of social development.

Third, they shared similar ideas and a vision about engagement with the State as part of the political processes. In their view, social justice was best realized by engaging directly with politics rather than being apolitical: 'Development is politics and there can be no development without political will' (*Lokayan Bulletin* 1996). This was abundantly clear in their motivation to set up base at Devdungri and evident in their strategy to work within the institutional and constitutional framework (this will be discussed in the next section).

When I met her in 2014, Roy explained the logic. 'What other option did we have but to engage with the State within the constitutional means? [Otherwise] in a scenario of direct conflict with the State we would be completely annihilated.'[2] In one of her earlier interviews in 2000, Roy stressed the importance of micro-level action.

[1] The role of the MKSS has been discussed extensively in the mainstream literature on the evolution of RTI. In fact, the starting point of the mainstream narrative is the MKSS.

[2] Interview with Aruna Roy, 30 April 2014, Devdungri, Rajasthan.

She pointed out: 'We can't all be Gandhi or Mao' (*Rediff* 2000). And yet, in a later interview in 2012, Roy stressed on alternate political formation citing the legacy of Gandhi and JP (*First Post* 2012). These were some of the ideas that provided activists the ideational basis to initiate a social and political process in rural Rajasthan. Roy confirmed that they drew upon the Gandhian ideology in their life and actions: 'Our notion of collective leadership, trusteeship, and simple frugal existence is derived from Gandhi.'[3] The forms of protests initiated by the MKSS followed the contours of the Gandhian ideology and social mobilization, which are akin to JP's mobilization around his clarion call of 'total revolution'. This formed the ideational base of leadership, which spearheaded the social mobilization in rural Rajasthan.

Initial Ideas on Access to Information: Emergence of Linkages

This section, while discussing the initial years of the grassroots-level struggles of the MKSS, examines three significant processes taking root.

First, the early social mobilization around the issue of land points towards a social process that revolved around the social formation, evident in the elite leadership of Roy and Dey. In a way, this intervention formed the 'core', which, on the one hand, challenged the socially dominant groups and the State and, on the other hand, mobilized the socially oppressed. Hence, different elements of society were both opposing and supporting the movement at the same time. Even within the core of the MKSS, Shankar Singh provided the 'local' element as the base set up in Devdungri was on the property of Singh's sister and brother-in-law. Singh was familiar with the social and political landscape of the area.

Second, I show the process of linkages being forged from both within and outside the State, giving a nascent shape to the still-developing 'epistemic community' that emerged in the mid-1990s. On the

3 Interview with Aruna Roy, 30 April 2014, Devdungri, Rajasthan.

one hand, mobilization was being shaped from above using the 'elite linkages', and on the other, social mobilization was being shaped from 'below' at the village level. The linkage formation both within State and society provided the legitimacy for the MKSS. Roy's IAS connection also added to this legitimacy and facilitated connections within the State. Additionally, the nature of the MKSS core enhanced its acceptability in society among the local residents of the village.

Third, the grassroots work of the MKSS around the issues of right to work, livelihood, and minimum wage resulted in the realization that these rights were inextricably linked to the access to official records at the village level. The official documents were necessary to support the demands of entitlement from the State. Hence, the grassroots mobilization was consequential in the recognition and realization of access to information.

These patterns were evident in the land struggle and minimum wage issue that the MKSS spearheaded in the late 1980s. For example, in 1988, the MKSS was requested to intervene in a local land struggle in the neighbouring village of Sohangarh. The local landlord, Hari Singh, had illegally claimed 25 hectares of forest area and was levying taxes on the villagers for the use of forest wood for fuel and charged a portion of the milk of their cattle as they used to graze in the forest land. Legally, the landlord could not lay claim to this land under the Land Ceiling Act. The three activists intervened and mobilized the villagers against the landlord.[4]

4 Interview with Shankar Singh, 29 April 2014, Devdungri, Rajasthan. The landlord had used force against the activists by physically assaulting Shankar Singh and Nikhil Dey. This acted as a trigger for villagers to mobilize as they saw it as an attack on the outsiders who were seen as 'do-gooders' helping the villagers. Finally, the police intervened to put an end to this. Dey also wrote about the incident:

> One day Nikhil and Shankar accompanied Surendra (a consultant appointed by the society), who was going to Sohangarh to make payments for construction works around the Bida. The *thakur*'s men waylaid them on the way back, and beat them up. Subsequently, people from three villages (Sohangarh, Kushalpura and Dhapda) took out a protest rally, marching to the sub-divisional headquarters of Bhim and raising slogans against the *thakur*. A decisive

The Sohangarh case was also the first time that access to information emerged as an issue. During the mobilization, the subdivisional magistrate (SDM) of the area was holding a public court to address the people's grievances in the nearby panchayat of Tal, as part of the State's initiative of village-level government. As a matter of framing the issue it was decided that a piece of land illegally possessed by the landlord would be identified. A 25-hectare grazing land was identified to nail the landlord. The question was, how would they get concrete evidence in the form of land records from the local land official called a *patwari*? A link was forged with a sympathetic *patwari* who provided the copies of the land records. This enabled the villagers to put forward their case in the SDM's court. The SDM ruled in their favour. Thereafter, the activists, along with the villagers, were able to mobilize the women's group to form a cooperative, which claimed the 25-hectare piece of land for forestation.[5] Meanwhile, in Sangwas, another neighbouring village of Devdungri, the group played an instrumental role in mobilizing the community against alcoholism and forced the authorities to close down the liquor shops in the village.

From these initial struggles, it is evident that linkages were being forged both within the State and society (with the local villagers). Socially dominant groups, such as the landlord in Sohangarh, were challenged and, on the other hand, oppressed social groups were mobilized.

During the same period, the issue of entitlement to minimum wage emerged at the State irrigation department work site of Dadi Rapat panchayat. Some residents from Sohangarh were employed at Dadi Rapat as well. Despite 140 workers having undertaken work diligently at the site, they were not paid the full amount. The minimum wage was INR 11 per day and they were being paid INR 6. In

---

'moment of transformation' in social and political consciousness took place when those returning from the rally stopped their bus in the *thakur*'s village and shouted slogans, loudly denouncing him in his own domain.' (Dey and Sampath 2005)

[5] Interview with Shankar Singh, 29 April 2014, Devdungri, Rajasthan. See also Mishra 2003.

protest, all 140 workers refused to accept the payment. Subsequently, the State famine commissioner and the executive engineer visited the site and declared that the work had been completed according to the measurements and directed the irrigation department to release the minimum wage of INR 11. The irrigation department offered INR 9 instead of INR 11. In protest, the MKSS mobilized these workers and organized a dharna (sit-in protest) along with a hunger strike in front of the SDM's office. The hunger strike was called off after the collector of the district intervened and assured the payment. Even after this intervention, no payment was released to the workers. Another hunger strike was organized in front of the SDM's office with twelve workers from Brar panchayat who faced non-payment of wages as well.

Meanwhile, petitions and notices were presented to the local authorities. With no response from the authorities, an indefinite hunger strike was organized in front of the SDM's office. By this time, workers from five other districts of Rajsamand, Pali, Ajmer, Jaipur, and Baran were mobilized to collectively protest against the non-payment of wages. Police initiated action against the protestors, which was followed by another hunger strike against the police atrocities.

Finally, the issue came to the notice of S.R. Sankaran, secretary of the Department of Rural Development, GoI, who categorically denied the Rajasthan government central assistance for the Jawahar Rozgar Yojana due to the violation of the Minimum Wages Act, 1948.[6] It is pertinent to note that S.R. Sankaran was known to Aruna Roy from her IAS days. Roy had admired Sankaran immensely for his sympathetic attitude towards the poor. The State government finally responded by releasing full payment to the twelve workers from Brar panchayat. S.R. Sankaran's appointment as secretary of the Department of Rural Development in the centre was part of the major bureaucratic shake-up initiated by the V.P. Singh government

[6] S.R. Sankaran was secretary at the Department of Rural Development, GoI. He later played a prominent role in the formation of a national campaign called 'People's Right to Know'.

(Maheshwari 1992: 339). The bureaucracy–activist network thus worked for the poor in Rajasthan.

These initial interventions helped the group to forge linkages with the local community on the one hand and with sympathetic bureaucrats within the State on the other. Seeds of the formation of a local network of individuals were also perceptible in this formative period. For instance, Lal Singh, a local resident, invited the activists to examine the issue of land in Sohangarh. Later, Lal Singh became a core member of the MKSS and played a major role in all the MKSS-led mobilizations.[7] Lal Singh shared with the three activists similar ideas and notions of social justice. Eventually, this led to the formation of a nucleus of likeminded individuals who would form the core of grassroots mobilization of the MKSS. It can be seen from the early struggles of the MKSS that even in the initial phase linkages were forged, which were both 'bottom up'—with likeminded local individuals such as Lal Singh—and 'top-down'—with sympathetic officials as seen in the case with sympathetic *patwari*, the SDM in Sohangarh, and intervention by the Rural Development secretary (S.R. Sankaran) in Dadi Rapat.

The formation of top-down linkages continued in later years. These linkages were not always unidirectional, where the MKSS sought State's intervention; at times the linkages were multidirectional, where State also sought guidance from the MKSS. For example, this linkage is reflected in an official communication (few years later) to Aruna Roy by Pritam Singh, an IAS officer who was posted as collector and district magistrate of Rajsamand district in 1996. In an official note dated 8

[7] Lal Singh is a local farmer who has been involved with the MKSS since its inception. He met the activists when he came to fix their kitchen door. This is when he requested the trio to intervene in the Sohangarh land issue. Lal Singh himself had an egalitarian outlook and had waged his own share of battles on social justice. Lal Singh was earlier a police constable and had mobilized a strike against the misuse of officials of lower rank for carrying out household chores for high-ranking officials. This mobilization had cost him his job. In this sense, Singh shared an ideational affinity to the core group of the MKSS (interview with Lal Singh, 30 April 2014, Devdungri, Rajasthan).

August 1996 (Letter from Pritam Singh (IAS), Collector and District Management, Rajsamand District, Rajasthan 1996), the officer assured Roy that he would look into the matters of irregularity and 'defalcation of funds in development works' as pointed in the MKSS's letter dated 4 July 1996 addressed to him. Interestingly, the officer also sought guidance and support from the MKSS in literacy, enrolment, immunization, and family-planning programmes of the GoI at the district level. Such multi-directional linkages were equally important for building the critical connections and opinions about the MKSS within the State, which in turn provided legitimacy to the core group of the MKSS.

There were multiple levels of linkages, which were forged both with the society and the State. At one level, the local links were established in the society as seen in the case of Lal Singh. At another level, local linkages within the State were established such as with the *patwari* and the district collector. At yet another level, linkages within the higher echelons of bureaucracy were activated at the national level, evident in the intervention by Sankaran in the Dadi Rapat minimum wage struggle. Connections at all these levels provided legitimacy to the sociopolitical processes initiated by the MKSS.

Roy acknowledged the importance of micro-level action being related to macro-level issues—'We have to work in a limited area. However, we have to understand how to relate our small work with big issues. Increasing this understanding is very important' (*Rediff* 2000).

These early interventions by the MKSS revolved around the legal entitlement related to land or wages but also underlined the significance of access to information. It was clear even in this nascent phase that the official records would support the demands for legal entitlements, such as the land records in the case of Sohangarh and the records of work undertaken in the minimum wage issue. Hence, the nature of both the linkages and the grassroots mobilization was ideational.

Process of *Jan Sunwayis* (Public Hearings): Framing the Demand for Access to Official Records

This section will discuss the process of *jan sunwayis* or public hearings established by the MKSS from the mid-1990s onwards. Two significant points emerge from this section. First, these public hearings resulted in the framing of issues on entitlement and wages as 'access or right to information'. Second, the public hearings also served as platforms where broader linkages were forged to deepen the public discourse around RTI. At one level the public hearings mobilized the subalterns and established local linkages and on another they established linkages with the elite such as the bureaucrats, legislators, journalists, academics, and writers, both within State and society.

How did the idea of *jan sunwayis* emerge as an integral part of the MKSS's work in the mid-1990s? In a way, the idea of public hearings was path-dependent on the MKSS's earlier engagement with issues of wage entitlement, drought relief, and food distributed through the PDS. These interventions also resulted in the conviction that access to official records were instrumental in exposing corruption and irregularity at the village level. Following the interventions in Dadi Rapat, the issue of minimum wage and workers' entitlement became the core focus of the MKSS in the coming years. A specific case of wage entitlement, which came before the MKSS in 1994, is worth discussing. An old man approached and requested the MKSS to intervene to help him get wages, which were long overdue. Workers from the MKSS went to the block office and were able to access and note down the records of work undertaken and wages distributed. The records revealed massive irregularities and corruption in funding and works executed (Ramon Magsaysay Award Foundation n.d.).

This specific case and earlier interventions in Sohangarh and Dadi Rapat convinced the MKSS to devise a methodology of *jan sunwayis* or public hearings to delve deeper into the problem. These hearings followed the methodology of collectively scrutinizing the financial and other related records of the public offices involved in the development work. The process entailed acquiring copies of relevant documents from some sympathetic bureaucrats (or known ones from Roy's network) and reading it aloud in front of the village at the level of Gram Sabhas. State officials were also invited to be part of the public hearing.

The hearings were presided over by well-respected individuals from within and outside the villages (Jenkins and Goetz 1999). In due course, this process exposed corruption and an exploitative nexus in the villages. The content of the public hearings was inextricably linked to the issue of access to information. Access to official records showing the financial details of the development work was necessary for the hearings. However, the norm of secrecy locked in at the systemic level hindered accessibility to these documents. Initially, progressive and sympathetic elements from within the State were instrumental in facilitating access to official records. Records revealed shocking corruption and misappropriation of funds. For instance, corruption in the muster rolls of the work sites was exposed during these hearings, which showed that wages were given to people who were not part of the work. Some names in the muster roll did not even receive the wage. It was discovered that toilets, school buildings, wells, and irrigation facilities were shown to be paid for but did not have a physical presence in the village. Between 1994 and 1995, five public hearings were organized, which exposed similar corruption at the local level (see A5 in book-end Appendices for a snapshot of the initial phase of public hearings).

The process of *jan sunwayis* was important from two perspectives.

First, the significance of access to official records was established through the *jan sunwayis*. The records (not open to the public) were the hard proof against the corrupt nexus and were inextricably linked to the legal entitlement of the workers and citizens. This led to the framing of issues such as 'access to information' as an important link in the development chain.

Second, the MKSS itself was forming its core by forging linkages with the likeminded part-time activists at the local level who shared the MKSS's idea of social justice. At another level, linkages were established with the progressive elements both within the State and society.

For instance, Roy's access within the government was consequential in obtaining the personal involvement of the BDO in the first public hearing. An early case of exposing corruption before the public hearing phase was undertaken by the MKSS with the help of a young IAS probationer, Nirmal Wadhwani. He was posted as a BDO in the Raipur block of Pali district. On the MKSS's request, the young

BDO visited one of the panchayats in Kot Kirana and read out the names in the muster roll in public, which to his surprise contained a significant number of proxy entries. He also discovered that the figures for the construction of panchayat building were augmented. He was reading out these details from the panchayat premise itself and could see for himself that the building accounted for in the papers was a half-built structure.

Later, on the request of Shankar Singh, Wadhwani agreed to share the copies of the muster roll, bills, and vouchers regarding the drought relief work. Junior colleagues of Wadhwani were not entirely supportive of the proactive BDO on his decision to open access to official records. In the face of opposition from his junior officers, Wadhwani asked Shankar Singh to copy all the records by hand. This was the record that formed the basis of the first public hearing in Kot Kirana. It can also be argued that sympathetic elements within the State were not only extending their support but also responding to the emerging social–political processes.

The connection with the government officials can be traced in the MKSS's formal engagement with other government institutions such as the LBSNAA and Roy's earlier background as an IAS officer. For example, the connection with the BDO was a result of a prior linkage, which was instrumental in forging a cooperative relation between the BDO and the MKSS. Nirmal Wadhwani had heard of and met Aruna Roy when he was a trainee at the IAS academy in Mussoorie. The linkage was rekindled when Wadhwani had assumed the role of BDO in Pali. In yet another example, in 1995, R.N. Mishra, a local schoolteacher, was removed from his position due to his association with the MKSS. Aruna Roy intervened by writing to Abhimanyu Singh who was the education secretary with the Government of Rajasthan. As a result, R.N. Mishra was reinstated in his job (Letter from Education Secretary, Abhimanyu Singh, Government of Rajasthan, to Gajanand Joshi, Deputy Director, Education Department, Udaipur 1995). These are the early signs of a network emerging from both within and outside the system, which played an instrumental role in the evolving discourse around the RTI Act. A process of State-in-society in a mutually empowering relationship takes root between the local MKSS and the sympathetic actors within the State bureaucracy.

The linkages deepened during the process of *jan sunwayis*. Formation of linkages can be seen at two levels—at one level links were establish with the bureaucrats and at another level prominent social actors were included in the process. Hence, the MKSS was able to mobilize elements within the State as well as the elites in the societal realm.

For instance, Wadhwa presided over the public hearing in Bori village as the collector of Rajsamand district. Linkages were also established with prominent people in the society. In the first public hearing at Kot Kirana, social worker and faculty at Kanodiya College in Jaipur, Renuka Pamecha; Bunker Roy of Social Work and Research Centre (SWRC); and Tilonia and Sawai Singh of Samagra Sewa Sangh, Jaipur, presided.

In all the subsequent public hearings, similar patterns of 'State and society' can be seen. The second hearing on 7 December 1994 at Bhim was chaired by the progressive poet of Rajasthan, Harish Bhadani. Similarly, in a later public hearing on 17 December 1994 at Vijaypura in Deogarh block, a young IAS cadre officer, Aditi Mehta, and *Lokayan* editor and social activist, Vijay Pratap, presided over the hearing in personal capacities.

The fourth public hearing at Jawajain Ajmer District on 7 January 1995 was attended by senior lawyers of the Rajasthan High Court and a faculty member from the National School of Drama as independent observers.

It is important to note that in all the public hearings the MKSS was able to establish linkages with facilitating bureaucrats who were either part of the enquiry or issued orders to the panchayats to provide the copies of the official records (Mishra 2003).

In a later public hearing of 1999 at Bori village, the collector of Rajsamand district, Nirmal Wadhwani; noted writer and Booker prize winner, Arundhati Roy; Madhu Kishwar, an academic and editor of *Manushi*; and noted SC of India lawyer, Prashant Bhushan, presided over the hearing (Sebastian 1999). The presence of academics, poets, social activists, journalists, and lawyers was an early sign of the emergence of an epistemic community at the sub-national level, which later got augmented at the national level.

The grassroots processes in the societal realm were taking shape in tandem with the policy and political processes at the State level. For instance, in 1995, CM Bhairon Singh Shekhawat announced in the legislative assembly that the State government would allow access to documents and photocopies of the records of rural development work undertaken between 1985 and 1995. The announcement coincided with the fifth public hearing of Bhilwara in 1995. I will discuss the background and context of the CM's announcement in the next section.

Political Commitment towards Access to Information

The evidence examined in this section traces the continuity of ideas expressed by the political leadership and establishes that the political leadership was not necessarily against the idea of access to information. This manifested in Shekhawat's formal announcement on 5 April 1995 in the legislative assembly that the State government intended to open the access of official papers related to the rural development work undertaken between 1985 and 1995 at the panchayat level to the citizens (State Legislative Assembly Debates 1995: 434–5). Additionally, I also establish in this section that this announcement was not merely a response to the emerging demands from the social forces. Instead, there was a continuity of ideas, which reflected in the thinking of political leadership. Hence, the CM's announcement has to be placed within the broader context of the ideational continuation.

Yet the demands articulated by the social actors were significant. Even though the leadership was committed in its political and policy intent to granting RTI, some segments of the permanent bureaucracy were hesitant and uncertain about pursuing the expressed intent by the political executive. This uncertainty was successfully challenged by the sociopolitical formations outside the State, which was instrumental in the mobilization to enact RTI in the State of Rajasthan. A similar process was visible at the central level too. These processes will be discussed in the subsequent sections. I establish that the demands around access to information emanating from the societal realm put pressure on the political leadership and acted as a catalyst. However, the ideas expressed by the political leadership and the political intent articulated in the CM's announcement were the central rallying points around which these sociopolitical processes took shape.

Let us examine the political context of the CM's announcement. Was it a response to the emerging social processes demanding access to official records articulated during the *jan sunwayis*? I argue that this singular deduction leaves significant gap to explore a more nuanced understanding of the political context behind the CM's announcement. The CM's announcement in the legislative assembly reveals two significant points. First, the announcement demonstrates the political will and intention of the leadership in the State. Second, one can see a direct continuity between earlier ideas on openness and access to information and the announcement by the CM in the legislative assembly. It is pertinent to note that Shekhawat was part of the Janata Party government in 1977, and was CM of Rajasthan from 1977 to 1980. As I have discussed in Chapter 1, the Janata Party government had expressed willingness to be more transparent and open about government affairs. Shekhawat's later articulation in the legislative assembly can be seen as an extension of Janata Party's position on openness. After assuming the office of CM in 1977, Shekhawat pushed for effective administration and change in attitude of the bureaucracy in dealing with public grievances. Additionally, he had also called for an effective control of the bureaucratic chain in the state to curb corruption (*ToI* 1977). During his second (1990–2) and third (1993–8) terms as well, Shekhawat had come to power with a strong anti-corruption agenda.[8] Shekhawat's stance on transparency and his announcement have to be placed within this broader political context rather than in isolation (Sawhney 1990).

[8] This is not to state, however, that the BJP government under Shekhawat was free of corruption and scams.

The impact of new social formations, which emerged during the public hearings organized by the MKSS, established direct causal linkage between the official records and corruption at the village level. This linkage between official records and corruption deepened the conviction of the political leadership, triggering the political announcement.

Internal papers of the MKSS reveal that the announcement was a result of the impact of public hearings, reflected clearly in the claim that 'the extraordinary achievement of this campaign was the announcement made by the CM of the State on the 5th April 1995 in Vidhan Sabha (legislative assembly)'.[9] However, the State refused to acknowledge the role of social actors. A press note issued by the government in May 1996 categorically refuted this claim, pointing towards internal conviction of the State and political leadership resulting in the announcement. It can be surmised that the policy outcome was a result of a combined impact of internal conviction within the State, which was evident in the CM's commitment as well as the political mobilization spearheaded by the MKSS. Sections within and outside the State needed to align their forces against those who gained from secrecy.

Emerging Social Demands: Society Holding the State Accountable

The announcement of the CM in the legislative assembly proved to be a rallying point around which the social forces outside the State mobilized and accentuated their demands for access to information. The initial *public hearings* between 1994 and 1996 had demonstrated that the grassroots governance and its effectiveness were inextricably linked to the access to official records. Moreover, political commitment and the positive intention displayed by the CM in the legislative assembly were not followed by a concrete policy to grant RTI to the people. Policy inaction was taken up by the MKSS for further mobilization to demand RTI from the state government.

[9] Public Statement, MKSS, 19 September 1995.

Within this context, this section will discuss the strategies through which these demands were articulated and communicated to the state government. This will also help us understand the emerging State–society dynamics around a policy choice about which the State was still hesitant despite the political commitment. Evidence examined in this section points towards two significant processes. First, mobilization for the demand for access to information was also used to forge linkages both with the grassroots and the elites. For instance, prominent journalists, jurists, former and serving bureaucrats, and other prominent actors were invited to be part of the meetings and dharnas that were organized all over Rajasthan to demand access to official records (as promised by the CM). Second, this was also an early phase of a deeper process that was set in motion later by progressive likeminded elements with similar ideas on transparency, openness, access, or RTI coming together for a common goal, that is, access to official records. In this phase early signs of confluence of ideas were visible.

On 25 September 1995, a public meeting was organized by the MKSS titled 'Transparency and Right to Information' in Beawar, a small town in Ajmer district in Rajasthan. Villagers, elected representatives of village bodies, members of mass-based organizations, lawyers, and academics participated in this meeting. The demand for orders to operationalize the CM's announcement was unequivocally expressed in the meeting. Crucially, a retired civil servant, K.R. Venugopal, was the chief guest and the keynote speaker in the meeting. Venugopal served as the additional secretary and secretary in the PM's office during 1990–5. These were early signs of two processes taking shape. First was the spread of transparency and access to information in an environment external to the State. Second, as evident in the participation in this meeting, linkages were being forged on a common issue area with a wide section of representatives, which included grassroots-level workers, common citizens, bureaucrats, activists, journalists, and the legal fraternity.

Subsequently, one year after the CM's announcement with a lack of follow-up by the administration on the issue, a dharna was organized under the umbrella of the MKSS in Beawar, from 5 April 1996. Crucially, this was also election time in the state. The dharna was strategically planned to coincide with the elections. The protest lasted for forty days in Beawar, which later extended to the state capital Jaipur on 6 May 1996. Notably, a day after the protest started in Beawar, the state government, on 6 April 1996, granted the right to inspect and copy development-related official documents at the village level. The government order also instructed the panchayat to publicly display the expenditure details related to development work on an information board. The order was promptly faxed to the SDM's office in Beawar, the place of the protest. This order was rejected by the MKSS on the grounds that it was incomplete as it failed to grant the right to photocopy the documents, backtracking on the declaration by the CM in the legislative assembly. The logic was that since most people in the villages could neither write nor read, they would not be able to inspect or copy the documents.

Hence, the dharna continued in Beawar and Jaipur. The mobilization in Beawar had the support of more than 400 signatories and by the time the protest extended to the state capital, Jaipur, it had the support of more than seventy people's organizations (see also Mander and Joshi 1998).[10] At another level, the dharna caught the attention of journalists, bureaucrats, and persons from the legal fraternity. For instance, the demand found sympathizers in eminent journalists such as Nikhil Chakravartty, Kuldip Nayar, Ajit Bhattacharjea, and Prabhash Joshi; political activists such as Swami Agnivesh; social activists such as Medha Patkar; and serving bureaucrats such as Harsh Mander as well as and former ones such as G.R. Khairnar.

While the pressure was deployed on the government from outside to issue an official order as a follow-up to the CM's announcement, internally within the State, dialogues were initiated to demand a prompt follow-up action by the government. This was reflected in a number of communications from the MKSS to the State government. Letters were promptly dispatched to both the bureaucracy and the political leadership. For instance, the MKSS wrote directly to the CM rejecting the government order, which granted permission to inspect and physically copy the official records related to development

[10] Interview with Nikhil Dey, 30 April 2014, Devdungri, Rajasthan.

work. The objection to the order was expressed in no uncertain terms in a letter to the CM dated 9 April 1996.[11] In the letter, the MKSS demanded the right to 'photocopy' the documents on the lines of the CM's announcement in the legislative assembly.

Later, a communication was sent to the chief secretary of Rajasthan, M.L. Mehta, on 11 May 1996, regarding the possibility of policy steps by the government to follow up on the announcement by the political leadership. It is noteworthy that the chief secretary was in 'sync' with the activities of the MKSS. In January 1995, a presentation was given to the chief secretary on the main findings of the public hearing in Jawaja. The communication by the MKSS was swiftly acknowledged by the chief secretary in his letter dated 12 May 1996, which was addressed to Aruna Roy. In the letter, he assured the MKSS that the state government had decided to form a committee to explore the possibility of operationalizing the access to official records at the village level in line with the CM's announcement.

This was followed by a formal press note issued by the state government on 14 May 1996. Interestingly, the press note categorically denied the role of social organizations in the initial steps towards RTI. The press note declared that since the CM and the state government itself had taken the initiative, there was no question of backing out from this commitment.[12] The official stance of internal conviction and initiative of the government was reflected in the views expressed within the administration. In an interview given in 2009, Chief Secretary M.L. Mehta corroborated this official stance. While acknowledging the 'good work' of the MKSS, he opined that the MKSS was not responsible for bringing about the idea of RTI, but that it was the government that played an instrumental role in giving 'birth' to the idea of RTI (Srinivasan 2001: 87).

11 The MKSS registered a formal protest to the CM via a letter dated 9 April 1996. The letter is addressed to the CM copied to the chief secretary, secretary-planning, inter-departmental commissioner, and SDM Beawar.

12 The title of the press communiqué was 'CM's announcement to disclose information regarding rural development work, no question of backing from the initiative'.

Additionally, the press note also formally announced the formation of a state-level committee under the chairmanship of Additional Secretary Arun Kumar. Professor V.S. Vyas, director of Institute of Development Studies (Jaipur), along with the development commissioner, district collector, secretary panchayati raj, and director of the Department of Rural Development who were the other members of this committee. The committee was directed to submit its report within two months of its constitution, which would form the basis for the policy operationalization of the CM's announcement in the legislative assembly.

Significantly, the only 'non-government' member of the committee, Professor Vyas, was a close ally and sympathizer of the MKSS. In fact, during the dharna in Beawar and Jaipur, Vyas often acted as a mediator between the administration and the MKSS. The linkage between Professor Vyas and the MKSS can be ascertained from the fact that in 1992, Aruna Roy, Nikhil Dey, and Shankar Singh (along with Anchie Singh) had authored a report on RTI for the Institute for Development Studies, Jaipur (Srinivasan 2001: 36).

Following this press release by the government, the dharna was formally lifted by the MKSS. The committee submitted its report to the government on 29 August 1996. The report was supportive of granting and operationalizing RTI at the panchayat level. It felt that 'transparency in development works done by the Panchayati Raj Bodies would ensure their effective execution'. Strangely, the report of the committee, even though it was examining the possibility of granting legal entitlement of right to know, was declared secret by the government, pointing yet again towards the hesitancy and polarity of the state government.

Irked by the government's decision to declare the report 'secret', V.S. Vyas, wrote a rather irate letter to the chairman of the committee, Arun Kumar, copying it to the chief secretary of the state. The letter demanded that the report be released officially.

> The report should be published and made available without any further delay. It is totally indefensible to make the report of a Committee constituted to strengthen and implement the right to information a 'confidential' document. This is making all of us associated with the

> Committee, and in fact the Government, a butt of ridicule. (Letter from Professor V.S. Vyas, to Arun Kumar, Additional Chief Secretary, Government of Rajasthan 1997)

Emanating from his prior linkages with the MKSS, Professor Vyas's stand was in line with the objections of the MKSS, who protested this move by the government.

The constitution of the committee and the submission of its report were not followed by any policy steps by the government to ensure access to information at the panchayat level. Another round of dharnas was organized between February and May 1997 to demand legal right to obtain copies of the documents related to development work in the panchayats as originally announced by the CM in the legislative assembly. Division-level dharnas were organized in five divisions—Ajmer, Kota, Udaipur, Bikaner, and Jodhpur. These dharnas culminated in a major dharna in Jaipur to articulate the demand. Starting from 14 July 1997 (a year since the Beawar dharna was lifted), this dharna lasted for fifty-three days from 26 May till 14 July 1997.

Incidentally, the political leadership was still committed to its intention to promulgate this legislation. This is evident from the fact that the CM during the Chief Ministers' Conference held on 24 May 1997 in New Delhi pointed out that the government had ensured transparent governance by passing an order that allows citizens to obtain photocopies of the records related to various departments at the panchayat level. The intention by the political leadership reflected in the CM's speech during the Chief Ministers' Conference on 24 May 1997:

> Access to information is key to people's power, for greater transparency and ensuring good quality work, we have recently issued instructions allowing people to take copies of documents related to all public works executed by local bodies and public works department. (Roy 1999: 34)

He assured the delegation led by veteran journalist Kuldip Nayar that the formal orders would be notified by 3 July 1997. On 3 July

1997 itself, a government subcommittee was constituted to look further into the matter. Clearly, the political intention was not in sync with the policy intentions of the government (*Lokayan Bulletin* 1999: 44). The dharna in Jaipur coincided with the Chief Ministers' Conference in New Delhi.

Subsequently, in a press conference called on 14 July 1997, the deputy CM declared that the Panchayati Raj Act was amended six months back to include provisions to obtain certified copies of documents related to panchayati raj institutions. That the order appeared in the government gazette six months back baffled the protestors and observers alike. The protest was called off after the gazette notification was made public.

Significant points emerge from the chain of events discussed in this section. As I have established, the idea of openness and access to information had by this time become part of the 'mainstream politics'. This is evident in the CM's announcement in the legislative assembly and his assurances, which followed the announcement. In this sense, there was both political commitment and policy intent.

The political commitment and intent did not translate in a concrete policy action. This meant that there were segments within the State that were still hesitant about granting right to access information. At the same time the political commitment remained constant throughout as part of the mainstream politics.

This uncertainty was challenged and eventually removed by social action. Epistemic linkages can be seen working from both within State and society, acting collectively to remove the persisting uncertainty regarding the norm of openness within the State. Actors forming these linkages point towards State and society working together in a mutually empowering relationship. The push of epistemic linkages converged with the mainstream politics eventually removing the underlying hesitancy within the State.

These processes form an important component of the final stages of *layering*. I establish in the subsequent sections that similar processes emerged at the national level, especially from the mid-1990's onwards, playing a significant role in the final stages of institutional change.

Emerging Linkages in the Societal Realm: Conflux of Progressive Elements

Outside the realm of dharnas and protests, broader processes were taking shape in terms of ideational linkages, which were forged around a common theme of transparency, accountability, and RTI. In this section we will examine the process of linkage formation. It points towards a confluence of progressive elements from the press, bureaucracy, judiciary, and social activists. In this light, I examine how these likeminded actors converged with common ideas on transparency and access to information. These linkages were also early signs of the formation of an epistemic network.

Journalists

The previous chapters show that the question of free press and its right to access to information deepened the ideational churning within the State. This pattern took yet another dimension when prominent journalists supported and displayed their solidarity in the Beawar dharna deepening the discourse further outside the State realm. In a sense, this was a continuation of earlier demands from the press for openness and access to information. The Beawar dharna provided them with a platform to express their views.

For instance, Prabhash Joshi, a respected senior journalist and thinker, visited Beawar during the dharna, and upon his return to New Delhi wrote a powerful editorial in a Hindi newspaper, *Jansatta*. The editorial titled 'Hum Janenge, Hum Jiyenge' (We Will Know, We Will Live) outlined the need for having the RTI (Roy, Dey, and Singh 2010).

Similarly, another distinguished journalist, Kuldip Nayar, upon his return from Beawar, wrote on RTI and the experiences of the MKSS in one of his regular columns in the English newspaper, *The Hindu* (Nayar 1997). Ajit Bhattacharjea, a senior journalist, on 16 December 1996 wrote in the English newspaper *Asian Age*, urging the government to honour its promise to enact RTI (Bhattacharjea 1996). This was followed by an editorial in the Hindi newspaper

Dainik Hindustan (Bhattacharjea 1997). Both the regional and national press carried the viewpoints of these prominent journalists—the mobilization in Beawar and Jaipur providing the context of the mobilization for RTI in Rajasthan.

Two significant points must be flagged here. First, the discourse attained a significant dimension and deepened further since these eminent journalists were raising the issue in both the English and vernacular press. On the one hand, they articulated and expressed their solidarity towards the demands expressed in Rajasthan on the issue of access to panchayat records, and, on the other, they held the national government accountable for its promise to promulgate the legislation on the freedom of information. This coincided with the second phase, which was characterized by hectic activity around the possible legislation on access to information both in terms of political commitment and policy movement within the executive as the idea of openness got embedded in mainstream politics (elaborated in Chapter 2).

Second, by virtue of their well-respected standing as journalists and public intellectuals, they had access to the political class, the executive, and important people from other fields. For instance, both Prabhash Joshi and Ajit Bhattacharjea had played an instrumental role in forging linkages with the PCI and convincing former chief justice P.B. Sawant to draft the proposed law on freedom of information. In another instance, Kuldip Nayar while expressing his solidarity led a delegation to meet the CM on the sidelines of the Chief Ministers' Conference to request him to issue executive orders for the implementation of his announcement to grant access to information in Rajasthan.

Bureaucracy

The progressive elements within the bureaucracy worked from both within and outside the State. For instance, Harsh Mander, an IAS officer, had extended his support to the demand for access to information in Rajasthan and had attended the Beawar dharna. A few months after his return from Rajasthan to Madhya Pradesh, Mander passed an executive order to grant RTI to the citizens of Bilaspur division in six government departments (elaborated in Chapter 2). Mander shared his executive order with Aruna Roy (through a letter dated 31 December 1996). In May 1996, he also shared the draft Madhya Pradesh Right to Information Bill with Nikhil Dey of the MKSS for his comments and suggestion (Letter from Harsh Mander, Professor, Public Administration, to Nikhil Dey, MKSS 1996). By this time Harsh Mander was posted as professor of public administration at LBSNAA, Mussoorie.

Later, in March 1997, Mander shared a note with the secretary, Department of Administrative Reforms and Public Grievances, to express his views on RTI in the light of the report of the H.D. Shourie Committee. Mander also articulated his views in the public domain through an article in an English newspaper. He wrote an article on corruption in an English daily *Pioneer* on 10 May 1996 (Mander 1996).

It is evident that Harsh Mander was working simultaneously from both within and outside the State, deepening the ongoing discourse within the executive and extending his support to the emerging discourse outside the State. The evidence also points towards the process where Mander in his capacity as a bureaucrat was acting as a bridging element between the State and society. This is apparent in that he passed the executive order on RTI in the Bilaspur division upon his return from the Beawar dharna. In a way it can be seen as a policy articulation of the ongoing demands on RTI in Rajasthan. On the other hand, he was sharing the policy steps within the State with social actors for their feedback and comments as evident in the letters written to the MKSS representatives. Later, Mander played an instrumental role in bringing together the progressive elements from both within and outside the State on a common platform.

Apart from Mander, other senior bureaucrats with progressive views on the issue of RTI also took keen interest in the emerging discourse on access to information and had active linkage with the developments in Rajasthan. Initial signs of these linkages were visible from the early 1990s onwards when a senior bureaucrat, S.R. Sankaran, was involved on the issue of payment of minimum wage in Brar panchayat, which was taken up by the MKSS. Later, Sankaran visited Devdungri.

On yet another occasion, a presentation was given to B.N. Yugandhar, former secretary of rural development, GoI, in February 1995 on the findings of the fourth public hearing in Jawaja.

Similarly, N.C. Saxena, who was also secretary at the Department of Rural Development, had active linkages with the MKSS since the early 1990s. N.C. Saxena was sympathetic to the demands to obtain photocopies of the documents related to development projects in the panchayats. In this light, he initiated steps within the government to ensure access to information at the panchayat level. As secretary, Ministry of Rural Development, Saxena, on 2 June 1997 wrote to all the state governments, directing them to pass orders to display the information related to expenditure and allocation of development work at the panchayat level on public noticeboards. Additionally, the communication also directed the state governments to ensure that the citizens have the right to inspect and photocopy all the documents related to development works at the panchayat level (discussed in Chapter 2). The issue was brought up again by N.C. Saxena in his communication with the chief secretaries of various states. In an official note dated 9 June 1997, Saxena provided policy recommendations for transparency and access to information at the panchayat level.

> There has to be a mechanism by which the poor people in a village know about the availability of funds with the gram panchayat; how they are being spent and what schemes are being funded … secondly, there should be a system by which information regarding availability of funds and its expenditure is displayed at prominent place in the village. (Internal Government Note to All Chief Secretaries 1997)

Significantly, Saxena, in his capacity as the director of LBSNAA, Mussoorie, along with Mander, organized a brainstorming meeting of these progressive elements at the academy. The meeting was instrumental in bringing together these actors on a common platform.

Incidentally, both Yugandhar and Saxena came from the IAS and also shared a similar legacy with S.R. Sankaran who was recognized and known for his pro-poor, pro-Dalit policies aimed towards the upliftment of excluded and marginalized groups. His pro-poor stance is reflected in one of his writings, 'There are laws which are enabling, empowering and facilitating mechanisms, which give sanction and authority to various public functionaries. They should be used as tools in favour of the poor to enhance the space for them' (Sankaran 2002: 364). Aruna Roy herself held Sankaran in high esteem.

> There were, however, two people whom she admired as model civil servants. One was S.R. Shankeran [Sankaran], a bachelor who was secretary of Rural Development to the Government of India. … The other was M. K. Bezboruah, who entered the civil service at the same time Aruna did and rose to Secretary to the Tariff Commission, Government of India. (Ramon Magsaysay Award Foundation n.d.)

As in the case of the press, traces of some segments of bureaucracy being in favour of greater openness regarding the affairs of the State were visible in early periods as well (discussed in Chapters 1 and 2). Hence, the views expressed at the present juncture were in continuation and extension of earlier ideas expressed on the issues of openness or access to information. The emerging processes outside and within the State deepened the ideational discourse further within the bureaucracy.

The prevailing mood of the bureaucracy is reflected in a contemplative piece authored by a former senior IAS officer, P.S. Appu, entitled 'Corruption and Criminalization' (P.S. Appu's Note on 'Corruption and Criminalization' 1996). While commenting on the exponential growth of criminalization in both politics and public life, Appu also provided policy prescriptions to tackle this menace. Among other policy recommendations, he called for 'drastic revision of the Official Secrets Act and abrogation of Section 5 [of the Act]' and 'the enactment of a new law guaranteeing the right to information' (Bhattacharya 2007). It can be surmised that like Aruna Roy, Appu's view on openness and transparency emanated from his own experience in the Indian Civil (administrative) Services.

Appu was a 1951 batch IAS officer from the Bihar cadre. After serving in both the state and central government, he became the director of LBSNAA in 1980. As the director of the IAS academy, he sought to take disciplinary action against a delinquent probationer who fired at his women colleagues during a field trip. He wrote to the Home Ministry seeking the probationer's removal from the academy. There was considerable political pressure on Appu to let go of the matter. In protest and on a matter of principle, he resigned from the IAS.[13]

Similar views on openness in favour of secrecy were expressed by B.G. Deshmukh, another 1951 batch IAS officer from the Maharashtra cadre, who was cabinet secretary from 1986 to 1989 and subsequently became the principal secretary of the PMO during the term of three PMs—Rajiv Gandhi, V.P. Singh, and Chandra Shekhar from 1989–91. As I have discussed in Chapter 2, the political and policy activities around RTI intensified during V.P. Singh's tenure as the PM. In this light, it is not surprising that the political will of the PM was echoed by his principal secretary, pointing towards similar ideas around openness within the State. B.G. Deshmukh commented in one of his writings,

> The Officials Secrets Act should he reviewed thoroughly and no privilege should be claimed by a bureaucrat or government for any document or information which is obligatory to place on the table of legislature. … We should seriously think of enacting a law for Right to Information. (Deshmukh 2009: 213–14)

Progressive ideas on transparency and RTI expressed by some segments of the bureaucracy emanated from their own experience of being in the IAS. This manifested in a number of cases. For instance,

[13] P.S. Appu's principled and ethical view regarding the IAS was marked by continuity and has been part of the ethical discourse within the civil services. Earlier in 1977, he was appointed as the chief secretary of Bihar. However, after a few months he resigned as his pre-conditions to accept the position of chief secretary, such as free hand in revamping the administration, building a team of his own choice, non-interference, and substantial delegation of powers, were not met. He joined another post with the GoI, which was not as significant as the position of chief secretary and even paid less (ATI Monograph 2005).

as discussed earlier, Aruna Roy's views were shaped by her own experience in the IAS. Similarly, some other serving and former bureaucrats such as S.R. Sankaran, N.C. Saxena, and Harsh Mander had expressed similar views favouring RTI. This trend is best reflected in one of the interviews of P.S. Appu that appeared in the news magazine *India Today*: 'This is a revolt against all that's wrong, but it's not enough,' said Appu. 'What we need is a mass movement to ensure radical political reforms' (*India Today* 1994).

The process of ideational intermingling is perceptible during this period, along with convergence of ideas. This can be ascertained from the fact that Harsh Mander shared P.S. Appu's writing on corruption and criminalization with the MKSS in April 1996. P.S. Appu's note was also circulated in subsequent meetings. As argued earlier (Chapter 2), by the early 1990s both the political and policy movement around RTI had been set in motion within the State. The role of these progressive bureaucrats is significant in this regard. With their involvement from both within and outside the State, the discourse around RTI intensified from within the State as well as outside it. This process took shape in cases of Harsh Mander and N.C. Saxena (discussed earlier). This was perceptible in other cases as well.

Judiciary

As I have discussed in the Chapter 3, interpretation of the constitution by the judiciary deepened the ideational discourse around RTI within the State. At this juncture actors from the judiciary joined in the emerging discourse outside the State around RTI. Justice P.B. Sawant stressed upon the need for legislation on RTI in his judgement of *S.P. Gupta* vs *President of India and Ors* (1982). Sawant, after his retirement and in his capacity as chairman of the PCI, formed linkages with the MKSS and other crucial actors.

Moreover, PCI played an instrumental role in extending its support to the emerging discourse outside the State. Similar to the bureaucratic actors, Justice Sawant was working from both within and outside the State. For instance, he shared the draft RTI legislation with the Shourie Committee constituted by the GoI in 1997.

At the same time, he shared it with other actors and opened it for wider discussion in public meetings. Subsequently, prominent lawyers such as Prashant Bhushan joined the discourse. It is pertinent to note that Prashant Bhushan played an instrumental role in a number of PILs around the issue of RTI, which was consequential in judicial pronouncements in favour of RTI.[14] Ideational confluence between Justice Sawant and Prashant Bhushan on the issue of RTI was established early. This is evident in a letter dated 20 August 1996 sharing the draft RTI Bill with Prashant Bhushan. The letter points towards a working relationship between the two on the issue of RTI.

Academia

Apart from the prominent journalists, grassroots and political activists, and judicial actors, academics with 'activist' inclinations displayed their keenness on the issue, which resulted in the formation of linkages with these actors. Formation of such linkages could be seen in the case of Professor V.S. Vyas (Institute of Development Studies, Jaipur) and the MKSS. Professor Vyas was also part of the government committee constituted by the Government of Rajasthan.

Likewise, mutual linkages were established with Professor Shekhar Singh who was a faculty member at the IIPA. Singh had a unique position: he was an academic and at the same time was also closely involved with the environmental movement. It was his involvement with the environmental movement that brought him closer to the issue of RTI. Apart from that he had close linkages with the government. In the early 1990s he was adviser, Planning Commission of India, and as a result had worked closely with then PM V.P. Singh. Hence, like the actors from bureaucracy, Professor Singh had active linkages within the State as well as with the movement or discourse outside it, in the social realm.

[14] Bhushan was the main petitioner in *People's Union for Civil Liberties* vs *Union of India*, where RTI was upheld and elevated to the status of human right (discussed in Chapter 3).

Conspicuously, even before the formation of the MKSS or the NCPRI, scholars were beginning to express their views on the right to know. For instance, in 1991, renowned legal scholar, S.P. Sathe, published a book on Right to know (Sathe 1991) opining that in a democratic government State as a privileged custodian of information should have a legal obligation to disclose it. Sathe recommended constitutional amendment to Article 19 (1) (a) and the provisions of the OSA.

Two points are discernible from the processes discussed here. First, the progressive elements from various segments from both the State and society, such as the social activists, journalists, bureaucrats, actors related to judiciary, and academics, were articulating ideas on transparency, openness of the government systems, and RTI. In some cases the ideas expressed were in continuation of the ideational journey from before, such as in the case of press, bureaucrats, and the judiciary.

Second, at this juncture one can see the convergence between progressive ideas as well as the actors expressing it. Meanwhile, the ideational churning within the State was an ongoing process, which intensified from the early 1990s onwards. At the same time, extraneous processes were beginning to take shape outside the State, in the societal realm, pointing towards an emerging State–society dynamic. At the State level, for instance in the case of Rajasthan, the new social and political formations outside the State had started putting pressure on the State's policy machinery, exacerbating the internal policy processes within the State.

Meetings, Seminars, and Workshops: Epistemic Evolution and Consolidation

The confluence of ideas took a definite shape in a series of meetings, conferences, and workshops. The meetings provided a space where linkages were forged with likeminded elements from varied backgrounds, such as bureaucrats, journalists, prominent political leaders, academics, and activists.

This was evident in a two-day workshop on RTI organized by LBSNAA on 6 and 7 October 1995. The workshop was organized on the initiative of N.C. Saxena, who was the Director of LBSNAA (Mussoorie) and Harsh Mander who was the deputy director of the academy.[15] The workshop was attended by progressive elements from various segments (discussed earlier)—activists, professional, and administrators—to work out a national agenda and formation of a national body towards the common goal of RTI (Singh 2011: 55). A draft bill was formulated in this meeting on the basis of the discussions.

Significantly, in this meeting, N.C. Saxena, on the issue of disclosure (or non-disclosure) of information, suggested that whatever can be shared in the parliament can also come under the purview of the RTI. This suggestion is often cited as a unique example of what came out of the Mussoorie meeting, in the dominant RTI narrative,

> This meeting produced one of the central provisions of the RTI Act 2005—a proviso in the law that prevents civil servants from misusing the exemption clause to restrict access to information. Dr. Saxena, the Director of the Academy, conceived the idea behind the clause. (Pande 2014: 122)

Interestingly, a similar view was expressed by the GoM constituted to examine the draft of the freedom of information bill in October 1997. The GoM was of the view that the disclosure should follow the general principle that what is disclosed in the parliament can be treated as information under the proposed legislation (Minutes of the Meeting of GoM 1997b). This points towards convergence of ideas within the State both at the level of the permanent and political executive.

[15] I interviewed Shekhar Singh on 25 March 2015 in New Delhi, during which he recalls that in the early 1990s (around 1992–3) Mander took a similar initiative before this meeting at LBSNAA, when like-minded individuals were brought together in a village in Chittoor district of Andhra Pradesh. These were activists, former and serving bureaucrats, and academics who were working on different issues but had common ideas around transparency, governance, and corruption. This points towards a confluence of ideas and Mander's instrumental role in bringing together these actors on a common platform. The LBSNNA meeting was, in many senses, a continuation from the Chittoor meeting.

Subsequently, on 21 and 22 July 1996, the Pink City (another name for the city of Jaipur) Press Club organized a meeting. Justice P.B. Sawant, Chairman of PCI, the CM of Rajasthan, government representatives, activists, senior journalists, and trade union representatives participated in the meeting. The two-day meeting discussed the possibility of legislation on RTI.

Following the meeting in Jaipur, a two-day meeting was organized by the PCI on 31 July and 1 August 1996. This was a high-profile meeting which saw the participation of Justice P.B. Sawant, Chairman, PCI; prominent journalists such as Nikhil Chakravartty, Prabhash Joshi, and Ajit Bhattacharjea; former PMs V.P. Singh and Chandra Shekhar; Attorney General of India; retired judge of Bombay High Court, V.M. Tarkunde; and constitutional expert and former secretary general of lower house of Indian parliament, Subhash C. Kashyap (Pande 2014: 127). Apart from these prominent participants, academics, activists, and journalists participated in the meeting.

This was followed by another meeting at the Gandhi Peace Foundation in New Delhi hosted by World Wide Fund for Nature (WWF), India. Like other meetings, the participants were from the media, former judges, activists, legislators, academics, and former and serving bureaucrats (Singh 2007: 43)

Formation of National Campaign for People's Right to Information: The Network of Epistemic Community

On the one hand, a series of frequent meetings brought various actors together on a common platform and also affirmed their linkages towards pursuing a common policy agenda, that is, the RTI. After the meeting at the Gandhi Peace Foundation, this agenda took formal shape as the NCPRI.

The founding members of the NCPRI were a mix of people comprising journalists, legal experts, activists, and academics. First, the members of the NCPRI came from various fields and brought expertise from different vantage points. For instance, journalists, by virtue of being in the media, knew how to create a discourse in the public domain.

This is evident from various articles written by prominent journalists during the Beawar and Jaipur dharnas. The legal experts brought inside knowledge of the judiciary and also the legalities involved with the proposed legislation on the RTI. Bureaucrats contributed with their inside knowledge of policy and political processes within the State. Academics contributed with their expertise on the subject, which came with their involvement and interaction with processes within the State and outside it. Activists pitched in with the perspective and experience of grassroots demands and subsequent mobilization.

Second, inter-linkages between these progressive elements was established early on, demonstrating a confluence of ideas. That these individuals might have been known to each other through their common links is incidental; it is their common interest and agenda around transparency, accountability, and the RTI, which is significant. Hence, this group was bound together by a common goal.

Third, by virtue of being experts in their profession or fields of activity, these actors had linkages both within and outside the State. This had a far-reaching impact on the core of the NCPRI, which eventually established a working synergy with the ongoing policy processes within the State and also created a discourse in the public domain.

How can this unique process be explained? Can it be explained by 'a small, intimate dense network' of people from the urban/upper caste/upper-middle-class, with common social, educational, and professional backgrounds having close connections with the political class (Sharma 2015)? Or does Bourdieu's idea of 'symbolic capital', where 'eminent activists' use their 'relevant capitals' collectively from the field of 'bureaucracy, politics and media' capture this process (Pande 2014: 146)? As argued earlier, while inter-personal connections might have facilitated the initial contact between these actors, a sustained working linkage can be better explained by their common interest around the idea of the RTI. A continuity of ideas around openness, transparency, accountability, and RTI was expressed by the press, political and permanent executive, and academia much before these individuals came together as the NCPRI. Hence, a dense, inter-personal network fails to explain this process. The commonality of ideas point towards an ideational linkage going beyond inter-personal linkages. Second, the symbolic capital of eminent activists enabling these actors to negotiate with the State does not explain the ongoing policy processes within the State. In fact, the group that emerged as the NCPRI was often working from both within and outside the State.

Moving beyond the arguments of a dense interpersonal network and symbolic capital, I propose two alternative arguments to explain the sociopolitical processes and the formation of the NCPRI. First, the role of ideas was paramount in bringing these actors together and the formation of linkages. The openness of government systems, State transparency and accountability, and citizens' RTI formed the ideational core around which this group emerged together as the NCPRI. If the political and policy processes within the State were the result of an ideational churning (discussed in the first three chapters), the formation of the NCPRI should also be treated as part of this ideational churning.

Second, I argue that the evidence examined earlier and the membership of the NCPRI point towards an emerging epistemic community (Haas 1992), which had expertise and knowledge not only in their own fields but also specifically on ideas on openness, transparency, and the RTI. The common agenda brought them together and enabled considerable policy coordination, both within and outside the State, eventually reducing the uncertainties within the State, which might have existed on a particular policy choice. My argument draws upon Haas's (1992) 'epistemic community' whose control over knowledge and information enables norm diffusion (at the international level). The epistemic characteristics of this community with its area of expertise resulted in policy coordination by reducing the perpetuating uncertainty within the system about a particular policy choice. Haas's notion of 'epistemic community' explains the sociopolitical processes taking shape with the formation of the NCPRI. In this sense, the NCPRI was an epistemic network and constituted a varied representation of an epistemic community. Table 4.1 provides the membership profile of the NCPRI. The profiles of the members reveal that each member had unique epistemic characteristics bound together with common ideas. On account of these epistemic qualities, members of the NCPRI were uniquely placed to bring in their

Table 4.1 NCPRI—Profile of Founding Members

Member	Background	Epistemic Characteristics
Aruna Roy	Activist and former bureaucrat	She was part of the MKSS with a deep knowledge about the grassroots and governance needs at the local level. As a former bureaucrat, she was familiar with what was happening within the State and had linkages with the bureaucracy. She was uniquely placed to work from both within and outside the system.
Pradip Prabhu	Activist and academic	He was an activist involved with tribal rights for more than three decades and was general secretary of Kashtakari Sanghatana, an organization of poor, landless, and marginal adivasi (tribal) people from north Maharashtra. He was part of a number of government committees including member of the Advisory Committee of the Planning Commission on the Implementation of Welfare Legislation. He was the former dean, Department of Rural Development, Tata Institute of Social Sciences. Like Roy, he had his ear to the governance processes on the ground and had connections with the State.
S.R. Sankaran	Former bureaucrat	He was a prominent bureaucrat and secretary, Department of Rural Development, GoI. He brought with him internal knowledge of the processes within the State as well as society. He was mentor to many bureaucrats with an activist bent of mind, including Aruna Roy.
Shekhar Singh	Activist and academic	An academic and activist, he was involved in the environmental movement since the early 1980s and was

Member	Background	Epistemic Characteristics
		a faculty member at University of Delhi; North Eastern Hill University, Meghalaya; and professor at IIPA. Notably, IIPA was the place for training many middle-level and senior bureaucrats. Singh was an advisor at the Planning Commission during V.P. Singh's government. He was uniquely placed with linkages at three levels—grassroots, academic, and the State.
K.G. Kannabiran	Human rights activist and lawyer	He was an ardent human rights and civil liberties lawyer and member of the national executive of People's Union for Civil Liberties (PUCL)[16] from 1995 to 2009. He wrote several books on civil liberties and human rights. He was uniquely placed within the NCPRI to provide legal and policy inputs. By virtue of being a prominent lawyer he had linkages with jurists and other lawyers.
Prashant Bhushan	Lawyer	Like Kannabiran, he was a civil rights lawyer who filed more than 500 PILs on a number of issues such as corruption, environment, and so on. He was also member of PUCL. With an astute legal mind, he was in a strategic position to not only provide legal and policy inputs but also pursue

(*Cont'd*)

16 PUCL emerged out of People's Union for Civil Liberties and Democratic Rights (PUCLDR) formed by JP in 1976 to defend civil liberties and human rights of citizens. As discussed in Chapter 1, JP was instrumental in the citizens' movement and formation of an anti-Congress coalition focusing on anti-corruption, transparency, and civil liberties. The coalition eventually formed the Janata Party government in the centre in 1977.

Table 4.1 (*Cont'd*)

Member	Background	Epistemic Characteristics
		the issue of access to information within the judiciary, which he eventually did in a PIL filed in the SC on the FoI Bill 2002.
Renuka Misra	Activist	She was an activist and had connections with the media as her husband was R.K. Mishra, owner of the English daily *Patriot.*
Prabhash Joshi	Journalist	A noted journalist, he primarily used to write in Hindi newspapers and was known to write scathing editorials on issues of corruption and human and civil rights. He was founding editor of a major Hindi daily, *Jansatta*. As a journalist, Joshi was also involved in the Janata Party movement as he was editor of the newspaper *Prajaniti* brought out in support of the JP movement. He had linkages with the political class and was close to former PM V.P. Singh. He was strategically placed to deepen the discourse around access to information in the public domain as well as to lobby with the legislators.
Ajit Bhattacharjea	Journalist	A veteran journalist, he was an editor of three major English dailies—*The Hindustan Times*, *ToI*, and the *Indian Express*—before retiring in 1983. From 1995 till 2004 he was the chairman of the Press Institute of India. He was closely involved with the JP movement and was editor of *Everyman's Weekly*, an English publication promoting the views of JP.[17]

[17] Ajit Bhattacharjea also wrote a biography of JP (see Bhattacharjea 1978).

Member	Background	Epistemic Characteristics
		As a senior journalist and a public thinker, he had close relations with the political class.
M.P. Parameshwaran	Scientist and activist	He was a scientist at Bhabha Atomic Research Centre from 1956 to 1975. In 1975 he joined Kerala Sastra Sahitya Parishad (KSSP), a people's movement to popularize science especially among the disadvantaged groups. He was a member of CPI-M and had close connections with the CPI-M leadership.
Bharat Dogra	Journalist	An independent journalist and a public intellectual who was well known as a writer on number of social issues.

Source: Author.

own knowledge within the NCPRI as well as to contribute to the ongoing policy processes within the State.

The epistemic community, which came together as the NCPRI, worked towards a common goal of legislation on RTI.[18] Significantly, one can also see a continuation of ideational churning in this epistemic formation. As discussed before, the political movement spearheaded by the JP movement and the Emergency provided the

18 This is not to say, however, that the NCPRI was devoid of any tension. Like any other sociopolitical process, there have been tensions related to ideology and viewpoints within the NCPRI, though it worked as a cohesive group. For instance, in 1997, Aruna Roy circulated a rather angry letter to the members of the NCPRI lamenting the fact that there was lack of participation and interest by the members especially during the dharna in Jaipur. Roy says in the letter, 'I want to say that such prolonged dharnas need energy to be "supplied" by friends & and their support. Campaign members have to give some time to think, critique and support. Without this the camping will and has probably already suffered in Rajasthan'. She further cast serious doubts on the efficacy of the NCPRI's strategy of networking and expressed her desire to re-visit her role within the NCPRI.

backdrop for the formation of the first anti-Congress government in the centre by the Janata Party in 1977. This was also the first time that the government had expressed political and policy will to re-examine the persisting norm of secrecy within the State. This idea extended further in the social realm and traces of its influence can be seen within this epistemic community.[19] The ideational continuity is evident in the involvement of both Prabhash Joshi and Ajit Bhattacharjea within the NCPRI who were closely involved with the JP movement and were editors of publications brought out in support of the JP movement (see Table 4.1).[20] Similarly, both K.G. Kannabiran and Prashant Bhushan were part of PUCL, which was originally founded by JP in 1976 to raise issues of civil liberties and democratic rights during the Emergency.[21] Hence, I argue that both the 'push' and 'pull' factors for the formation of the NCPRI was ideational rather than the interpersonal connections with common backgrounds.

[19] As discussed in this chapter, Kuldip Nayar was a distinguished journalist who supported the MKSS and NCPRI's cause in Rajasthan, nationally opposed Emergency, and was sympathetic to the JP movement when he was working with the *Indian Express*. In fact, during the Emergency, he was arrested under the MISA, 1971. See Noorani 1978.

[20] The JP movement created public discourse on issues through two publications—*Everyman's Weekly* and *Prajaniti*. Ajit Bhattacharjea was in charge of the English journal and Prabhash Joshi was editor of the Hindi publication. The journals carried articles on the movement from different states. Publications were used to highlight the growing discontent against the Congress government and its leader Indira Gandhi. Both these publications were closed down during the Emergency.

[21] In the backdrop of large-scale civil and human rights violations during the Emergency, a conference was organized on 17 December 1976 in which JP took the initiative of forming PUCLDR. In 1977, the Emergency was lifted; however, with the reports of young boys labelled as Naxals being killed led to the re-christening of PUCLDR as PUCL in a conference held in 1980. Subsequently, leading jurists, public intellectuals, and lawyers such as V.M. Tarkunde (1982–4); Rajni Kothari (1984–6); and Rajindar Sachar (1986–95) provided leadership to PUCL. K.G. Kannabiran was president of PUCL from 1995 to 2010.

Interventions by the NCPRI: Advocacy, Discourse Creation, and Providing Legal–Policy Inputs

In this section, I examine the strategies adopted by the NCPRI to intervene in the process of policymaking at the central level. The strategies in turn are reflective of how the linkages worked within this epistemic community and how each node of this network contributed from the vantage of their epistemic characteristics.

The internal papers of the NCPRI and the MKSS point towards three interrelated areas around which the NCPRI concentrated its efforts. First, advocacy was carried out at different levels of the government both within the political class as well as within the executive. This was especially significant, in the light of the fact that the actors had linkages and interconnections with segments both within and outside the State.

The second area of activities clustered around deepening the discourse around RTI in the public domain. This took shape of meetings, seminars, and articles in the media to name a few.

Third, the NCPRI focused on providing policy inputs on the proposed legislation on the RTI. This objective was approached at two levels. First was the inputs provided to the policy processes within the State as external actors. For example, policy suggestions and inputs were provided as testimonies during various meetings of the parliamentary committees constituted to examine the legislation on RTI. Second, the policy intervention occurred from within the State. This process manifested more directly after the formation of the NAC by the UPA government in 2004. Significantly, some actors of NCPRI were part of the NAC when it was constituted. Hence, it can be argued that the NCPRI was working in tandem from both within and outside the State.

The three-pronged approach discussed here emerged clearly in the first internal meeting of the NCPRI held on 11 August 1996.

Advocacy

In terms of advocacy it was decided that parliamentarians and leaders of the opposition would be approached. Additionally, a declaration by the NCPRI was circulated to be signed and endorsed by the parliamentarians. An exhaustive list of parliamentarians from across party lines was drawn up for advocacy. For instance, former PMs H.D. Deve Gowda, V.P. Singh, and P.V. Narasimha Rao were part of the list. Specific responsibilities were distributed among the working group to contact parliamentarians known personally to them. Prabhash Joshi and Renuka Mishra were entrusted with the task of establishing contact with parliamentarians from Janata Dal and Congress Party. Aruna Roy on the other hand was supposed to initiate contacts with the CPI-M. Regional parties such as TDP and Samajwadi Janata Party (SP) were also targeted. K.G. Kannabiran was given the task of contacting the TDP and Prashant Bhushan was to contact the SP.

The focus of the NCPRI on advocacy with the political class emerges clearly from its first meeting. In the first meeting decisions were taken to start lobbying 'with the parliamentarians and leaders of the political parties and getting them to sign the declaration'. They further decided, 'Other members of the working group and the campaign who already had contact with the parliamentarians and political party leaders (the political executive) should also take the initiative and lobby on behalf the national campaign' (Minutes of the Working Group Meeting 1996). This strategy took definite shape in establishing long-term linkages with political leaders such as the former PM V.P. Singh. This was evident when the PCI organized a meeting in 1996 to discuss the draft RTI Bill. Former PMs V.P. Singh and Chandra Shekhar participated in this meeting (discussed earlier). Additionally, BJP leader Atal Bihari Vajpayee also extended his support to the meeting. Similarly, the NCPRI established connections with Dr Manmohan Singh in December 1998. In a letter to him dated 8 December 1998, the NCPRI expressed its concern over the delay in the passage of the proposed FoI Bill and requested a meeting with him. Significantly, Manmohan Singh was to become the PM later during the UPA government.

In addition, the NCPRI established contacts with the bureaucracy. Shekhar Singh and Harsh Mander initiated contacts within the administration and established relations with government institutions such as the LBSSNA and IIPA. Similar to the processes in Rajasthan, at the national level as well the NCPRI involved itself regularly with the ongoing policy processes within the State. On 8 February 1997, the NCPRI communicated to the additional secretary, Department of Administrative Reforms and Public Grievances, informing him about the activities of the NCPRI and that a note on the proposed FoI would be sent to the department and circulated to the Shourie Committee. Similarly, a note from the NCPRI working committee was shared with the cabinet committee constituted on the RTI in 1998. In the note, the NCPRI registered its appreciation for the PM's announcement that a bill on FoI would be introduced in the parliament. Additionally, some policy inputs were also provided to the cabinet committee on the proposed FoI Bill on including the private sector and NGOs within the ambit of the proposed law, provision for penalties, and the limitation and appellate mechanism outlined in the bill.[22] Often, advocacy would be accompanied by providing policy inputs. The strategy to contact specific parliamentarians from different parties and the permanent executive personally known to the working group points towards a broader process of episteme taking root within the policy processes of the State. The prominent position and collective knowledge base of the NCPRI, which represented different fields, enabled the NCPRI to access other prominent actors, which in this case belonged to the political and administrative classes. In this initial phase, the epistemic network imparted their collective knowledge to remove any policy uncertainty within the State on the issue of RTI. It may be noted that by 1996 the policy processes around a possible legislation on the access to information had already taken root within the State (discussed in Chapter 2).

Deepening the Discourse

The strategies discussed within the NCPRI also aim towards deepening the discourse in the public domain. In the first meeting itself,

[22] The letter was signed by Justice P.B. Sawant, Aruna Roy, Prabhash Joshi, and Ajit Bhattacharjea on behalf of the NCPRI.

the NCPRI adopted the approach of forming active linkages with the media. For instance, Ajit Bhattacharjea, who was the chairman of the Press Institute of India, formed an information cell within the institute to coordinate the flow of information from the NCPRI to the media. Additionally, he proposed to bring out a twelve-page monthly newsletter on RTI.

Prominent journalists such as Prabhash Joshi and Ajit Bhattacharjea were asked to organize their established contacts in journalism to highlight the issue in the public domain. Vernacular and regional press was also targeted. For example, Om Sharma, a freelance journalist from Rajasthan, was given the responsibility of galvanizing journalists' unions all over Rajasthan. A series of meetings and public hearings were planned to deepen the discourse in the public domain. Five public hearings were organized in Bhim, Jawaja, Devgarh, Mandal, and Alwar in Rajasthan between August and September 1996. Additionally, public hearings were organized in Madhya Pradesh and Maharashtra during this period.

The discourse was further extended by establishing linkages with likeminded organizations: trade unions, national networks, students' organizations, and human rights organizations. For instance, in Maharashtra, a meeting was organized with Shoshit Jan Andolan on 30 and 31 August 1996. Another meeting was organized at Makhan Lal Chaturvedi National University in 1996 in Bhopal, Madhya Pradesh. Linkages were established with organizations and networks such as Manav Hakka Abhiyan, Committee for Protection of Democratic Rights (CPDR), Jan Mukti Andolan, Tribal Joint Action Committee, PUCL, National Committee of Construction Labour, and Bombay Union of Journalists, to name a few.

In September 1996, Shekhar Singh organized a panel discussion at IIPA with the intention to initiate a dialogue with administrators. Prominent members of the NCPRI such as Aruna Roy, Ajit Bhattacharjea, and Prashant Bhushan were part of the proposed panel. It can be surmised that the various actors of the working group with their own set of linkages and knowledge base were working in tandem. This is evident from the fact that in September 1996 Shekhar Singh was invited by the LBSNAA to deliver the Srinivasan Memorial Lecture for the year 1996. Singh, in this lecture titled

TABLE 4.2 Meetings on RTI Organized at the NCPRI's Initiative

25 September 1995: Rajasthan State Level Convention on the RTI in Beawar. Demanded that an order be issued on the CM's statement in the state assembly in April 1995. K.R. Venugopal, Former Secretary PMO, was the chief speaker in the meeting.
6–7 October 1995: National meeting in the LBSNAA in Mussoorie. The academy gives a commitment on the issue.
4–6 June 1996: Meeting titled 'Living by (One's) Values, and Follow Up on Right to Information' in Dahanu, Maharashtra.
21–22 July 1996: Meeting in Jaipur on the RTI called by the Pink City Press Club. Participants: CM, Justice Sawant of PCI, journalist unions, senior activists, and others.
10 August 1996: PCI holds a high-powered meeting on the RTI with the participation of former PM V.P. Singh, CMs, the attorney general and other legal luminaries, media persons, activists, and others. Formation of core to draft the bill on the RTI.
30 September–2 October 1996: An NGO named Bharat Gyan Vigyan Samiti (BGVS) organized a three-day national convention on RTI at Pendra, Bilaspur, and Madhya Pradesh. Significantly, S.R. Sankaran was the chairperson of BGVS and Dr M.P. Parameswaran was the vice chairperson.

Source: Author

'Right to Information and the Environment' brought in his own experience from the environmental movement and RTI. Similarly, Prashant Bhushan shared the booklet prepared by the Press Institute and a note prepared by Shekhar Singh during a meeting on judicial accountability held in September 1998. Several meetings on RTI were organized on the initiative of the NCPRI to create a public discourse on the issue of RTI (see Table 4.2).

Policy Interventions: Providing Policy and Legal Inputs

The third objective of the NCPRI was to provide policy and legal inputs on the proposed legislation. The formation of the NCPRI in

1996 coincided with the PCI's initiative to draft legislation on FoI. Justice P.B. Sawant was the chairman of the PCI. Though he was not part of the working committee of the NCPRI, he had close linkages with the NCPRI. The NCPRI established contacts with Justice Sawant regarding the draft legislation and it was decided that a committee would be formed by the PCI to work out a draft.

Apart from Justice Sawant, Prashant Bhushan and Shekhar Singh were part of this drafting committee. Significantly, both Shekhar Singh and Prashant Bhushan were formally part of the NCPRI. In the second meeting of the NCPRI held on 31 August 1996, Prashant Bhushan shared some provisions of the draft bill worked out by the PCI. The PCI bill was further circulated to the Working Committee on Right to Information and Transparency constituted in January 1997, headed by H.D. Shourie.[23] Often, this took the shape of both advocacy and providing policy inputs. For instance, in 1998 Shekhar Singh on behalf of the NCPRI wrote to the president and then PM Atal Bihar Vajpayee, expressing concern on the delay in enactment of the proposed FoI law. Additionally, the letter urged the government to enact the legislation and requested time from the president and the PM for a meeting with the NCPRI delegation.

State–Society Engagement: 'Together' in the Policy Processes

By 2000 a more formal and structured State–society engagement can be seen emerging around the policy processes within the State. This reached a threshold during the UPA government with the formation of the NAC. This engagement points towards two processes taking root. First, it points towards the emerging epistemic community

[23] This is not to claim, however, that the Shourie Committee based its recommendations on the PCI bill. The PCI bill was one of the important documents that the committee studied in addition to the CERC draft bill of 1993, existing freedom of information laws in other developed and developing countries, and the internal note of GoI. This evidence is extensively laid out in Chapter 2.

around the issue of access to information. Second, the epistemic community was engaging formally with the State, contributing towards the ongoing policy processes at the State level.

This is reflected in the formal engagement with the policy processes within the government. For instance, the role of the 'epistemia' was evident in the depositions before the DRPSC-HA to examine the FoI Bill tabled by the NDA government in the parliament. The same process of 'State–society' engagement could be seen in the meetings of the DRPSC on Personnel, Public Grievances, Law and Justice constituted during the UPA regime to examine the amendments proposed in the FoI law of 2002. Finally, the constitution of the NAC when the UPA formed the government at the centre points towards the role of the epistemic community. In fact, the membership of the NAC is a clear pointer of that.

The DRPSC-HA considered the bill in five sittings during which they heard the testimonies of both government and non-government representatives. In its second meeting on 24 January 2000, the DRPSC engaged in representations by Maja Daruwala, Abha S. Joshi, Bimal Arora, and Deepika Mogilshetty of the CHRI;[24] Madhav Godbole, a senior IAS officer who retired as home secretary of the central government in 1993; A.G. Noorani, a senior advocate; and Manubhai Shah, Director of CERC—which was the first NGO to have drafted the FoI Bill in 1993. The profile of this group, which testified before the DRPSC, points towards two significant points. First, the group was part of the epistemic community with intra-linkages pointing towards an epistemic network. Second, typical of the epistemic network discussed here, each individual from this group forged with their own set of epistemic characteristics along with their own views on openness and access to information. Let us examine the profile of the individuals and

[24] CHRI worked with the NCPRI, and Maja Daruwala, director of CHRI worked closely with the NCPRI working group. Significantly, in 1999 Abha S. Joshi, who was working with CHRI, co-authored a paper with Harsh Mander, who was part of the NCPRI, on 'Movement for Right to Information in India'.

organizations who deposed before the DRPSC as witnesses. The profile would help us establish the epistemic characteristics of the group and would also show the continuity of ideas on openness and access to information expressed by some witnesses before the deposition by the DRPSC.

The CHRI is an international organization set up in 1987 mandated to work on the issue of human rights. It was based in London until 1993, when it shifted to Delhi. Maja Daruwala took over as its director in 1996 and decided to have three focus areas—RTI, police, and prison reform. CHRI, being an international human rights organization, was also keyed in to the emerging discourse on FoI laws globally. Nationally, it was engaged in the policy process as well. This is evident in two publications by the CHRI in 1999. The first publication provided comments and recommendation on the 1997 draft bill of the Shourie Committee (CHRI 1999). The second publication authored by V.K. Chand[25] examined the existing drafts of the FoI Bill such as the Shourie Committee bill, the CERC bill of 1993, and the PCI bill of 1996 (Chand 1999). The paper drew upon international FoI experiences from the USA, the UK, Ireland, South Africa, Canada, and Australia. This publication was supported by Friedrich Naumann Sttifung. Again, in 1999, Abha S. Joshi who was project-coordinator with CHRI co-authored a paper with Harsh Mander titled, 'Movement for Right to Information in India'. Importantly, Harsh Mander was part of the working committee of the NCPRI. Maja Daruwala herself worked closely with various elements involved formally with the NCPRI. This points towards the intra-linkages among the epistemic community.

Another witness before the DRPSC was Madhav Godbole. Like some other members of the NCPRI, Godbole was a Maharashtra cadre IAS, a former bureaucrat, and had his own experience with the IAS—that eventually convinced him to resign from his position

[25] Chand represented the epistemic community as well. V.K. Chand holds a PhD from Department of Government, Harvard University. In 1999 he was associate professor at CPR and subsequently started working at the India office of the WB.

as home secretary in April 1993.[26] Apart from being a bureaucrat, Godbole was also a public intellectual and had written six books on numerous subjects related to development and governance. Similar to other cases, Godbole's view on openness, transparency, accountability, and access to information emanated from his own experience in the IAS. For instance, in 2000, Godbole authored two articles in the *Economic and Political Weekly* (*EPW*) demanding an early enactment of the proposed bill and pointing out the deficiencies and omissions in the FoI Bill 2000 (Godbole 2000a; 2000b). The views expressed in the *EPW* article are elaborated again in a book published in 2003 authored by Godbole, *Public Accountability and Transparency*. In this book Godbole discussed the culture of secrecy emanating from outdated laws such as the OSA. Additionally, on the lines of his *EPW* articles in 2000, Godbole, discussed the deficiencies and omissions of the FoI Bill, 2000, enacted by the NDA government in December 2002 (Godbole 2003). Madhav Godbole was also part of the Government of Maharashtra committee constituted to examine the revision of the Maharashtra FoI Bill of 2000. Godbole's deposition before the DRPSC echoed the same views expressed in his writings such as the use of 'right to information' instead of 'freedom of information', the inclusion of the penalty clause, and the reduction of the twenty-five-year rule applicable to disclosure of government documents to fifteen years to name a few (DRPSC-HA 2001).

A.G. Noorani was another member of the group who deposed before the DRPSC. A.G. Noorani is a prominent lawyer and Constitution expert who practised both at the Bombay High Court and the SC. Noorani's view on RTI emanated from his experience of working with the judiciary. He wrote a series of articles in *EPW* on the issue of secrecy and the RTI. In an article in 1990, he discussed the report entitled 'Freedom of Information and Expression

[26] Godbole was the home secretary when he resigned from the IAS. His resignation was purportedly triggered by the rift between two ministers in the Ministry of Home—the senior home minister, S.B. Chavan, and the minister of state, Rajesh Pilot. Godbole was viewed as Chavan's man since he belonged to the Maharashtra cadre (*India Today* 1993).

in India' published by the International Centre on Censorship. In this article, Noorani discussed the government's inaction to address the culture of secrecy by not repealing the OSA (Noorani 1990a). In yet another article in 1990, he writes on the topic of 'Press Freedom and Right to Privacy' (Noorani 1990b). In December 1996, Noorani expressed his views on the PCI draft bill on FoI in *EPW* and commented that the media should study the bill closely and called for a wider public discussion on the draft bill. He suggested some legal improvements in the bill and pointed out that the bill should take into consideration earlier judicial verdicts in which RTI was considered inherently part of the Indian Constitution (Noorani 1996). In 1998, Noorani, argued that it was an opportune time to draft an FoI Bill which should be an amalgam of the bill prepared by the Shourie Committee in 1997, the Karnataka bill of 1988, and the Tamil Nadu RTI Act of 1997. He opined that it was the lack of 'political will' that was precluding the government to enact the bill: 'There is ample material for any good draftsman to draw upon. The Bill is not difficult to draft, either. What is lacking is political will and courage' (Noorani 1998). Noorani also articulated his views on RTI in a chapter of an edited book, *Corruption, Political Interference and the Indian Civil Service*, where he discussed about the ongoing policy process on RTI within the State and discussed some significant judicial cases which interpreted the constitutional provisions in line with the RTI (discussed in Chapter 3) (Noorani 1997). Incidentally, Madhav Godbole also contributed in the same volume (Godbole 1997). It is evident that Noorani, as a legal and constitutional expert, provided policy and legal inputs on the proposed legislation and also contributed to the policy discourse in the public domain.

Another testimony before the DRPSC was from Manubhai Shah, who was the managing trustee of the CERC. Notably, as discussed in Chapter 2, in 1991 Shah had undertaken a study tour of the USA, Canada, and the UK to learn about the international experiences of FoI laws. The learning and experiences from these tours was published in a two-part article in a journal named *Consumer Confrontation*. Subsequently, CERC drafted an FoI Bill in 1993.

Apart from the testimonies discussed here, six representatives from the MKSS deposed before the DRPSC in its fifth meeting held on 8 February 2001. Nikhil Dey, Prabhash Joshi, Neelabh Mishra, Kavita Shrivastava, Jahrana Jhaveri, and Anuraj Singh spoke with the DRPSC. This was a mixed group of journalists and activists associated with the MKSS and the NCPRI. Prabhash Joshi and Neelabh Mishra were journalists. The rest were activists and were closely associated with the MKSS. Additionally, Justice P.B. Sawant, who was the chairman of the PCI and had drafted the legislation on FoI in 1996, deposed before the DRPSC as well, as a representative of PCI. Justice Sawant's progressive views on RTI were all too well known by this time, first as a chief justice of the SC and then as the chairman of the PCI. As discussed earlier, Justice Sawant had close linkages with various actors of the NCPRI as well (DRPSC-HA 2001).

In May 2004, the government in the centre changed after the general elections. The UPA—a coalition of parties—formed the government. The UPA was a coalition of left and regional parties with the Congress Party at its helm. Amidst much political drama and speculation of accusations by opposition parties regarding the foreign origin of the president of Congress Party, Sonia Gandhi eventually refused to assume the position of PM. Manmohan Singh, the architect of the 1991 economic reforms, assumed the office of the PM when the UPA came to power.

Two significant points emerge regarding the policy processes around the RTI at this juncture. First, there is a continuation of both political and policy intent by the UPA from the earlier regimes. This was outlined in the CMP of the new government. Second, the UPA government can be treated as a watershed in the convergence of ideas on access to information between State and society. The epistemic community had a more direct and participatory role in the ongoing policy processes on the issue of openness, transparency, accountability, and access to information within the State. This manifested itself in the form of the NAC—an extra-constitutional body that was not officially mandated but served as an internal think tank (of sorts) to the current government.

State–Society Constituting Each Other: The National Advisory Council

The processes within the NAC demonstrate how the State and society work together on a common issue often constituting each other. The NAC was a broader platform where this process was most visible. In a sense, the NAC was an extension of 'State in society'. The membership of the NAC points towards the significant role of an 'epistemia' in guiding and shaping the State's policy preferences.

In 2004 the NAC was constituted to monitor the progress and implementation of the CMP, to provide policy inputs to the government, and also provide support to the legislative business of the government (Government Order No. 631/2/1/2004-Cab).

The PM in consultation with the chairperson of the UPA constituted the membership of the NAC, which consisted of representatives from the civil society, academia, legislators, and bureaucrats—both former and serving (see A6 of book-end Appendices for membership profile of the NAC). Sonia Gandhi served as the chairperson of the NAC. Each member was included in the NAC keeping in mind their expertise and knowledge base and the objectives of the CMP. For instance, the membership of the NAC included educationists, technocrats, activists, policymakers, and former bureaucrats (see A6 of book-end Appendices). This demonstrates that the NAC was a representation of an epistemic community, which provided policy inputs to the government. The NAC represented State-in-society, a space where both State and non-State actors deliberated on policy issues, the conclusions of which were relayed back to the executive—a process that worked out well in the initial phase of policymaking related to social welfare.

The NAC played a pivotal role in the framing of the draft RTI Bill and in the process of the passage of the final bill. This is the space where State–society synergy can be seen at work in all its practical policy imports. The membership of the NAC is an exemplar of an epistemic community working in tandem with the government, providing policy inputs to remove any uncertainty that the political and permanent executive might have regarding a policy choice (Haas 1992). Significantly, some members of the NAC such as Aruna Roy,

Jean Dreze, and N.C. Saxena were part of the NCPRI and shared common ideas on access to information.

The process of epistemic State policy formulation was perceptible in the case of RTI. In the first meeting of the NAC held on 17 July 2004, Aruna Roy shared a formal statement by the NCPRI on the RTI (NCPRI 2004).[27] While welcoming the political commitment made by the government for more progressive participatory and meaningful legislation on RTI, the NCPRI had some specific policy recommendations. The NCPRI suggested moving beyond the FoI Bill, 2002, of the previous government and provided the legal modifications in the proposed law given in Table 4.3.

At the same time, CHRI shared its own set of recommendations improving upon the existing FoI Bill of 2002 (CHRI 2004). The recommendations, in the form of a paper published in July 2004, were in many ways a continuation of the CHRI's earlier publication

Table 4.3 Policy Recommendations by the NCPRI

Broad definition and scope of RTI
Non-court independent appeal mechanism
Provision for penalties
Exemptions within the scope of Article 19 (1) and Article 19 (2)
Disclosure of even exempted information in the light of 'public interest'
Applicability of act to all persons
Extension of applicability of act to all bodies performing public functions including private bodies
Suo motu (voluntary) disclosure
Act should override all existing laws
Body to monitor the implementation of the act
Provision for whistle-blower protection
Existing State laws should be in place

Source: NCPRI Internal Papers, 16 July 2004, New Delhi.

27 Statement of the NCPRI, 16 July 2004, New Delhi. Available at: http://www.humanrightsinitiative.org/programs/ai/rti/news/statement_ncpri.pdf (accessed 7 April 2020).

from 1999 (discussed earlier). This paper was shared with the members of the NAC and prior to the first meeting of the NAC was also circulated to the MPs.

Between the second and the third meetings of the NAC, on 30 July and 14 August 2004 respectively, several rounds of draft recommendations were circulated back and forth between social actors and the NAC. Table 4.4 captures the activity around RTI within and outside the NAC.

Meanwhile, a PIL came up for hearing in the SC regarding the notification of rules for the enacted the FoI Bill of 2002. The PIL was filed by Prashant Bhushan on behalf of the NCPRI and the Centre for PIL in 2002. In its order of 20 August 2004, the SC ordered the government to implement the FoI Bill, 2002, by 15 September 2004. The SC ruling had an impact on the ongoing policy process within

TABLE 4.4 Policy Activity on RTI outside the NAC

17 July 2004	In the first meeting, the NCPRI statement containing policy recommendations improving upon the existing FoI Bill was shared with the NAC.
17 July 2004	The CHRI shared its recommendation with the NAC and also circulated the recommendations to the cabinet ministers prior to the meeting.
17 July 2004	The NAC requested the NCPRI to submit amendments to the FoI Bill of 2002.
31 July 2004	Suggested amendments to the FoI Bill of 2002 were prepared by the NCPRI and submitted to the NAC for consideration.
31 July 2004	The NAC issued recommendations and sets of amendments on FoI Bill, 2002, based on the amendments suggested by the NCPRI.
14 August 2004	The CHRI submitted another set of recommendations based on the NAC draft amendments—the NAC finalized the recommendations.
14 August 2004	Sonia Gandhi, chairperson of the NAC, forwarded the NAC draft to the PMO.

Source: Derived from NCPRI 2004.

the State. This revealed itself in an internal government note of the DoPT in which there is a clear direction from the PMO that the draft rule for the FoI Bill, 2002, should be finalized by 15 September 2004 (the deadline set by the SC). Nevertheless, the DoPT internally decided that since too many modifications were suggested by the NAC in the present FoI law, the notification of rules should be put on hold (Internal Government Document 2004).

The NAC draft was forwarded to the PM and the government tabled the bill in the winter session of the parliament on 23 December 2004. The bill was then referred to the DRPSC on Personnel, Public Grievances, Law, and Justice. The committee heard the representations from both the social and State actors and submitted its report on 21 March 2005. Subsequently, the new RTI Act, 2005, was passed by both the houses of the parliament on 11 and 12 May 2005. The Act received the presidential assent and formally came into force on 12 October 2005.

Similar to the State–society processes that took shape when the DRPSC-HA was constituted earlier to examine the FoI Bill 2002, the DRPSC constituted in 2005 (under a different government) also points towards the role of epistemic community. The DRPSC was constituted to examine the amendments in the FoI Bill, 2002, and the new law on RTI proposed by the NAC. By this time a formalization of institutional engagement of social actors with the State through the NAC was established. This was evident in the testimonies presented before the DRPSC. The DRPSC heard the deposition from a wide range of actors such as the activists, legal experts, representatives of the political parties, and the bureaucracy. In some cases, the representations were an extension of the nature of membership of the NCPRI consisting of activists, lawyers, journalists, academics, and bureaucrats. On 14 February 2005, the committee heard depositions from this group. Table 4.5 provides a snapshot of these depositions before the DRPSC.

Even while the policy processes were set in motion within the State, catalysed by the recommendations from NAC, another set of processes were taking shape outside the NAC. For instance, on 5 December 2004, a delegation from the NCPRI met the PM to express their concern regarding the delay in the introduction of the bill in

Table 4.5 Depositions before the DRPSC

Aruna Roy	MKSS and NCPRI activist, former bureaucrat, and member of NAC
Jean Dreze	Part of the NCPRI and an academic member of the NAC
Angela Rangad	NCPRI representative
Prashant Bhushan	Lawyer and member of the NCPRI
Nikhil Dey	Activist, part of the MKSS and NCPRI
Harsh Mander	Former bureaucrat, activist, and member of the NCPRI; director, Centre for Equity Studies
Anna Hazare	Prominent anti-corruption activist from Maharashtra; played a prominent role in the Maharashtra RTI Act; had active linkages with the NCPRI
Prakash Kardale	Well-known journalist and resident editor for the *Indian Express* (Pune, Maharashtra); known as ally of Anna Hazare in the anti-corruption movement; known linkages with the NCPRI
Shekar Singh	Convener of the NCPRI, academic, and activist
Shailesh Gandhi	Fellow, Indian Institute of Management Ahmedabad, academic-activist, known linkages with Maharashtra RTI Act and the NCPRI
Maja Daruwala,	Director, CHRI
Charmaine Rodrigues	CHRI
Venkatesh Nayak	CHRI; all three CHRI representatives had linkages with the NCPRI
N. Jaya Prakash	Convener of Lok Satta Party

Source: Author.

the parliament. Former PM V.P. Singh, Aruna Roy (also part of the NAC), and Shekhar Singh represented the NCPRI in this meeting. At the same time, the NCPRI initiated a process of organizing support letters from individuals and organizations addressed to the PM, extending their support to the amendments suggested by the NAC in the FoI Bill, 2002. Former PM, V.P. Singh, was part of this process. In a letter dated 6 November 2004, which was sent to some prominent citizens from both within and outside the State, V.P. Singh, urged them to extend their full support to the NAC amendments, requesting them to write to the PM. Prior to the meeting with the PM in December 2004, the NCPRI had written to the PM in October 2004 urging him to facilitate the legislation without diluting the amendments suggested by the NAC. Letters with similar content urging them to support the NAC amendments were sent to the representatives of the left parties, namely CPI-M. Notably, CPI-M was part of the UPA coalition. In yet another letter from November 2004, Aruna Roy on behalf of the NCPRI wrote to Sonia Gandhi (president of the Congress Party and the chairperson of the NAC). Roy urged Gandhi to set up an expert group under the NAC to work out a policy to handle the problems faced by the 'whistleblowers' that expose corruption.

Intervention by the NCPRI both from within and outside the NAC was visible after the RTI Bill was tabled in the parliament. The bill tabled in the parliament was a diluted version, which was only applicable to the agencies of the central government. The State-level agencies were excluded from its purview. Further, the bill had envisaged a strict penalty clause, which was weakened in the version tabled in the parliament. These changes were not part of the discussions within the NAC or even during the DRPSC meetings. Aruna Roy on behalf of the NCPRI promptly dispatched a strong letter to Sonia Gandhi on 18 January 2005 expressing the NCPRI's shock and dismay, and requesting urgent action to address the dilutions introduced in the legislation. Sonia Gandhi, chairperson of the NAC, on her part, communicated with the PM, expressing her concern on the dilution of these significant amendments originally introduced by the NAC and requesting the PM to 'have these issues looked into, on priority basis' (From Sonia Gandhi (Chairperson of NAC) Addressed to the PM 2005) (see A3 of book-end Appendices). This convinced the PM and he directed the DoPT to re-examine these amendments in the law (PMO ID No. 600/40/C/5/04-ES-II) (see A4 of book-end Appendices). As a result, the government constituted a GoM in January 2005 to examine the issue (Internal Government Communique Notifying the Constitution of GOM 2005) (discussed in Chapter 2).

***

As I have argued in the first three chapters, the ideational churning within the State around the norm of openness and access to information had started immediately after Independence, much before the discourse started emerging in the societal realm. This happened in two layers. In the first layer, from 1947 until 1989, nascent ideas on openness and transparency emerged on the policy fringes of the State, primarily as part of opposition politics. Our second and final layer starts from 1989, when these rudimentary ideas become embedded into mainstream politics. By the early 1990s, when the NF formed the coalition government, the initial ideas on the norm of openness had overwhelmed the locked-in norm of secrecy, finally *layering* it out in 2005. This was evident in both the political and policy commitment showed by the coalition governments at the centre since the 1990s. The processes in the societal realm discussed in this chapter coincided with the final layer of political and policy processes around RTI or FoI. This is evident from the formation of the MKSS in the early 1990s and of the NCPRI in 1996. In the latter half of the final layer, progressive elements from both the State and society forged ideational linkages and came together as an epistemic community that engaged structurally with mainstream politics and the ongoing policy processes within the State. This manifested in the depositions in various DRPSCs and, finally, through the NAC. This convergence pushed the ongoing churning to the 'tipping point' of institutional change.

How did the process deepen the ongoing 'powering and puzzling' of the State leading to the 'tipping point' of institutional change? On the basis of the evidence presented, I argue that the social and political processes surrounding the MKSS and the NCPRI exacerbated the ongoing ideational churning within the State. They played a significant role in deepening the discourse and provided policy inputs from both within and outside the State. Extending the discourse in the public domain outside the scope of the State removed the procedural and legal uncertainties that might have existed at the political and policy level within the State. In this sense, I argue that it was not the case where demand from society results in the creation of new policy space within the State. The processes analysed in this chapter point towards State and society constituting each other in a mutually empowering relationship. Admittedly, the relationship between State and society was contentious and cooperative at the same time. This was evident in the case of Rajasthan where the dharnas to demand policy action on the basis of the CM's announcement were contentious in nature and yet elements both within the State and society were negotiating with each other.

Similarly, this was seen in the final passage of the bill when the dilution of the proposed bill occurred within the policy machinery. This resulted in the NCPRI sending a strong letter to Sonia Gandhi and as a result steps were taken by the political leadership to address this omission. This chapter illuminates on this complex process of State and society constituting each other, rather than the simplistic State vs society view, which argues that social demands put pressure on the State to demand policy change. Additionally, I also argue that it was 'State in society'—the NAC, which was formed as an extra-constitutional body acted, in fact, as an extension of the State, and played a consequential role in the final passage of the RTI Act. In doing so, I problematize the people's or social movement view of institutional change, which claims that societal interests shaped the policy choices within the State.

Second, I argue for the primacy of ideas rather than interests shaping up the State's policy preferences. The evidence examined in this chapter points towards the paramount role of ideas around the norm of openness, transparency, and accountability and the access to information. For instance, in the case of Rajasthan, the idea was that official documents would reveal anomalies or irregularities at the panchayat level, which in turn would help the village residents secure their right to fair work and livelihood. This led to the demand by the MKSS for access to information at the local level. The same ideational push convinced the political leadership to make the policy commitment towards that goal as is evident in the announcement made by the CM in the legislative assembly. In this light the Habermasian public sphere does not explain the significance of *jan sunwayis* or public hearing (Pande 2014). The significance of *jan sunwayis* resided in the fact that they highlighted and escalated the idea that access to official documents are important and this idea was consequential in shaping the discourse around access to information at the State level. Hence, in this case ideas shaped the interests. It was also the commonality of ideas on access to information that brought different actors from varied fields together as the NCPRI. This manifested in individuals from varied backgrounds such as the journalists, legal activists, jurists, academics, politicians, and bureaucrats with similar ideas coming together to work towards a common goal. It was the ideas that brought and bound them together as the NCPRI rather than the interpersonal connections such as the common services background, same college, or similar social class category of belonging to the middle-class elite (Sharma 2015). In this sense, the NCPRI represented a confluence of progressive ideas and cannot be explained by middle-class elite interconnections. To provide an example, this confluence and commonality of ideas manifested in the testimonies during the DRPSC and the policy inputs provided by these actors, especially since 2000. A common legal framework and imperatives are expressed throughout, of which four legal inputs can be identified as follows:

1. 'Freedom' of information should be replaced by 'right' to information, as a legal right.
2. Penalty provisions ought to be included in the legislation for the erring officials who do not disclose the information requested.
3. There should be maximum disclosure and minimum exemptions.
4. There should be independent appellate authorities or independent appeal mechanisms.

These imperatives eventually find their way inside the legislation during its final passage in 2005.

Third, how do we conceptualize the phenomenon of progressive elements working from both within and outside the State? How can one understand the linkages and connections between the agents who played a significant role in the process of institutional change? Can one conceptualize and understand this on account of common background and interpersonal linkages resulting in a 'dense middle-class elite network' (Sharma 2015)? Or was it because of the collective social capital of eminent people (Pande 2014)? Neither of these arguments capture the process of progressive elements coming together in affecting institutional change. Instead, the membership of the NCPRI, depositions of the social actors before the DRPSC, and the profile of the NAC point towards the role of epistemic community (Haas 1992). As I have explained and argued in this chapter, the profile of the group involved in the process of institutional change from both within and outside the State possess significant epistemic characteristics. Their epistemic characteristics enabled them to move freely between the boundaries of the State and society, working from both within and outside the State. For instance, Aruna Roy is an activist and yet she understands the way State works, as she was in the IAS and had continuous interactions with the State due to her activist work. To take yet another example, Shekhar Singh was an important part of the NCPRI. He is an academic and environmental activist, and was also part of the State as adviser, Planning Commission. Each of these agents had linkages with the State as well as society and had recognized knowledge and expertise over policy domain. This positioned them strategically to work in tandem from both within and outside the State. Epistemic characteristics helped in advocacy with the political class and the executive and discourse creation in the public domain, and enabled them to provide informed policy and legal inputs in the formulation of the draft legislation.

Lastly, I would like to propose a conceptual nuancing of the sociopolitical processes discussed earlier. Rather than explaining the phenomenon through social movement or people's movement or grassroots movement, an elite network (Sharma 2015), or as part of the symbolic capital of eminent activists (Pande 2014), it can be better captured by terming it an epistemic network. This is because of several reasons. First, the linkages between these actors were more ideational rather than interest- or class-based. It was the epistemic nature of this group that brought them together on a common platform. Second, as I have shown, the individuals in this network were from varied backgrounds, which consisted of a wide array of people not only from the grassroots but also government officials, lawyers, jurists, academics, journalists, former bureaucrats, and even some legislators. Each one of them brought in their own knowledge base contributing towards a common goal. The diverse nature of issues and socio-economic and political linkages provided the basis and context for the creation of this epistemic network. This network had formal and informal linkages with the State. It exemplifies the process of diverse actors coming together for a common cause, interest, policy intervention, and outcome. The evidence examined in this chapter demonstrates that this was an epistemic network as they had formal or informal linkages, shared common beliefs, ideas, causes, or interest, exchanged information and communicated through vertical and horizontal channels, were driven by a moral sense of right, and most importantly had multiple linkages from both grassroots and people outside the system as well as linkages within the State apparatus at the same time.

5 Do Global Norms Matter?[1]

I have argued that institutional change in the form of the RTI Act was the result of a multi-layered process. I show that the cumulative and incremental role of ideas on openness, transparency, and access to information played an instrumental role in this institutional change. Ideational churning occurring endogenously within the State since Independence shaped the discourse in the formative years and challenged the nested norm of secrecy, eventually displacing it in 2005 with the promulgation of the RTI Act. From the mid-1990s, progressive elements from both within State and society deepened the ongoing policy discourse within the State.

There is yet another dimension, of global norms, which has been ignored or parsimoniously treated in the mainstream literature. This chapter examines the role of global norms in this narrative of institutional change and establishes that these global norms had a demonstrative as well as operative impact on the ongoing endogenous discourse on transparency and openness (Jha 2019). I proposes two arguments supported by evidence. First, the global norms informed and influenced the ongoing discourse at the national level along with considerable demonstrative influence, in what I term as 'norm demonstration'. Second, drawing upon Acharya's (2004) argument of 'norm localisation', I postulate that the global norms were not adopted by the State as 'passive learners', but rather they were

[1] This chapter has drawn on arguments offered and empirical material in Himanshu Jha. 2019. 'Untangling Global–Local Linkages: The Case of the Right to Information Act in India'. *India Review* 18(1): 32–53.

actively drawn upon and adapted at the national level in accordance with the ongoing policy discourse and processes. Significantly, I conceptualize that both 'norm demonstration' and 'norm localisation' can be adapted and used in various ways at the national level, going beyond arguments that suggest that the national norm is often forced to follow the path of global norms. In this case, norm diffusion was not part of the coercive conditionalities of multilateral agencies but was adapted at the national level in conjunction with the ideational churning occurring at the national level (see Jha 2019).

The evidence examined in the current chapter shows that the impact of global norms coincides with the process of layering that has been laid out in the first four chapters. In the first layer, 'norm demonstration' was reflected in the nascent ideas of 'openness' articulated in phase I from 1947 onwards. Even though 'norm demonstration' complemented the nascent ideas on openness during this period, it was insufficient to convince the State to adopt the norm of openness. Instead, during this period, an intensification of the State's policies towards secrecy occurred, manifesting in the 1967 amendment of the OSA. However, in the second phase starting from the early 1990s, both demonstrative and operative impacts of the role of global norms intensified as the endogenous processes reached a critical mass. The trajectory of global norms along the two distinct layers shows that its role needs to be seen within the broader context of the emerging endogenous discourse and processes.

The RTI Act legislated in 2005 coincided with the global trend of promulgation of similar laws on information disclosure. Globally, seventy-six countries adopted laws on the FoI or RTI. This signified an incremental move towards enhancing transparency and accountability within their established governance apparatus. Out of those seventy-six countries, sixty-four enacted laws on access to information between 1990 and 2010, and forty-two between 2000 and 2010 (Banisar 2006). Enactment of the RTI Act in India coincided with this broader global context. Hence, the significance of such a coincidence needs deeper analysis (see Figure 5.1).

Additionally, one can also see the convergence of the 'good governance' agenda of the International Monetary Fund (IMF) and the WB and the global proliferation of laws on transparency. The focus

FIGURE 5.1 Number of Countries That Promulgated FoI or RTI Laws

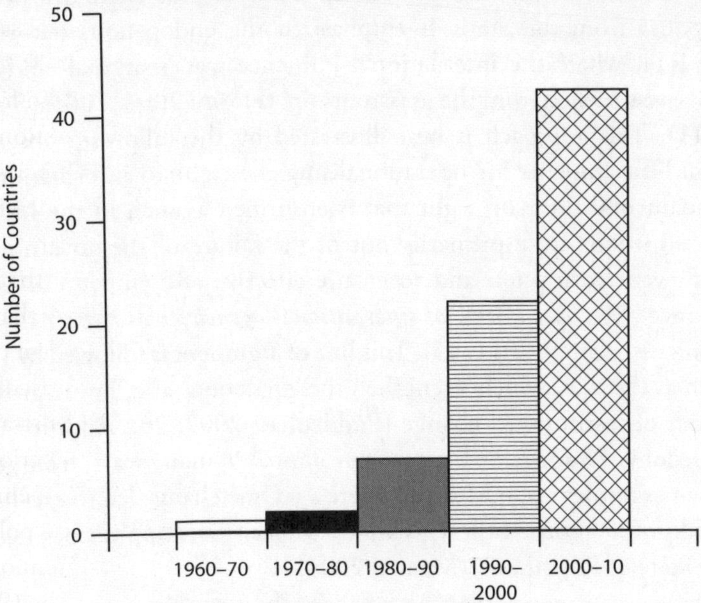

Source: Author.

of these international financial institutions (IFIs) was on transparent and accountable government as a part of the conditionality of their structural adjustment programs (SAPs) initiated in the 1990s. The convergence of SAPs with the global move towards the enactment of laws on access to information suggests the role of exogenous factors. Was this true of institutional change in India as well? Did exogenous factors such as the global policy stimulus around transparency and accountability (discussed earlier) play an instrumental role in the institutional change?

Global Norms: Missing and Marginalized in the Literature

As elaborated in the introduction, the mainstream literature that deals with the evolution of the RTI regime in India suggests that institutional change was primarily an endogenous 'bottom-up' process, and the result of a bottom-up demand that elicited a policy response from the State. It emphasized the endogenous nature of the RTI, where the international influence was 'marginal' and the 'drive was fuelled from the grassroots up' (Florini 2007: 10; see Singh 2011). This approach is best illustrated by the following observation: 'The impetus for operationalising the right to information, a fundamental (human) right that is enshrined as such in the Indian Constitution, arose primarily out of the failure of the government to prevent corruption and to ensure effective and empathetic governance. *The role, if any, of international agencies was marginal* [my emphasis]' (Singh 2011: 45). This line of argument is followed by IFIs such as the WB, which strengthen the 'grassroots' and 'home-grown' aspect of institutional change (Puddephatt 2009: 25). Additionally, 'Freedom of information laws are promoted in many ways, from top-down examples (as in Mexico, where a regime change led to excellent freedom of information legislation) to grassroots approaches (as in the State of Rajasthan)' (Mendel 2004).

However, some scholars have flagged this issue but have not examined this further. For instance, Baviskar (2007) raises a pertinent though insufficiently elaborated question of global influence and effect of 'transnational institutions and processes' on the evolution of RTI.

To be sure, this question has been examined in relatively recent scholarship, which acknowledges the significance of the international influence (Mathur 2015; Sharma 2015). It is argued that the information laws established globally were often invoked during policy discussions over the need to have an RTI in India, as it had instrumental and symbolic value in achieving the State's aspiration to be seen as an 'advanced democracy'. Second, this line of argument adds credence to the role of international institutions such as the WB, ADB, and WTO and the new good governance agenda that emanated from these institutions. Third, this was due to the adoption of liberalization policy at the national level.

In continuation of this line of scholarly argument, it is pertinent to examine the role of global norm diffusion in institutional change.

Within the context of the consequential role of the State and policy discussions internal to the State, this chapter seeks to examine the role of evolving global norms on the process of norm formation at the domestic level. I explore the process of norm diffusion from global to the local and examine how 'home-grown' the process was (Singh 2011; see also Sharma 2015). More specifically, the current chapter engages with two questions: (*a*) What was the degree of 'norm diffusion' that took place? and (*b*) How much of a role did exogenous factors, which include global norms, have to play in the institutional change?

Explanations of Global Norm Diffusion: Addressing the Gaps

Scholars have examined the process of transnational norm diffusion from various vantage points. Risse, Ropp, and Sikkink (1999) explore the 'conditions under which principled ideas and international norms affect domestic institutional change', which 'depends on the establishment and sustainability of networks among domestic and transnational actors who manage to link up with international regimes, to alert western public opinion and western governments' (Risse, Ropp, and Sikkink 1999: 4–5).

Finnemore and Sikkink (1998) present three stages of adoption of norms: (*a*) 'norm emergence', where the framing of the norm takes place by 'norm entrepreneurs' at the global level, and if enough States adopt the norm it reaches the tipping point leading to the next stage; (*b*) 'norm cascade', where States adopt the norm under international pressure even if there is no domestic pressure; and (*c*) the last stage is of *norm internalization*.

Keck and Sikkink (1998) view the transnational advocacy networks as catalysts of global norm diffusion, where a policy block at the domestic level is unblocked by means of transnational advocacy through these networks.

In explaining the case of Association of Southeast Asian Nations (ASEAN), Acharya (2004) examines the spread of ideas and norms at the transnational level through norm localization, 'a dynamic congruence building process' that stresses the 'agency role of norm takers'.

The global–local interplay of ideas in the case of the RTI Act points towards a similar process of norm diffusion from the global to the domestic. However, as I have argued, a policy discourse was already taking place endogenously regarding possible legislation on the access to information right since Independence. In this sense, it was not a case of 'policy blockage' at the domestic level, which necessitated domestic actors to forge linkages globally to 'unblock' this 'blockage'. Instead, the State and society were puzzling and debating internally on this policy question. This problematizes the role of norm entrepreneurs and advocacy networks with transnational linkages.

Therefore, it is necessary to examine the role of global norms from a nuanced perspective. I place my analysis within the broader context of the ongoing ideational churning taking place endogenously, and trace the degree and extent of global norm diffusion from two perspectives. First, I examine the demonstrative impact of global norms. Second, I probe the role of global norms from the standpoint of drawing upon established legal provisions from existing international laws on access to information.

This chapter is divided into two sections. The first section deals with phase I, discussed in Chapter 1, where nascent ideas on 'openness' emerged on the fringes, even though the State was pushing towards greater secrecy. In this phase, we find the convergence of global patterns and narratives on the domestic discourse. The global trend has had a demonstrative impact, manifesting itself in study tours, conferences, reports, and the role of international agencies. However, consistent with the endogenous ideas on 'openness', the global norms remained on the fringes as well. This is the first layer of institutional change, in which rudimentary ideas on openness emerged on the fringes of the persisting institution of 'secrecy'.

In the second section, I establish that while the endogenous processes intensified within the State and became part of mainstream politics, the demonstrative and operative value of the emerging global norms and best practices on the ongoing discourse intensified as well. I show that as various governments initiated the policy processes, the process of international FoI laws that contributed to the content of the Indian bill had also started. This is the final layer of institutional change where the policy process drew upon global norms. In this sense, one can see an operative impact of norm diffusion on the policy framework at the domestic level.

Phase I (1947–80): Global Norms on the Fringes—Through Reports, Seminars, and Conferences

In this section, I examine the role of reports, foreign tours, conferences, and seminars. The evidence examined in this section shows that the emerging ideational churning even in the initial phases was well informed about the emerging global norms and was in congruence with the global discourse on FoI. However, in this phase, the institution of secrecy was further intensified within the State. Hence, the impact of global norms was limited to the segments where the first nascent ideas on 'openness' emerged.

This is evidenced by earlier reports from State institutions on 'government and administration', which reflected on the culture of secrecy prevalent within the State. This internal reflection was a significant dimension that added to the ongoing ideational churning within the State. The discourse and arguments emerging from these reports were often informed by the emerging and established norms globally. Additionally, the evidence also shows that while the State was 'in sync' with the ongoing global discourse on FoI, its domestic policy trajectory was going in the other direction, towards 'secrecy' (as shown in Chapter 1). This is evident in the earlier seminars organized by the GoI.

As discussed in Chapter 1, the Press Law Enquiry Committee was constituted in 1947 to examine the laws regulating the press and to review the existing laws in the context of fundamental rights and provide appropriate recommendations to the government (Press Law Enquiry Committee 1948). The report of the committee published in 1948 deemed it necessary to have the OSA in operation to protect national interests. However, such faith in the State was not shared by two members of the committee, namely S.A. Brelvi and K. Srinivasan. They offered a note of dissent on the subject, objecting to the blanket application of the OSA to make most issues secret. The international influence was clear in their argument that the Act must remain 'confined, as *the recent Geneva Conference on Freedom of Information (FOI)* [my emphasis] has recommended, only to matters which must remain secret in the interest of the national safety' (Press Law Enquiry Committee 1948: 31). This shows that the weight of prevailing ideas within the State was in opposition to the idea of 'openness' but that supporters of 'openness' invoked global norms.

Later in 1948, in his capacity as editor of the *Bombay Chronicle*, Brelvi attended the UN Conference on FoI as part of the government delegation. He stressed on the need for the FoI in an article in the *ToI* by providing a synopsis of the conference's recommendations (Brelvi 1948).

Yet another important link pointing towards the role of international agencies can be seen in one of the earlier critical reviews (in 1953) of public administration in India. The Ministry of Finance and the Ford Foundation invited Paul H. Appleby to survey and study the way public administration was carried out in the country (Appleby 1953; *ToI* 1953). Among other recommendations on improving efficiency, Appleby briefly touched upon the lack of openness and related issues of record keeping in the Indian administration. In the context of Appleby's own background of administration and academia in the USA and Ford Foundation's involvement in inviting Appleby, the report can be treated as part of global norm diffusion. Possibly Appleby's idea on openness was inspired by his own experience of the ongoing discourse on administrative openness in the USA. The Appleby report demonstrates that there was global support in a domestic environment that supported secrecy.

As discussed previously, the emerging discourse during this period points towards the polarity of ideas. While on the one hand, the State pushed towards 'secrecy' domestically, it extended support to the idea of 'openness' at the global level. This is evident in the Indian government's support and convergence with the emerging policies of FoI within the United Nations (UN). Brelvi's stance within the Press Law Enquiry Commission favouring openness and objecting to the blanket application of the policy of secrecy emanated from his engagement with the UN Conference on the FoI in 1948.

The Indian government's support to the UN's stance on the FoI stemmed from its belief and conviction regarding the international FoI discourse and independent of international pressure, because at the domestic level it continued with the persisting norm of 'secrecy' operationalized through the OSA and other laws. This was evident in 1952 when the UN suggested in the Social Committee of the General Assembly that a new approach should be adopted to formulate the proposed convention on the FoI. This was to be achieved by hiking the quantum of technical aid to underdeveloped countries to improve their media of information. Despite the fact that the UN draft treaty on the FoI was opposed by the USA, India went against the USA's stance and supported the draft FoI treaty (among other supporters from emerging nations such as Egypt and Indonesia). The Indian representative said that '[The] FOI stands in the degree of importance on the highest list of priorities' (*ToI* 1952).

Later in 1962, the GoI and the UN organized a joint seminar in New Delhi (see UN 1962a: 55, 1962b). The vice-president of India during this period, S. Radhakrishnan, inaugurated this seminar and PM Nehru addressed it (*ToI* 1962b). The vice-president's speech at the seminar was not ostensibly against the idea of FoI. He noted that the FoI was essential to maintain 'liberty, justice, fellowship, and fraternity' and stressed the significance of Indian democracy, which stood for individual freedom and social justice. Additionally, he called for maintaining a judicious balance between the freedom of press and censorship (*ToI* 1962b). The union law minister, A.K. Sen, pointed towards the role of the judiciary in promoting the FoI by rejecting some restrictive legislations to uphold the freedom of expression and speech provided in the Constitution of India. However, paradoxically, the policy action was just the opposite, evident in the 1967 amendment of the OSA.

A session in this seminar chaired by the joint secretary at the Ministry of Information and Broadcasting discussed the issue of striking an equilibrium between the restrictive role of the State and the free expression of an individual (*ToI* 1962b). The nominated member of the Indian delegation for this seminar, J.P. Chaturvedi, raised the issue of the privileges of the judiciary and the parliament in relation to the press and urged that these privileges should be clearly defined. A joint secretary with the Ministry of Law underlined the need to check the concentration of ownership (or 'monopoly') to ensure greater and effective FoI (*ToI* 1962a).

The stance of both the political and permanent executive expressed in this seminar stress three significant points. First, it shows that there were elements of the political leadership who were in favour of greater openness of the State. This sentiment was articulated by some segments of the bureaucracy, as seen in the case of interventions by the joint secretaries (discussed earlier). Second, it demonstrates that the GoI was in sync with the discourse emerging globally around the FoI and within international institutions. Third, it is pertinent to note that five years later, in 1967, the government decided to amend the OSA to an even stronger version. This pointed towards the polarity of the Indian State, which supported the FoI globally and pushed for greater secrecy domestically. This global–domestic polarity might have emanated from the international compulsions of the Indian State to be viewed and accepted as a mature and advanced democratic polity. It is possible that the supporters of greater openness and transparency were in a minority during this phase, which necessitated their engagement with the global norms consistent with India's image as a democracy.

Global norms were manifested in reports of the early 1980s, which directly challenged the nested norm of secrecy (discussed in Chapter 1). One of the significant interventions on the issue of secrecy came in the form of an edited book titled *Secrecy in Government* published by the IIPA in 1980 (Chaturvedi 1980) (elaborated in Chapter 1). Notably, the IIPA was set up on Appleby's recommendations. Apart from raising some critical concerns and providing recommendations to deal with the prevailing culture of secrecy within the State, the book also drew abundantly from established global practices. The report juxtaposed the prevailing legal framework in India against the legal precedents in other countries by bringing in the Freedom of the Press Act of Sweden; FoI Act of USA; Access to Official Information Act of Canada; Access to Official Information Act of Australia; FoI Bill of Australia; and Access to Administrative Information Bill of the Netherlands (Chaturvedi 1980).

Phase II (1980–2005): Demonstrative and Operative Impact of Global Norms

As discussed in Chapter 2, this phase is the final stage of layering where the incremental weight of ideas became part of mainstream politics, eventually aligning with the emerging epistemic network. Hence, there was a convergence of the State and society. In this layer, the norm of 'openness' reached a 'tipping point' of institutional change with the enactment of the RTI Act 2005. As the endogenous processes became part of mainstream politics and policy processes, demonstrative and operative impact of global norms escalated as well. This is evinced in the reports, conferences, workshops, and the policy processes examining the legal provisions of the proposed legislation on the FoI or RTI.

Workshops, Study Tours, Seminars, and Conferences

During the NF government, in March 1990, a workshop was organized by the CPR at New Delhi on 'Freedom of Information and Official Secrets Act' under the aegis of the MHA. The government officials, legislators, academicians, journalists, and senior civil servants from the MHA, Ministry of Information and Broadcasting, MPPP, and MEA attended this workshop. Significantly, the existing FoI laws in Australia, Sweden, Canada, and the USA were discussed at length in this workshop (CPR 1990).

During the same period, in 1991, the MHA set up an Inter-Ministerial Task Force to examine the feasibility of enacting legislation on the public access to government information. The task force visited the UK, Sweden, the USA, and Canada to study the functioning of FoI laws in those countries. The task force submitted its report to the MHA on 31 May 1991 (MPPP 2001).

Again in 1993, CERC a consumer rights group in Ahmedabad, took significant initiative by producing a draft of the access to information bill, under which citizens were granted right to access information from the government and government undertakings (Gandhi 1996; Girimaji 1994). The bill was the result of an international workshop organized by the CERC in 1993. Prior to this, in 1991, Manubhai Shah, managing trustee of CERC, and Preeti Shah, deputy manager of CERC, had undertaken an educational trip to the USA, Canada, and the UK to learn about the FoI laws of those countries. The trip was funded by the International Development Research Centre (IDRC), Canada, and produced a paper entitled 'A Study on the Access to Information in US Canada and UK', published in the journal *Consumer Confrontation* by the CERC in 1991–2 (Shah and Shah 1991–2).

Similarly, in 1996, under the aegis of the CPR, B.G. Verghese (a prominent Indian journalist and public intellectual) conducted a survey of FoI laws in countries such as the USA, Canada, Sweden, and Australia to explore their potential to serve as a model to be adopted in India (Kirpekar 1996a). The pattern of drawing from the existing FoI laws in other countries has been a constant in the process of the evolution of RTI.

This pattern is significant from two standpoints. First, the international experience gained from study tours and conferences was drawn from to bear upon the ongoing discourse at the domestic level. International agencies such as the Ford Foundation and the IDRC played a significant role in initiating the dialogue on transparency and openness. Second, the international discourse on the FoI had a demonstrative impact on the discourse on openness evolving within the country. This was consistent with the deepening of the endogenous processes domestically around the RTI. In the subsequent section, I establish that the reports, international study tours, conferences, and seminars provided the context for further policy discussions within the State.

Demonstrative Impact of the Emerging Global Norms

The previous section shows that the global discourse had a demonstrative impact on the emerging discourse at the national level. In this section, I show that the ideational churning emerging within the State often converged with the global trend on the access to information. This process can be clearly seen in the internal government discussions on the possibility of legislation around access to information. The laws on transparency and access to information in other countries provided the milieu for the policy discussions. Additionally, the worldwide trend of transparency laws held demonstrative value during policy discussions.

In January 1997, the cabinet secretary constituted a nine-member Working Committee on the Right to Information and Transparency (also known as the Shourie Committee; MPPP 1997). The committee was constituted with the objective of examining the feasibility, applicability, and operationalization of the 'full-fledged Right to Information Act or its introduction in a phased manner to meet the needs of open and responsive government'. To be sure, global norms provided the context for discussions within the committee on the proposed FoI Bill (Internal Government Communication 1997). This is evident from the fact that a major portion of the background material shared with the committee was on laws on access to information in other countries. For instance, a note titled 'Transparency in Government' prepared by Kiran Aggrawal (a member of the 1964 IAS cadre and a secretary-level officer at the Department of Supply), which was shared with the committee, contained brief notes on the laws on access to information in New Zealand, Canada, the UK, Malaysia, and the USA. Additionally, the working group was provided with copies of the British and US FoI Acts and an article by A.G. Noorani titled 'The Right to Know', which traced the legal origins of the US FoI Act. Besides, the study published by CERC on access to information in the USA, Canada, and the UK was shared with the committee.

The discussions within the committee drew abundantly from the experiences of the FoI laws in other countries. This pattern emerged in the first two meetings of the working group when Soli Sorabjee, a committee member, drew upon the experience in the USA and Australia and stressed the strengthening and capacity building of related institutions and procedures concurrently with the framing of law. The working group took into consideration the FoI Acts of USA and Australia, Access to Information Act of Canada, the Official Information Act of New Zealand, and Code of Practice on Access to

Government Information of the UK (Working Group on Right to Information and Promotion of Open and Transparent Government 1997).

The initiatives adopted around the FoI legislations in the developing world were cited to argue for similar legislation in India, such as the FoI Ordinance in Pakistan, the New South African Constitution, which provided the RTI in its Bill of Rights, and the Malaysian database system of civil services link, which enabled citizens to access information regarding the functioning of the government (Working Group on Right to Information and Promotion of Open and Transparent Government 1997: 3). The committee viewed transparency and access to information as prerequisites for democracy. Similar practices in other countries were drawn upon while setting the context for FoI legislation in India, as 'openness and accessibility of people to information about the government's functioning is a vital component of democracy' and that the veil of secrecy from the government activities was being 'progressively lifted … in most democratic countries' (1997: 3). The report of the committee added that 'it is not only the developed countries that have enacted freedom of information legislation. Similar trends have appeared in the developing countries as well' (1997: 3).

In 1998, the newly elected NDA, led by the BJP, constituted a GoM to examine the proposed FoI and finalize its recommendations.[2] In a background note prepared by the DoPT for the GoM, the international trend of FoI laws was cited yet again to provide the context for a similar legislation in India. The DoPT note pointed out:

[2] The GoM was constituted on 27 April 1998 through an office memo (Cabinet Secretariat, GoM 1998), cabinet secretariat, GoI. Members of the GoM were L.K. Advani, minister of home affairs; George Fernandes, minister of defence; M. Thambi Durai, minister of law, justice and company affairs, and minister of surface transport; Sushma Swaraj, minister of information and broadcasting and minister of communications; Vasundhra Raje, minister of state in the MEA; and R. Janarthanam, minister of state in the MPPP.

> There is a *worldwide trend* [my emphasis] in democratic countries to have legislation for assuring to the citizens the right of access to information of the public authorities as part of the effort to promote openness, transparency and accountability in the administration and to ensure greater participation of the people in the decision-making. (Internal Note for the GOM 1998)

The stress on the worldwide trend appears repeatedly in government papers. This was reiterated in an internal note prepared by the DoPT in January 1998 for the approval of the cabinet of the proposed FoI Bill. The government note justified the proposed FoI Bill in India in line with the worldwide trend, and viewed transparency as a 'vital element of good governance advocated by agencies and citizens' groups alike' (Internal Government Note for the Cabinet, DoPT 1998).

The 'worldwide trend' was referred to yet again in the 78th report of the DRPSC-HA (2000), which cited legislation in other democratic countries such as the 'USA, Japan, Ireland, the Netherlands, Australia, Canada, France, the UK, New Zealand, and South Africa' (DRPSC 2000).

Similarly, in 2005, a background note prepared for the DRPSC, DOPT, provided the context of the 'worldwide trend' of 'new era of government transparency', especially as 'over 55 countries have adopted comprehensive laws to facilitate access and many more are in the process of doing so' (Internal DoPT Note to Rajya Sabha Secretariat 2005).

The tendency of citing international trends continued until 2005 even during the final passage of the RTI Bill. When the bill was referred to the DRPSC on Personnel, Public Grievances and Law and Justice (DRPSC 2005). While acknowledging the significance of access to official information, the DRPSC pointed towards the 'worldwide trend' of 'fifty-five countries enacting comprehensive laws' on access to information, and specifically mentioned Sweden, Australia, Canada, New Zealand, Belize, Pakistan, South Africa, Trinidad and Tobago, the UK, Zimbabwe, Jamaica, and the USA (DRPSC 2005).

As discussed, the global norms often provided the reference for ongoing policy discussions. This was evident during the debates in the parliament on the draft FoI Bill, 2000, and the RTI Bill, 2004. For instance, while moving the FoI Bill, 2000, in the lower house, Vasundhara Raje, minister of state in the MPPP placed the Indian bill within the international context:

> The idea of this bill basically is to promote openness, transparency and accountability … in the administration and to ensure a greater participation of the people in decision-making, *and also to maintain consistency with the worldwide trend in democratic countries to have a legislation* [my emphasis] for giving the citizens the right of access to information, to transactions of public authorities. (Lok Sabha Debates 2002)

In the same discussion, another MP, Ramesh Chennithala of the Indian National Congress, supported the FoI Bill and contexualized the global trend of promulgating FoI laws:

> Effective and responsive governments are a necessity in today's world. It is because the mankind is progressing and also the concept of free society is existing in today's world. Governments must be more transparent. Governments must be more accountable to the public … *there is a worldwide trend, in almost all democratic countries in the world, to have right to information* [my emphasis]. The United States of America passed a legislation in this regard in 1966. Countries like Japan, Ireland, The Netherlands, Australia, Canada, France, UK, New Zealand and South Africa have enacted similar legislation to enforce transparency. In Australia, the Freedom of information Act, 1982 gives its citizens the right to see personal files primarily held by Social Security and Tax Departments. The South African countries also are following this path. (Lok Sabha Debates 2002)

This was evident during the debate on final passage of the RTI Bill in 2005 as well. While moving the RTI Bill, 2004, minister of state of MPPP, Suresh Pachouri, said:

> I believe that the provisions of the bill will be a watershed in the evolution of the right to information in our country, and *will bring India at par with only a handful of the countries which have enacted*

> *such legislations* [my emphasis] … It is coming just in time when India is *emerging and claiming its rightful place, as a major global player in the comity of nations* [my emphasis]. (Lok Sabha Debates 2005)

The process of citing global trends had an impact at four levels. First, the best practices were always cited, which was perceptible even during the first phase. However, their salience increased with greater domestic political and policy mobilization favouring RTI. Second, citing the international trends provided demonstrative value and justification for the ongoing discourse within the country. Third, repeated reference to the growing global trend around access to information norms strengthened and deepened the internal policy discussions within the executive. Fourth, the examples of transparency and accountability as an integral part of democratic deepening and the sheer number of countries enacting legislations on access to information provided both context and urgency at the policy level. This is reflected in the government papers, which repeatedly touched upon the 'worldwide trend' and cited the increase in the number of countries that had enacted FoI laws.

Drawing on International Best Practices: Shaping the Law

Global norms and international best practices contributed at the domestic level by playing a crucial role in providing a template for the legal specificities in India. The FoI laws in other countries provided both content and context for the Indian law. Specific clauses from the FoI laws of other countries were cited and drawn upon in a clause-wise discussion of the proposed FoI Bill in India.

For example, in 1997, while considering the disclosure clause, the Shourie Committee unanimously agreed that inter- and intra-departmental noting should be excluded from the disclosure, as it would affect the decision-making of civil servants, citing the case of the USA where this clause applies only to files in the pre-decisional phase (Report of the Working Group 1997). Similarly, on the question of whether the draft FoI Bill should have an overriding clause as against the other laws, the committee examined the FoI laws of the

USA, Canada, and Australia, which contained such clauses (Report of the Working Group 1997: 8).[3]

The Shourie Committee's discussions on the issue of disclosure of information were informed by the existing FoI laws in other countries. This was evident from the fact that the committee directed the DoPT to provide a comparison of the categories of information exempted in international FoI laws (Internal Government Note 1997a). In response, the DoPT provided a comparison of relevant provisions from the Australian FoI Act, 1982; Canadian Access to Information Act, 1980; the UK's Code of Practice on Access to Information, Second Edition, 1997; and the USA's FoI Act, 1966 (amended and codified at 5 USC Section 552). The role of global norms on the access to information reflected during the committee's discussion on the review mechanism of the information appeal. The legal statutes of the USA, UK, Canada, Australia, and New Zealand were provided as a template to reach a considered decision on the question of a review mechanism (Internal Government Note 1997b).

Global precedent reflected in the inter-governmental response to the draft FoI Bill of the Shourie Committee as well. For instance, in response to the draft FoI Bill, the MHA expressed that the information related to 'scientific, economic and technological' matters should be included in the list of restrictive items, *which was also the case with the US FOI law* [my emphasis]'. Additionally, concern was also raised on the financial costs involved in the implementation of the FoI Bill; the cost of 65 million dollars incurred by the USA in 1989 and the 5 million dollars spent by Canada were cited (D.O. No. II/21011/54/96-is/us.D.II). The Shourie Committee considered these issues in its third meeting on 19 February 1997. International precedents are reflected in the discussions of these meetings. On the issue of disclosure of internal government files, inter and intra-departmental file noting, and correspondence, the US law was cited where this provision protected files in the pre-decisional phase. Clause 3(2) was borrowed from the US law where only the available information needed to be disclosed: 'The

[3] The committee finally decided to have a non-obstante clause in the bill as Clause 18, which gave the Act an overriding effect.

bill should not result in an obligation to create records where none was operationally necessary-on the analogy of the FOIA of the US' (third meeting of the working group, 19 February 1997).

In yet another example of drawing upon legal frameworks from other countries, the FoI laws of the USA, Canada, and Australia were taken into consideration on the question of whether to include private bodies within the ambit of the proposed legislation. Finally, these were excluded. The FoI legislations in the USA, Canada, Australia, and New Zealand were again drawn upon to shape the clauses related to the disclosure of information. On the basis of the clauses of the FoI laws in these countries, a negative list was provisioned in Clauses 8 and 9 of the proposed bill, which contained the categories of information exempted from disclosure (DRPSC-HA 2000: 5).

Notably, earlier in 1997, a group of civil servants had visited the USA, Canada, New Zealand, and Australia to study the citizen's charter in operation in these countries, and also examine the FoI laws. The report of this study group was later used by the DoPT for discussions within the GoM in 1997 (Internal Government Note 1998). This is evident in the GoM's demand for FoI legislations from other countries for their discussions; the GoM '*desired that copies of similar legislation in advanced democracies may be obtained* [my emphasis]'.[4]

Access to information laws from the USA, Canada, and Australia, and a white paper of the British government on FoI law provided the background and context for the first meeting of the newly constituted GoM by the NDA government in 1999 (Cabinet Secretariat 1999).[5]

[4] An internal note of the DoPT provides evidence for such demands from the GoM. The note mentions, 'In their meeting held on 18 December 1998, the Group of Ministers considered the legislative proposal for freedom of information and *desired that copies of similar legislation in advanced democracies may be obtained* [my emphasis].' This was pursued by the DoPT and action was taken (Internal DoPT Note 1998).

[5] The NDA had come back to power in 1999 after the 13th general elections. The previous GoM of 1998 to examine the proposed FoI law was expanded to include Ram Jethmalani, minister of law, justice and company affairs; Arun Jaitley, minister of information and broadcasting; and Jaswant Singh, minister of external affairs.

The background note for the GoM had a detailed discussion on various exemptions in the FoI laws of these countries (Government Background Note for the Group of Ministers 1999). The GoM's directive to the DoPT to redraft Clauses 8 and 9 of the proposed bill in accordance with Articles 19(1) and 19(2) of the Constitution of India was guided by the international legal precedent of allowing free access to information with certain specific exemptions and without any positive list:

> The GoM noted that while there were differences in the individual acts of parliament belonging to different countries, a perusal of the available information indicated that by and large, the advanced countries were also allowing free access to information with certain exceptions and there was no positive list in the statues of other countries as all information was available subject to specific exceptions. (Minutes of the Meeting of GoM 1999)

The influence of existing global norms on access to information was evident during the clause-wise discussion on the draft FoI Bill, 2000. The DRPSC invited the views of individuals and organizations and forwarded these to the DoPT for the government's response. While responding to these concerns, the DoPT cited existing global norms extensively (Table 5.1). Prior to the DRPSC meetings, a comparative statement and notes on the provisions of the proposed FoI Bill, 2000, with other countries such as the New Zealand, Ireland, the USA, Japan, Australia, Canada, and the Netherlands was provided to the Rajya Sabha Secretariat (MPPP 2001). Most of these clauses were retained in the RTI Act, 2005.

The influence of global norms continued during the final passage of the bill. In the previous chapter, I discussed the consequential role of the epistemic network in the promulgation of the RTI Act. This network was actively consulting global laws and often drew upon these. For instance, Shekhar Singh, one of the founders of the NCPRI, was invited by Joseph Stiglitz to be part of the 'transparency taskforce' of the Initiative for Policy Dialogue (IPD). In 2000, Stiglitz had initiated a policy dialogue on development issues and brought together experts from various countries to participate (also

TABLE 5.1 Drawing on International Laws

Clause	Global Norms
Naming the title of the bill as RTI Bill keeping in mind the fundamental right granted in the Constitution.	Government in its response cited that Australia (1982), Ireland (1997), the USA (1966), the UK (2000), Canada (1985), New Zealand (1982), and the Netherlands (1991) have named their legislations as FoI as well.
Extent and coverage of the bill to all persons including the citizens.	Acts of the USA, the Netherlands, the UK, and Canada provided as examples to justify the objective that access to information should be extended to all citizens including persons who are present in the country.
Private bodies should be covered by the Act.	Laws of the USA, Canada, and Australia cited for not including private bodies within the ambit of the law.
Response time to provide information.	Thirty- days of response time in the proposed bill was in the light of thirty days in Canada, twenty working days in New Zealand, thirty days in Australia, twenty days in the USA, twenty-eight days in Ireland, and twenty days in the UK.
Disclosure of information on international relations.	Non-disclosure of information related to international relations in the proposed Indian FoI Bill was not an 'exception' in relation to similar provisions in Australia, New Zealand, Ireland, the Netherlands, the USA, France, and Canada.
Inclusion of information related to the deliberative process of the government.	Government held the view that records of internal discussions, advice (including legal advice), opinions, and recommendations made by the officers would not be covered under the law in relation to similar practices existing in the UK, Australia, New Zealand, Ireland, the Netherlands, the USA, France, and Canada.
Time of 50 days to invite third-party representation.	Universal practice of third-party intervention is cited along with the time period of sixty days for third-party intervention as provided in the Canadian law.

(*Cont'd*)

TABLE 5.1 (*Cont'd*)

Clause	Global Norms
Provision for protection of action taken by any person in 'good faith'.	Yet again the universal practice of such a provision is cited along with similar provisions in FoI laws of Canada, Australia, New Zealand, and Ireland.
Exclusion of organizations from the law.	Exemption of thirteen organizations in the Australian Act cited in favour of similar provisions.

Source: Rajya Sabha Secretariat 2001.

see Sharma 2015).[6] Singh, along with Ann Florini, chaired the transparency task force of the IPD. As part of this task force, Singh forged linkages with transparency experts in other countries. When the final version of the RTI Bill was being worked out within the NCPRI, Singh often consulted with these linkages, and drew upon laws from other countries. For instance, there was much discussion on the inclusion of the private sector within the ambit of the proposed legislation in India. The decision to exclude the private sector from the draft law was guided by the South African example. Singh's email exchange with the South African connection revealed that this provision was ineffective in South Africa. Similarly, the Australian law was consulted during the discussions on various provisions of the draft bill.

The evidence examined in this chapter points towards the convergence of global norms and the ongoing policy discussions in India. This was a continuous process, starting right since Independence until the promulgation of the RTI Act in 2005. Therefore, one can see an imprint of global best practices and established principles of transparency on the Indian law. These principles emanated from the established international declarations on the freedom of expression and speech and FoI. The UN had recognized the FoI in the

[6] Interview with Shekhar Singh, 10 April 2015, New Delhi.

first session of its General Assembly by adopting resolution 59 (1), which stated, '[The] Freedom of Information is [a] fundamental Human Right ... the touchstone of all the freedom to which the UN is consecrated'. In continuation of this resolution, the Universal Declaration of Human Rights (UDHR) adopted by the UN General Assembly in 1948 in Article 19 guaranteed and ensured freedom of expression and speech: 'Everyone has the right to freedom of opinion and expression; this right includes freedom to hold opinions without interference *and to seek, receive and impart information and ideas through any media and regardless of frontiers* [my emphasis]'. Additionally, the legally binding treaty of the International Covenant on Civil and Political Rights, adopted in the UN General Assembly, also recognized freedom of expression and speech on the lines of the UDHR. Early ideas on openness expressed in India were informed and influenced by the ongoing global discourse on the FoI, especially from the UN. This was evident in 1962 when the UN and the GoI jointly organized a seminar on FoI. Moreover, Article 19 of the Constitution of India is in line with Article 19 of the UDHR. Significantly, as established in Chapter 3, the judiciary so interpreted Article 19 of the Constitution of India in a number of cases and upheld the freedom of expression and speech. This interpretation later evolved as the 'right to know' inherent in Article 19 of the Constitution of India.

On the basis of these early international norms on FoI and freedom of expression and speech emerging from the international institutions, global best practices have been examined and laid out by the scholars (Article 19 1999; Mendel 2008). National laws are often juxtaposed in relation to these best practices, which should conform to the template of these desirable principles. A deeper examination of the RTI Act, 2005, and these principles show that the Indian law is in line with these global principles (Sharma 2015). This congruence of global principles with the Indian law was a result of the cumulative impact of a continuous synergy of global norms and the ongoing ideational churning at the domestic level. This is evident if the global principles are juxtaposed in terms of the specific clauses of RTI Act (Table 5.2).

Table 5.2 Reflection of Global Principles on the Indian Law

Global Principles	RTI Act, India
Maximum Disclosure: This implies that the scope of the law should be as broadly defined as possible to include a range of information, coverage, and its accessibility by individuals.	In terms of its scope, the RTI Act applies to the entire country. The Act also applies to all levels of the government—both central and the state governments and covers all public bodies, including bodies that the government funds. Private institutions are not included in the ambit of the law. The law also broadly defines the categories of records and information.
Obligation to Publish: This means proactive disclosure by the public authorities by publishing and disseminating information.	This is reflected in Section 4 (b) of the RTI Act, which stipulates the public authorities for suo motu disclosure of information.
Promotion of Open Government: This means that the public authorities should actively promote open government.	Section 26 of the RTI Act directs public authorities at both the central and the state levels to promote RTI.
Limited Scope of Exceptions	Section 8 of the RTI Act provides a list of exemptions from disclosure. Subsection 2 of Section 8 provides an override clause where the information can be disclosed if the public interest outweighs the non-disclosure of information.
Processes to facilitate Access: Rapid and fair processing of requests for information with independent review mechanism.	Section 7 of the RTI Act provides that the information should be given to the applicant by the public authorities within thirty days of receiving the application. Additionally, provision for a twin-level independent appellate mechanism is provided to appeal in case of non-disclosure or unsatisfactory disclosure.

Global Principles	RTI Act, India
Costs: Excessive costs should not deter the access to information.	The Act states that the cost of application should be not excessive. Most central and state governments have fixed the cost for application at INR 10. Information-seekers below the poverty line are exempted to pay any cost. Additionally, INR 2 per page is charged for the photocopy of the documents provided as part of information. This is, however, not applicable if the information is not provided within the stipulated time period of thirty days.
Open Meetings: Meetings of the public bodies should be open to public.	The RTI Act does not address this specifically. However subsections vii and viii of Section 4 of the RTI Act provides for publishing the details of the public consultation with public in relation to any policy formulation and implementation and statement of the boards, councils, and committees. Also, minutes of the public authorities should be accessible and open to public.
Precedence of Disclosure: Other existing laws that come in conflict with the principle of maximum disclosure should be repealed and amended.	Section 22 of the RTI Act, in all its practical policy import, has the power to override the other existing laws which might come in direct conflict with the RTI Act such as the OSA, 1923; Sections 1, 2, and 3 of the Indian Evidence Act; and Civil Services Conduct Rules. Section 22 of the RTI Act states: 'The provisions of this Act shall have effect notwithstanding anything inconsistent therewith contained in the Official Secrets Act, 1923, and any other law for the time being in force or in any instrument having effect by virtue of any law other than this Act'.

(*Cont'd*)

TABLE 5.2 (*Cont'd*)

Global Principles	RTI Act, India
Protection for Whistle-blowers: Individuals who disclose the information exposing wrongdoings such as corruption should be protected.	No provision for whistle-blowers' protection is provided in the RTI Act. However, in 2011, the Indian parliament promulgated the Whistle Blowers Protection Act, 2011, 'to establish a mechanism to receive complaints relating to disclosure on any allegation of corruption or wilful misuse of power or wilful misuse of discretion against any public servant and to inquire or cause an inquiry into such disclosure and to provide adequate safeguards against victimization of the person making such complaint'.

Source: Adapted from Mendel 2008: 31–40; *The Right to Information Act, 2005*, as published in Gazette of India, Part II Section I, 21 June 2005 (see also Sharma 2015; Shreyaskar 2013).

***

Some notable points are discernible from the evidence presented in this chapter.

First, the evidence examined establishes the role and influence of global norms in the institutional change in the transparency regime in India. Substantive portions of the policy discussions within the state point towards a process of global norm diffusion. However, despite the international influence, institutional change in the form of the RTI was due primarily to endogenous pulls and pressures, rather than to exogenous factors. This was evident in the way global norms were dictated by the domestic policy discourse and is consistent with the two-layered process of institutional change. In the first layer, the global norms had a limited role to play, which was consistent with the emerging domestic discourse within the State. This was the phase where some ideas on openness emerged on the fringes while the institution of secrecy persisted and was even reinforced within the State. However, during the second layer, while the initial ideas were becoming embedded in the State thinking and its policy intent, global norms were often cited and liberally borrowed from since the early 1990s. Global norms played a more important role in the second phase because domestic constituencies had evolved in that direction. In this sense, the role of global norms was contingent upon the trajectory of endogenous ideas and processes.

It can be concluded that global norms deepened the ongoing churning of ideas on openness at the national level. However, it was part of the broader endogenous processes that were taking shape internally. The global norms had demonstrative as well an operative impact, which deepened the discourse within the State and society. This deepening can be seen in the process of the clause-wise discussion on the draft FoI Bill, which drew extensively upon global best practices in the FoI laws of other countries (a process similar to the making of the Constitution of India, which borrowed extensively from the constitutions of other countries, although both the thrust and conviction of the discussions were entirely endogenous).

An ideational churning on the issue of openness in government affairs started right since Independence, eventually reaching a tipping point in 2005. This was a multi-layered process, where the cumulative push of emerging ideas played a consequential role. The interplay of global norms at the national level has to be seen within this broader, multi-layered churning process. The evidence examined in this chapter points towards the process of norm diffusion, in which emerging global norms had a demonstrative effect on policy discourse. In this light, I argue that the process can be understood in terms of 'norm demonstration'. This can be seen manifesting at two levels: first was the demonstrative element of transparency and accountability as an integral part of the process of democratic deepening, and at the second, FoI laws being adopted by more than fifty countries having a demonstrative impact on the prevailing thinking within the State.

Second, the evidence establishes a process of 'norm localisation' (Acharya 2004), where the emerging ideas and norms at the domestic level are strengthened or justified by drawing upon the established norms at the global level. In the case of the RTI Act, the norm diffusion globally had a demonstration effect on the ongoing discourse in India. In India, the RTI Act was not a result of 'exogenous' influence. Instead, the endogenous movement of ideas on openness and transparency was instrumental in affecting norm change at the institutional level. The international FoI laws and the global trend on transparency deepened the ongoing discourse within the State. This is evident often during the discussions in government committees, which quoted the existing international norms in other countries as justification for enacting a similar law in India. As argued by Acharya (2004), domestic actors in this case were not passive learners of transnational norms, but 'actively borrowed and modified' the global norms 'in accordance with their pre-constructed normative beliefs and practices' (2004: 269).

It is argued that the policy imperatives of transparent and accountable government, which came attached with the SAPs of the WB and the IMF, had a role in effecting institutional change (Sharma 2015). However, between 1991 and 1996, when the liberalization policy unfolded during the Congress government, one not only finds a hiatus of activities around the access to information at the level of the political and permanent executive but an effort to sustain the norm of secrecy by amending the Manual of Departmental Security Instructions in 1994 (discussed in Chapter 1). Moreover, as discussed earlier, the churning process on the openness in government affairs within the State had started much earlier. Hence, policy moves around transparency and accountability and the role of IFIs do not seem to have directly shaped each other. However, it cannot be ruled out that the view of IFIs mattered in the discussions within the executive. The discussions show that the executive machinery is concerned over how policies are calibrated with the institutional imperatives of IFIs. This is evident in an internal government discussion regarding the Country Policy and Institutional Assessment (CPIA) of the WB, which determines the individual country allocation by the International Development Association (IDA). The concern was expressed in a letter to the MPPP by the Ministry of Finance on CPIA ratings on three indicators: property rights and rule-based government; quality of public administration; and transparency, accountability, and corruption in the public sector (DO no.

2/1/2003-FB-II). The CPIA rating on the indicator of transparency, accountability, and corruption was three and a half for the years 2002 and 2003. In its response to the CPIA, the MPPP was rather apologetic with 'no comments to offer' and having 'no quarrel' with the CPIA putting India's performance between moderately unsatisfactory to moderately satisfactory (Internal Government Communication from Joint Secretary, DoPT 2004). The role of international agencies, if any, at best has to be seen within the broader context of norm localization and norm demonstration.

Conclusion

In this book I capture the process of institutional change in the 'information regime' in India by tracing the passage of the RTI Act, 2005. At the beginning, I posed the institutional change in the information regime as a research puzzle. Prior to the RTI Act, the details and process of governance were shrouded in secrecy and limited to the offices of public authorities. Access to information was governed by legal norms that weakened the information regime.

I unravelled the puzzle of institutional persistence and change by casting light on the why, how, and what of institutional change. In the first three chapters, I brought in new evidence to show that the institutional change was a result of, primarily, a long-drawn process of ideational churning from different segments of the State. In Chapter 4, I acknowledged and explored the complementarity of society and the State, and showed that actors from both society and the State with progressive ideas on openness, transparency, and access to information forged linkages and caused an epistemic network to form. This network worked from both within and outside the State to deepen the ideational churning ongoing within the State. These processes were consequential in institutional change. Additionally, I examined the role of global norms in Chapter 5 and showed that global norms had a demonstrative as well as an operative effect at the domestic level, in the form of what I argue was 'norm demonstration' and 'norm localization'.

Four broad conceptual points are discernible:

1. the role of ideas and the layered tipping point, that is, a multi-layered process of institutional change;
2. the role of the State;
3. the complementarity of the State and society; and
4. the role of global norms through demonstration and localization.

The Role of Ideas and the Layered Tipping Point

How do we explain and capture institutional change? I argue that we need to understand this process through the 'layered tipping point' model of institutional change, which suggests that institutional change is an incremental, cumulative, slow-moving process driven substantially, and endogenously, through the increasing political power of ideas. This argument gives primacy to the role of ideas as instrumental factors that lead to a tipping point of institutional change. The primacy of ideas helps in shaping interests. The evidence examined in this book shows that institutional change in the case of the RTI in India is an incremental and gradual process of ideas emerging from within the State that reached a tipping point in 2005. The first three chapters showed ideas that emerged cumulatively and incrementally shaped concrete norms and policies. Eventually, this cumulative and incremental push of ideas became embedded in State thinking, and led to a change in the State's policy choices and preferences, and therefore to institutional change.

My argument draws upon established scholarship in the field that uses the tipping point model to understand institutional change (Hall 1993; Jha 2018b; Mukherji 2013; 2014a). For instance, the mainstream diagnosis of the reasons for institutional change in Indian economic policy in 1991 is the alliance of prevalent dominant business interests and exogenous pressures. But Mukherji (2013; 2014a) argues that the institutional change was actually the result, or the tipping point, of the incremental causal effect of endogenous ideas that had long taken root among technocrats and the political class—exogenous pressures from the IMF merely created an opportunity for the already persuaded technocrats to negotiate with and convince the political class. Similarly, Hall (1993) uses an ideational lens to explore the adoption of neoliberal policies in Great Britain—a policy shift. Hall provides a framework of ideas (a paradigm) that structures the actor's perception of problems and solutions, and dictates the instruments to be used to reach policy goals.[1]

The institutional change from the norm of secrecy to the norm of openness in this case occurred in a 'layered tipping point'. Layering is a process in which a new legal structure with a new set of norms is placed atop an existing structure and, eventually, wears it out. I argue that the process of institutional change was two-layered in the case of the RTI Act too, although the layering occurred in the ideational realm and not as a legal structure. It is seen initially at the level of ideas, and eventually in policy processes.

In the first layer, ideas of openness emerged in a very rudimentary form at the periphery; at the same time, the norm of secrecy was being institutionalized. In this polarity of ideas, the narrative was being pulled in favour of both secrecy and of openness. This is the beginning of the ideational churning within the State. After the National Emergency imposed in 1975 and the Janata party government in 1977, the nascent ideas on openness became nuanced. The polarity remained but the ideational churning within the State deepened and found expression in political commitment articulated through election manifestos, policy pronouncements, public statements, election manifestos, studies, and reports from within the legislature (such as private members' bills). In this layer, the idea of 'openness' was primarily part of opposition politics. Some technocratic elements within the State too questioned the prevailing 'secrecy' and favoured greater openness of the State. The judicial interpretation of Article 19 (1) (a) upholding free speech (discussed in Chapter 3) converges with the first layer.

In the second layer, the nascent ideas on 'openness' became part of mainstream politics. Statements made by PMs of various governments, beginning with the NF government in 1989, corroborate this. The policy processes began to reflect the ideas and the political

[1] Admittedly, in Hall's account it is unclear whether the entry of Margret Thatcher was a critical juncture or a tipping point (Blyth 2002; Mukherji 2014a).

commitment—the political and permanent executive were working in tandem to formulate a specific legislation on the FoI or RTI. This development was evident also in the formation of government committees, inter-ministerial task forces, and the constitution of GoMs to explore the possibility of legislation on access to information. The latter half of the second layer, starting from the mid-1990s, is significant in completing the layering process. This was evident when the NDA government promulgated the FoI Act, 2002. However, this Act did not come into force, which indicates uncertainty within the State over replacing the existing institutional framework. In the context of Article 19 (1) (a), the progression of the judicial stance from free speech to the 'right to know' inherent in the fundamental right to freedom of expression and speech was consistent with the policy processes initiated in the second layer.

Significantly, it was during this period that State–society synergy took a more structural form, which culminated in the formation of the NAC during the UPA government in 2004. This was instrumental in removing any uncertainty that the State might have had regarding the policy choice in favour of RTI. At the same time, the SC of India also directed the UPA government to operationalize the law that was enacted in 2003.

This was similar to the case of institutional change in the telecommunications sector in India. The Department of Telecommunications (DoT), the regulatory authority at that time, favoured government-owned telecommunications companies. When the Telecom Regulatory Authority of India and the Telecom Dispute Settlement Appellate Tribunal were set up, a level playing field was created for private players (Mukherji 2014a). The setting up of the NAC and the direction of the SC has to be seen in a similar light in the case of the RTI Act. The NAC brought on board ideas from both the State and society, worked in tandem with the PMO to work out the legislation on the RTI, and played an instrumental role in removing any political and bureaucratic uncertainty. Eventually, the RTI Act 'layered over' the 'nested rules'. At this point the transparency 'tipped' from the norm of 'secrecy to 'openness'. Section 22 of the RTI Act, which overrides all other laws, completes the layering process. The process of layering can be seen in Table C1.

Table C1 Process of Layering

Layer I (1947–89): Polarity of Ideas—Narrative Pulled Both Ways between 'Secrecy' and 'Openness'	
Institutionalization of Secrecy	Nascent Ideas on Openness
OSA and 1967 amendment of OSA reinforced by other laws such as Civil Services Conduct Rules, 1964, Sections 1, 2, and 3 of Indian Evidence Act, 1842, and Manual of Office Procedures—'locked-in nested rules reinforcing secrecy'	Nascent ideas on openness emerge on the fringes of the persisting institution of 'secrecy'. • Narrative on 'openness' as part of *opposition politics.* • We see a demand for openness from opposition parties and some technocratic elements within State challenging the nested norm of secrecy. This manifested in parliamentary debates, reports of the government committees, political commitment by the Janata Party followed by limited and aborted policy steps, public statements, and limited policy initiatives adopted at the State level. Judicial stance on free speech contributes to the emerging ideational churning around 'openness'.
Layer II (1989–2005): Institution 'Tips' Over from Secrecy to Openness—Incremental Weight of Ideas Result in a Transition from the Layer I to Layer II	
The Final Layer System Tips Over	Transition of Ideas and Norms
Final stages of layering: norm of 'openness' layered out the nested norm of 'secrecy' by 2005.	Transition of ideas from *opposition politics* in layer I to *mainstream politics* in layer II Ideas on openness get rooted in the State thinking displacing the institutional gridlock of secrecy, reflected in • political and policy intent, followed by the policy processes initiated to

	legislate FoI/RTI. This was evident in the formation of internal government committees; GoMs, DRPSCs; and RTI Acts promulgated at the sub-national level from 1997 onwards. • Additionally, judicial interpretation of the Constitution of India transitioned from free speech in layer I to 'right to know' in layer II as an inherent part of the Article 19 (1) (a) of the Constitution of India. • Actors from both within State and society forge ideational linkages to form an epistemic network; State–society synergy emerges in a mutually enforcing relationship (for example, NAC) in the final stages of the RTI Act.

Source: Author.

It is difficult to point out the exact threshold of when the tipping point will be reached. If a certain threshold of ideas is reached and gains enough critical mass to cause a norm change, the system can be said to have tipped over. Even for the seismologists (a more accurate science than social science) it is impossible to predict the exact time of the earthquake; however, tracking the shifts in the tectonic plates might indicate a likelihood of an earthquake.[2] Explaining institutional change by tracing shifts in ideas across time is somewhat like predicting earthquakes.

Why should 2005 be considered a tipping point? First, the RTI Act signifies an institutional rearrangement evident in the norm shift from 'secrecy' to 'openness'. The RTI Act introduced openness and this new norm replaced the nested norm of secrecy, which had been persisting since the colonial period. Section 22 of the RTI Act, which says the Act supersedes any Act in conflict with it, completed the process of institutional change. The supremacy of the RTI Act over

[2] I am thankful to Professor Rahul Mukherji for this discussion on the threshold of tipping point.

other laws was an advancement of similar clauses in earlier bills such as clause 26 of the FoI Bill (2000) introduced by the NDA government. This was a slow-moving progression of earlier ideas reaching a threshold in 2005.

Second, the political and policy movements prior to 2005 show that the idea of openness emerged cumulatively and incrementally shaping concrete norms and policies starting from the NF government in 1989. The RTI Act, 2005, in this sense represented advancement of earlier ideas elaborated in the two layers. Hence, the change of government itself does not explain institutional change. The frenetic political and policy movements prior to the UPA government show that the incremental weight of ideas had reached a threshold to arrive at a tipping point in 2005. The gradual movement towards institutional change is evident in the way ideas emerged on the fringes in the first layer, evolved over time, and, in the second layer, tipped the system over in 2005 (see Jha 2018b).

The tipping point argument is different from other arguments such as the 'critical junctures' that suggest that the path of a historically persistent institution is altered by 'exogenous shocks' that impact the institutional path and lead to institutional change. This argument follows the 'punctuated equilibrium' model, which suggests that institutional change occurs through path-altering shocks. These are, as Capoccia (2016: 89) puts it, 'distal historical causation': 'events and developments in the distant past, generally concentrated in a relatively short period, that have a crucial impact on outcomes later in time'. For instance, Krasner argues that because institutions are path-dependent in nature and, hence, durable, there has to be fundamental discord with the existing social and economic conditions, or a dramatic, exogenous shock, to change the prevailing static configuration—'short bursts of rapid institutional change followed by [a] long period of stasis' (Krasner 1984: 242). In this crucial period, termed a 'critical juncture', the old traditional institutional configuration collapses, and this collapse makes several new policy choices possible (for a short duration). Similarly, Acemoglu and Robinson (2012) hold that present institutions are shaped by critical junctures in history, such as colonialism and revolutions. International pressure and domestic economic crises are seen as critical junctures in changing the policy choices of countries such as Singapore, Taiwan, Hong Kong, and South Korea from import substitution to export-substituting industrialization (Haggard 1990). The changes in the legal and regulatory structures of the USA after 9/11 constitute a more dramatic example of a path-altering exogenous shock that causes a critical juncture which, in turn, leads to institutional change (Parry 2007). Likewise, new regulatory structures were imposed on the global airline industry (and the US Federal Aviation Authority was revamped), although the airline industry, consumer organizations, and safety activists had traditionally opposed those structures for decades (Niles 2002).

Additionally, the tipping point model challenges interest-based arguments as well, which hold that interests—not ideas—are important. This line of argument posits the primary role to dominant interests that play the pivotal role in institutional change. The argument is that societal interests (or demands) play a consequential role in determining and guiding the State's policy preferences. An example of the interest-based argument is the mainstream literature that deals with institutional change in the form of the RTI, which holds that societal interests or social pressures are consequential in shaping the State's policy choices and that these demands were articulated through social mobilization in the form of a 'people's movement'.

Contrary to the critical junctures and interest-based arguments, the evidence examined in this book persuades us to adopt the 'tipping point' argument, which views institutional change as a slow-moving, endogenous process, in which ideas shape interests. The 'critical junctures' argument is found wanting in explaining the institutional change in the information regime in India, which was neither sudden nor the result of an exogenous shock. Similarly, the view of social or people's movements in pressurizing the State to yield to the demand of institutional change can only partially explain the change, as the empirical evidence examined in this book shows that the push for change was from both within and outside the system, where ideas on openness were paramount. Furthermore, one can see the role of an active network, from both within the State and society, where actors forged ideational linkages around the common goal of the RTI.

In this light, I problematize the prevailing interest-based argument and present an alternative argument of the layered tipping point to understand the institutional change. I stress the incremental causality of ideas. In the case of the information regime in India, we see ideas on openness emerging incrementally within the State and playing a consequential role in shaping concrete norms and policies. Institutions tend to persist and the related norms locked in within the State create powerful ideas around themselves. The norm of secrecy was locked in within the Indian State and created powerful ideas in its favour. However, the counter-norm of openness emerged from various segments of the State and accumulated enough power to displace the 'locked-in' norm of secrecy. I show that the norm of openness was on the periphery in the early years, but shifted slowly to the policy centre stage, and eventually displaced the locked-in norm of secrecy in a long-drawn process of endogenous ideational churning. This led to change in the State's policy choices and preferences, which reached a tipping point in 2005.

The churning of ideas can be seen in different phases since Independence. In the first phase, although the norm of secrecy is institutionalized within State systems, ideas on openness emerge from within the State. In the second phase, the ideas become embedded within the State; such embeddedness can be seen in the moves to explore the possibility of concretizing the emergent ideas as norms in the legislature, in the constitution of government committees, and in the demands from State institutions. Such institutions include the PCI, Law Commission of India, and the IIPA. In the third phase, the State takes initiatives to channelize the embedded ideas to form a concrete policy and make institutional change ineluctable.

The long-drawn churning process of ideas provided an ideational base for future norm change and the final push towards institutional change. I present evidence to support the argument that the counter-ideational narrative created pulls and pressures, and caused the institutional path to break away from the persisting norm of secrecy and adopt a counter-norm of openness. In this sense, the institutional change that occurred in 2005—marked by the passing of the RTI Act—is path-dependent on the emerging ideational narrative. The ideational move around openness and transparency gradually and cumulatively shaped the interests of both the political and permanent executive in favour of access to information or RTI. The continual chain of judicial verdicts adds credence to our point on endogenous, slow-moving institutional change taking root in the interpretation of the Constitution of India from the early phase. Linkages can be established between the movement of ideas within the judiciary and the ideational patterns emerging in other segments of the State. For instance, Justices A.N. Sen, K.K. Mathew, and P.N. Bhagwati later became chairmen of the PCI respectively. As a result, the judicial interpretation of the Constitution found expression in ideas articulated continually by the PCI. In 1996, this manifested in the draft RTI Bill prepared by the PCI under Justice P.B. Sawant, which formed the basis for future policy discussions around the RTI Act. Additionally, from the judicial verdicts we see clearly how ideas around openness gradually evolved as the interpretation of Article 19 (1) (a) of the Constitution of India moved categorically towards citizens' (fundamental) rights and the notion that the right to know and to information were integral to the freedom of expression and speech. Judicial verdicts contribute towards a gradual diffusion of norms; such diffusion complements the process through which ideas on openness are embedded as norms in State thinking. Culpepper (2008) describes the nature of this type of institutional change best: 'Observing how ideas become shared is much like watching grass grow: nothing seems to be happening in the short term, but one day a former patch of mud is suddenly green.'

The Role of the State

Second, this book necessitates deeper engagement with the role of the State. Based on the evidence explored, I suggest a 'statist' turn in explaining institutional change, and challenge the mainstream argument, which posits the primary role to the social or people's movement, and treats 'bottom-up', grassroots demands as the primary causality that played an instrumental role in demanding the RTI. It is essentially a societal-based argument, where demands are articulated through social and political mobilization, and pressurize the State to yield a desired policy or institutional space. Instead, this book demonstrated the crucial role of the State and the emerging ideas from within its different segments to capture the incremental shift in policy processes and preferences. The evidence examined showed the role of the State and emergent ideas rather than societal interests singularly. This aspect is conspicuous by its absence in the mainstream literature that explains institutional change in the information and transparency regime in India (through RTI Act).

I argue for 'bringing the State back in' (Skocpol 1985) with regard to its thinking and will—and not only in terms of its autonomy or capacity. This argument establishes the crucial role of State thinking and political will shaped by the incremental push of ideas on openness from within the State. If one discusses 'institutional change or transformation', it is not merely State autonomy or capacity (Skocpol 1985) but also the degree of autonomy and capacity of State thinking that shapes emerging policy and institutional contours. In this case, the degree of autonomy and the capacity of the State have to be seen in the light of pursuing certain ideas, such as the norm of openness. Political will and State thinking are, then, contingent upon these ideas.

The historical evidence examined demonstrates that in the case of the RTI Act certain elements of the State started articulating the ideas on the desired norm of openness much before such ideas emerged in the societal realm; the idea originated within the State. This view treats State thinking as a significant variable and provides an alternative argument—the State is an important source of ideas and pre-empts societal interests. The pronouncements and policy moves by various governments, starting with the Janata Party government, point towards the significant role of political will. This was also reflected in the personal interest taken in the passage of the bill by various heads of government, from the NF government to the NAC, which provided the legislation with the final push.

Social forces played a crucial role, especially in the latter half of our second phase, where I show considerable State–society synergy. However, the cumulative push of ideas and the consequential policy initiatives from within the State cannot be neglected and had already attained critical mass prior to the emergence of these social impulses. Hence, I argue that it is necessary to understand the ideas that shaped State thinking and political will to understand the process of institutional change.

I do not claim absolute autonomy for the State where it pursues an agenda independent of society. For example, Krasner (1984) uses the foreign policy of a State and a case study of investment in raw materials to show that the State has an autonomous agenda insulated from societal pressures. For Krasner, States are formally 'defined as central decision-making institutions and roles' (Krasner 1984: 12). In the USA, this definition translates into 'the President and those bureaus relatively insulated from societal pressures' (Krasner 1984: 62); 'the most important institutions are the White House and the State Department' (Krasner 1984: 11). I do not claim autonomy for the State when it formulates and pursues policies that are not 'reflective of the demands or interests of social groups, classes or society' (Skocpol 1985). A State's autonomy lies in its capacity to pursue certain ideas. This is evident in the continuity of ideas on openness being articulated by segments within the State: the ideas that emerged outside the State in the societal realm were in line with the ideas on openness expressed from within it right since Independence. The sociopolitical processes deepened the ongoing ideational churning. From the mid-1990s, elements from both the State and society forged linkages to work towards a common goal. This necessitates deeper engagement with the State-and-society argument, which I discuss in the subsequent section.

In his study of State thinking in Britain and Sweden on the old age pension and unemployment insurance programmes, Heclo (1974) stresses economic growth as the necessary condition in both countries and argues that the role of ideas and, therefore, these policies were part of 'social learning'. The State not only powers but also puzzles; 'policy making is a form of collective puzzlement on society's behalf; it entails both deciding and knowing' (1974: 305). Learning involves drawing lessons from previous policy failures and forming new policies to address these. The central role for civil servants (or bureaucrats) is to insulate the process from politics and interest groups and play 'a leading part in identifying these conditions and framing concrete alternatives to deal with them on behalf of the society' (1974: 301–2). Drawing upon Heclo's proposition in this case, I describe the ideational churning around the norm of openness within the State as representative of the 'powering and puzzling' of the Indian State. This can be seen happening in different stages—a norm emerges, then takes root in State thinking, and finally assumes policy centre stage and eventually 'displaces' the locked-in norm.

Complementarity of State and Society

I propose a rethinking of the 'State vs society' argument, which is that the contestations or pressures from the societal level convince the State to adopt a certain institutional path (for such an argument, see Hasan 2018). The view that the people's movement led to the RTI Act is in line with this 'State vs society' argument. I propose neither to reify the State or society, nor see either as a monolith, but nuance the argument and argue that the State and society complement each other. I suggest that the synergy of the State and society working mutually and in tandem shaped the ideas about a specific policy choice. This is similar to the State-and-society arguments proposed in the scholarship dealing with the State–society dichotomy, which views this dichotomous relationship in the light of the two realms constituting each other (Evans 1997; Migdal 1988; 2001; Migdal, Kohli, and Shue 1994).

The process of institutional change in the case of the RTI Act is reflective of the State–society synergy. The State–society argument needs to be placed in the broader context of the long-drawn ideational churning within the State that had been taking place since Independence. Progressive elements from both within the State and society with similar ideas on transparency, openness, and legislation on access to information forged linkages and worked for a common goal. This complemented the ongoing policy process within the State that was put in motion by the political leadership from 1989. It took concrete shape in the form of the NCPRI, an epistemic community with its own special knowledge, which deepened the discourse ongoing within the State and society. The formation of such an epistemic community outside the State created an environment conducive to the norm of openness. This network worked from both within and outside the State to remove the uncertainties about a specific policy choice, and eventually brought about institutional change. The government formed the NAC, a think tank representative of both the State and society and uniquely placed to calibrate the discourse from both sides. In 2005, this process resulted in the promulgation of the RTI Act.

The Global–Local Linkages

Although the journey of the ideas from nascent norms to institutional change was endogenous in nature, exogenous factors such as global transparency norms and the concept of the FoI did affect the ongoing ideational discourse. I establish that the role of global norms was in the form of 'norm demonstration', in which global norms and laws were often cited as justification for a similar law in the country. This demonstrative value of global norms deepened the endogenous process. In addition, specific provisions from existing laws in other countries significant in the broader Indian context were actively drawn upon. Acharya (2004) terms this 'norm localization'. However, global norm diffusion did not force domestic policies to change; instead—similar to the process of the Constitution of India—it deepened and complemented endogenous processes.

***

The RTI Act has opened a space for accountability between the State and the citizens. In this accountability continuum one end is of the information givers and at the other end are the information seekers (Jha 2018a). The relationship between the two is often tumultuous. The culture of secrecy still prevails within the bureaucracy, and is evident in their hesitancy to share information. The official view of information seekers is unfavourable. There have been attempts to weaken the law. After the enactment of the RTI Act, both the UPA and the NDA governments have attempted to dilute the law. Political parties across lines have resisted coming under the ambit of the RTI Act. In 2013, an amendment to the RTI Act was proposed to grant immunity to political parties.

Perhaps one of the most powerful and equally contested dilutions to the RTI Act came fourteen years after it was first promulgated in 2005. The amendment passed by both the upper and the lower houses of the parliament in July 2019 entails two changes on tenure and emoluments of the information commissioners. First, the fixed five-year tenure of the information commissioners will now be prescribed by the central government. Second, salaries, allowances, and other related benefits will also be stipulated by the central government. Relevant subsections of Sections 13, 16, and 27 dealing with the terms of office and conditions of service were amended (see Table C2).

Principal opposition to these amendments is that it will take the autonomy of the information commissioners and put them in greater control under the State. This will impact the adjuratory role of the information commissioners who are supposed to act as independent and neutral regulators of the transparency and information regime.

TABLE C2 RTI Act, 2019, Amendments

RTI Act 2005	RTI (Amendment) Bill 2019
Section 13 stipulates that the information commissioners shall hold office for the fixed tenure of five years and shall not be eligible for reappointment.	This amends the five-year tenure stipulation to include tenure prescribed by the central government.
Subsection 5 of section 13 states the salaries and allowances of the information commissioner's equivalent of the election commissioner of India.	The amendment bill stipulates the salaries and allowances of the the information commissioners to be fixed by the central government.

Source: Right to Information Act 2005 and Right to Information (Amendment) Bill 2019.

In that sense, these amendments can also be construed as efforts to weaken the regulator to wield greater control on the flow of information. Significantly, the RTI amendment bill was neither referred to the parliamentary standing committee, nor put in the public domain for wider consultation as is the norm for bills introduced in the parliament. The justification provided by the government, on the other hand, is that since the mandate of the information commissioners and the election commissioner is different, the status and the salary needs to be rationalized.

What will be the impact of these amendments? Ever since the inception of the RTI Act, it was often the norm that the information commissioners at both the central and state levels were former bureaucrats. A 2006–7 study by the Society for Participatory Research in Asia (PRIA—a Delhi based non-government research organization) revealed that a retired bureaucrat headed at least fifteen state information commissions. The study showed that out of fifty-two commissioners in twenty state information commissions studied, twenty-seven were former bureaucrats (PRIA 2007). There was always the likelihood that the commissioners would be sympathetic to their genus and will often shield the executive. Indeed, citizens and activists constantly opposed the capture of information regime by bureaucrats. Clearly, even prior to the 2019 amendments the information regime was susceptible to greater control by the State since the commissioners were formerly part of the State. Despite this, the RTI Act has been extensively used across the country (24.4 million requests filed between 2005 and 2016 according to a modest estimate). My own study of the state of Bihar shows that against all odds RTI Act as an institution has substantially progressed, evident in its extensive use (Jha 2018a). Based on these field insights, I am inclined to argue that institutional change still holds valid, as the recent dilutions have not countermanded the norm change from the previously locked-in norm of 'secrecy' to 'openness'. Constitutionally granted rights such as the RTI, cannot be withdrawn but can be consciously blunted. This is evident in the recent amendments, which do not directly alter the power of the information commissioners, but merely introduce changes in their service rules and salaries.

Clearly, the stage after institutional change is riddled by yet another kind of ideational contestation. The relationship between the information givers and information seekers is often tumultuous and multi-hued. For example, on the one hand the legal tool of the RTI successfully reveals the cost of foreign travels by the PM and the council of ministers (see *Business Line* 2019), while on the other hand the RTI faces a negative response on the educational degrees of the PM and some of the cabinet ministers. Nevertheless, the pressure and the scrutiny on the State to disclose information by its citizens could not have been possible in the absence of institutional change that occurred in 2005. Veritably, the State itself reveals crucial information about the processes within the State—such disclosure was unimaginable in the pre-RTI period. For example, recently the DoPT made public the file notings showing that the government had proposed an ordinance to fulfil the objective of the RTI amendment bill, 2019, a policy initiative not accepted by the PMO (DoPT F. No: 4/9/2018-IR).

Similar initiatives are perceptible at the sub-national level even in the wake of the 2019 amendments. In Rajasthan, the State and the social actors conceptualized and, in 2019, launched the Jan Soochana Portal (public information portal) and mobile app, which gives access to real-time information about various public policy programmes in the State. Similarly, much before Rajasthan, Bihar introduced an ICT-enabled call centre called Jankari in 2007 enabling citizens to file an RTI application by placing a call to the call centre (Jha 2018a). In the absence of institutional change it could not have been possible to have these governance innovations to seek or voluntarily divulge information from within the State. The change is both de facto and de jure. Legal and policy regimes are seldom perfectly executed on the ground, contestations are omnipresent. Nevertheless, institutional change in the form of RTI has bestowed a legal right to the citizens to demand transparency and accountability from the State. It is in this vein that citizens' groups such as the NCPRI in response to the recent amendments have launched a national campaign to 'Use RTI, to save RTI' urging citizens to constantly seek information from the State (NCPRI Press Release 2019).

Indeed, the question mark that is put on the greatness and revolutionary aspect of the RTI in terms of its potential to deepen democracy and development still remains even after fifteen years of its promulgation (Roberts 2010). The institutional progression is not complete; it is, at best, partial and still evolving. Despite this, the institutional change that grants citizens the RTI has led to extensive use of the RTI, and has in turn pressurized the hesitant public authorities to grant citizens their rights. Despite their hesitancy, the bureaucracy is mindful of the RTI in its daily functioning (Jha 2018a). Similar to the ideational churning I have traced in this book, yet another churning is taking place in the process of institutional progression.

Appendices

A1 Speaker's Ruling in 1965

The Speaker delivered a detailed seven-point ruling.

1. A member can ordinarily quote from document that is created by the government as secret or confidential and which the government has not disclosed in the public interest.
2. The government is not obliged to lay such a document on table of the house, and the chair cannot compel it to do if it continued to hold the view that it is not in the public interest to do so.
3. It is for the government to consider whether the document, copies of which have been circulated among members and which have appeared in the press, wholly or partially, shall still be treated as secret or confidential and not laid on the table.
4. While the government cannot be compelled to admit or deny the correctness of any alleged copy of a document, which is classified as secret or confidential, it necessary for the member who quotes from such a document to certify that he has verified from his personal knowledge that the document is true copy of the original with the government, and the member will do so on his own responsibility. In case the member is not prepared to give a certificate in these terms and he insists on quoting from such document, that chair may find out from the government about

the authenticity of such a document and the facts placed by the government before the chair will be final in determining whether such a document is genuine or not. Where the government declines to admit or deny the correctness of any alleged copy, the chair will allow the member to proceed and it will for the government to give such answers as it thinks fit and the house possesses ample power to deal with the matter under the Constitution and the rules.

5. Normally, a member is not expected to spring a surprise on the speaker, the house and the government by quoting from a document, which is not public. In fairness to all, and in accordance with parliamentary conventions, the member should inform the chair and the government in advance so that they are in a position to deal with the matter on the floor of the house when it is raised. If this requirement is not complied with, the chair may stop the member from quoting from such a document and may ask the member to make available to the chair a copy before the chair allows the member to proceed with any quotation from it.
6. A document, which is treated by the government as secret or confidential, can be obtained through leakage or stealth or in an irregular manner, but the chair would not compel the member to disclose the source from which copies have been obtained by the member.
7. The member has a right to quote from such a document subject to conditions specified (*ToI* 1965c).

A2 Comments on the Draft PCI Bill Were Received by Secretary, MHA; Discussed in the Shourie Committee

1. Since the Bill pertained to both state and central levels, it would be prudent to seek the views of the State before the Bill is enacted.

2. Section 2 C(ii) of the Act proposed including public authorities, companies, corporations, societies, firms, or cooperative societies owned or controlled by private individuals within the ambit of the Act, which was not concurred by the MHA as the private bodies were governed by different sets of laws and statutes. In the view of MHA this would be problematic in implementation.
3. Inter-departmental and intra-departmental noting should not be included with the purview of the law (incidentally this was much debated and discussed when the RTI Act was enacted in 2005, an aspect which would be discussed later).
4. Circulation of budget issues should be restricted before the budget is presented.
5. Scientific, economic, and technological matters should be included in the lists of restrictive categories.
6. The provision for parliamentary privileges should be defined clearly.
7. Section 8 of the draft bill of PCI provides for personal responsibility of the officers not furnishing the information which might pose serious problems in implementation (this was also discussed extensively in later discussion on the law).
8. Lastly, concern was raised regarding the financial implication of operationalizing the proposed law.

Source: Comments on the Draft Bill on the FoI by the MHA 1997.

A3 Sonia Gandhi's Letter to the Prime Minister Requesting GoI to Prioritize RTI Bill, 2004

No. 410/CP/NAC/2005

SONIA GANDHI
CHAIRPERSON
NATIONAL ADVISORY COUNCIL

2, MOTI LAL NEHRU PLACE
NEW DELHI - 110 011
PHONES : 011-2301 8669
011-2301 8654
FAX : 011-2301 8646

January 14, 2005

Dear Prime Minister,

The National Common Minimum Programme, as you are aware, pledges "to provide a government that is corruption-free, transparent and accountable at all times". Towards this end, the National Advisory Council had examined the Freedom of Information Act, 2002 with the objective of making it more progressive, participatory and meaningful. I had forwarded the recommendations of the Council on 16th August, 2004.

2. Subsequently, after close examination of the Right to Information Bill, 2004 (as introduced in the Lok Sabha on 24th December, 2004), the NAC have unanimously felt that this Bill overlooks certain crucial recommendations that makes the law less effective than it was intended to be.

3. The Right to Information Bill, 2004 proposes to cover only the Offices of the Central Government and the Union Territories, leaving most public authorities and matters of relevance to common citizens such as State and District Authorities and Local Self-Government, outside the ambit of the Bill. I am informed that there is conflicting legal opinion about whether the Central Act can legislate for the officers and authorities under the State Governments and local bodies and if so, what would be the status of the Right to Information Acts already existing in several States. The NAC would like to suggest that the possibility of treating the Right to Information Bill, 2004 as an enactment under entry 97 of List I of the VIIth Schedule to the Constitution may be speedily examined by the Group of Ministers set up for this purpose. The Group of Ministers could look into this matter immediately and not wait for the tabling of amendments during the discussion of the Bill in Parliament. If the option suggested above is found to be feasible and legally tenable, it could be moved as a Government amendment to the existing Bill.

Contd..............2

PM may wish to see pl.

(Cont'd)

SONIA GANDHI
CHAIRPERSON
NATIONAL ADVISORY COUNCIL

2, MOTI LAL NEHRU PLACE
NEW DELHI - 110 011
PHONES : 011-2301 8669
011-2301 8654
FAX : 011-2301 8646

: 2 :

4. It is also found that the penalty provisions have been significantly diluted with the prescription of a procedure which restricts the effectiveness of the office and institution of the Information Commission. It is felt that the Information Commissioner should at least be given powers to prosecute and file charges against offending officials.

5. The National Advisory Council's draft had also suggested that in order to make the Right to Information accessible to the common citizens, the fees for procuring information should be reasonable. The Right to Information Bill, 2004, however, allows the Government to prescribe the fees at any level. It is felt that an appropriate amendment in this clause is necessary.

6. I would request you to kindly have these issues looked into, on priority basis, so that amendments to the existing Bill could be prepared before the Bill is taken up for discussion and passing in the Lok Sabha.

With regards,

Yours sincerely,
Sonia Gandhi

Dr. Manmohan Singh
Prime Minister of India
South Block
New Delhi

Source: Author (procured through RTI).

NAC Member	Educational Qualification	Profession	Profile
Jairam Ramesh	Bachelor's degree in engineering from IIT Mumbai, India, double masters in economics and public policy from Carnegie Mellon University, Pennsylvania, USA, and Massachusetts Institute of Technology, USA	MP, cabinet minister, and economist	Held number of important positions such as adviser to the PM, adviser to the finance minister, adviser to the Planning Commission, economic advisor to some state governments, and MPs in 2004 from Congress Party. He became a cabinet minister in 2011.
Jayprakash Narayan	Trained physician	Former bureaucrat and founder of Lok Satta Party	He was a former IAS officer and now a politician and founder of a political party called Lok Satta. He was member of the 13th legislative assembly in Karnataka. He works on political and democratic reforms through his organization, Foundation for Democratic Reforms. He was also member of the second Administrative Reforms Commission of GoI.

NAC Member	Educational Qualification	Profession	Profile
V. Krishnamurthy	Technocrat familiar with both private and public sectors	Doctor of sciences and doctor of letters from India and honorary doctorate in economics from the Academy of Sciences of the Soviet Union, Moscow, Russia	Long-standing engagement with public-sector undertakings and held important positions such as chief of planning of Bharat Heavy Electricals Limited (BHEL) in the 1960s and 1970s; vice chairman of Maruti Udyog Ltd in 1982; chief of Steel Authority of India Limited (SAIL) in 1985 after which he became the board member of leading private companies such as United Breweries (UB) group, DCM, Escorts, and Flakt. He was secretary of industry in GoI and member, Planning Commission. Considered to be close to the Gandhi family though he held important portfolios in other governments as well starting from the Janata Party in 1977. Conferred with three top GoI civilian honours—Padma Shri (1973), Padma Bhushan (1986), and Padma Vibhushan (2007).

NAC Member	Educational Qualification	Profession	Profile
Mirai Chatterjee	Bachelor's degree from Harvard University, Massachusetts, USA, and masters from Johns Hopkins University, Maryland, USA	Activist	Worked in area of public health and is director of SEWA, a non-profit organization working on issues of public health, women's welfare, livelihood issues, and rural development.
Madhav Chavan	Bachelor's degree in chemical engineering, Institute of Chemical Technology, Mumbai, India, and PhD from Ohio State University, USA	Social entrepreneur	Worked in the area of education and is founder of Pratham, a non-profit organization working on providing quality education for poor people.
A.K. Shiva Kumar	MBA, Indian Institute of Management Ahmedabad, India, and masters in economics from Bangalore University, India; PhD in economics	Development economist	Worked in the area of human development and was on advisory panel and senior adviser to the UNDP Human Development Report Office. He has contributed to various human development reports published by UNDP and also the national HDR

NAC Member	Educational Qualification	Profession	Profile
	from Harvard University		published by national governments. Taught economics and public policy at Harvard Kennedy School, Massachusetts, USA, and Indian School of Business, Hyderabad. Was closely associated with GoI programme of Sarva Shiksha Abhiyan on providing universal education.
D. Swaminadhan	PhD from Liverpool, England	Educationalist and scientist	He was additional secretary in the University Grants Commission, New Delhi; member, Planning Commission, GoI; and vice chancellor, Jawaharlal Nehru Technological University, Hyderabad. He was also United Nations Educational, Scientific and Cultural Organization (UNESCO) chair professor.
Sam Pitroda	Masters in physics and electronics from India and masters in electrical engineering from Illinois Institute of Technology, USA	Entrepreneur and technocrat	In 1984 he was invited by the PM to improve telecommunications in India and set up C-DOT, a telecommunication development centre. In 1987, he became the advisor to the PM and is credited for revolutionizing telecommunication in India. Considered close to Gandhi family.

Bibliography

Books and Chapters in Edited Volumes

Acemoglu, Daron, and James A. Robinson. 2012. *Why Nations Fail: The Origins of Power, Prosperity and Poverty*. New York: Crown Business.

Aggarwal, S.K. 1989. *Media Credibility*. India: Mittal Publications.

Agrawal, S.P., and J.C. Aggarwal. 1990. *Lok Sabha and Vidhan Sabha Elections, 1989–90: Process and Results with Comparative Study of Manifestos*. India: Concept Publishers.

Ahuja, Sangeeta. 1997. *People, Law and Justice: Casebook on Public Interest Litigation*, volume II. India: Orient Blackswan.

Bardhan, Pranab. 1984. *The Political Economy of Development in India*. New Delhi: Oxford University Press.

Bhattacharjea, Ajit. 1978. *Jayprakash Narayan: A Political Biography*. India: Vikas Publishing House.

Bhattacharya, P., ed. 2007. *The Appu Papers: Writings of Padma Bhushan P.S. Appu, IAS (Retd.)*. India: Sahitya Samsad.

Blyth, Mark. 2002. *Great Transformations: Economic Ideas and Institutional Change in the Twentieth Century*. Cambridge: Cambridge University Press.

Blyth, Mark, O. Helgadottir, and W. Kring. 2016. 'Ideas and Historical Institutionalism'. In *Oxford Handbook of Historical Institutionalism*, edited by Orfeo Fioretos, pp. 142–62. New York: Oxford University Press.

Brass, Paul R. 1974. *Language, Religion, and Politics in North India*. Cambridge: Cambridge University Press.

Capoccia, Giovani. 2016. 'Critical Junctures'. In *Oxford Handbook of Historical Institutionalism*, edited by Orfeo Fioretos, pp. 89–106. New York: Oxford University Press.

Chand, Vikram K. 1999. *Legislating Freedom of Information: India in Comparative Perspective.* New Delhi: Commonwealth Human Rights Initiative (CHRI).

Chandra, Kanchan. 2004. *Why Ethnic Parties Succeed: Patronage and Ethnic Head Counts in India.* Cambridge: Cambridge University Press.

Chatterjee, Partha. 2011. *Lineages of Political Society: Studies in Post Colonial Democracy.* New York: Columbia University Press.

Chaturvedi, T.N., ed. 1980. *Secrecy in Government.* New Delhi: Indian Institute of Public Administration.

Corbridge, Stuart. 2009. 'The Political Economy of Development in India since Independence'. In *Routledge Handbook of South Asian Politics: India, Pakistan, Bangladesh, Sri Lanka, and Nepal*, edited by Paul Brass. Routledge, pp. 318–36. Abingdon, UK: Routledge.

Corbridge, S., and J. Harriss. 2000. *Reinventing India: Liberalization, Hindu Nationalism and Popular Democracy.* Cambridge, UK: Polity Press.

Corbridge, S., J. Harriss, and C. Jeffrey. 2013. *India Today: Economy, Politics & Society.* Cambridge, UK: Polity Press.

Corbridge, Stuart, Glyn Williams, Manoj Srivastava, and René Véron. 2005. *Seeing the State: Governance and Governmentality in India.* Cambridge: Cambridge University Press.

Dahl, Robert A. 1970. *Modern Political Analysis*, Second Edition. Englewood Cliffs, NJ: Prentice-Hall.

Della Porta, Donatella, and Mario Diani. 2006. *Social Movements: An Introduction*, second edition. USA, UK, and Australia: Blackwell Publishing.

Desai, A.R. 1994. *Rural Sociology in India.* India: Popular Prakashan.

Drieberg, Trevor, and Sarala Jagmohan. 1975. *Emergency in India.* India: Manas Publications.

Eckstein, Harry. 1975. 'Case Study and Theory in Political Science'. In *The Handbook of Political Science*, edited by F.I. Greenstein and N.W. Polsby, pp. 79–138. Reading: Addison-Wesley.

Erdman, Howard, L. 1967. *The Swatantra Party and Indian Conservatism.* Cambridge: Cambridge University Press.

Evans, Peter B. 1995. *Embedded Autonomy: States and Industrial Transformation.* Princeton, NJ: Princeton University Press.

———, ed. 1997. *State–Society Synergy: Government and Social Capital in Development.* Berkeley: International and Area Studies, University of California.

Falleti, Tulia G. 2010. 'Infiltrating the State: The Evolution of Health Care Reforms in Brazil, I964–1988'. In *Explaining Institutional Change:*

Ambiguity, Agency, and Power, edited by J. Mahoney, and K. Thelen, pp. 38–62. New York: Cambridge University Press

Florini, Ann, ed. 2007. 'Introduction'. In *The Right to Know: Transparency for an Open World*, pp 1–16. New York: Columbia University Press.

Frankel, Francine R. 1978. *India's Political Economy, 1947–77: The Gradual Revolution*. Princeton, New Jersey: Princeton University Press.

———. 1989. 'Introduction'. In *Dominance and State Power in Modern India: Decline of Social Order*, volume I, edited by Francine R. Frankel and M.S.A. Rao, pp. 1–20. India: Oxford University Press.

———. 2005. *India's Political Economy, 1947–2004: The Gradual Revolution*, second edition. New York: Oxford University Press.

Garg, Vivek. 2012. *PMO to Delhi Secretariat: RTIs Expose Commonwealth Scam*. New Delhi: Manas Publications.

George, Alexander L., and Andrew Bennett. 2005. *Case Studies and Theory Development in the Social Sciences*. Cambridge, Massachusetts: MIT Press.

George, Alexander L., and Timothy J. Mckeown. 1985. 'Case Studies and Theories of Organizational Decision Making'. In *Advances in Information Processing in Organizations*, edited by Robert Coulam and Richard Smith, pp. 43–68. Greenwich, CT: JAI Press.

Ghosh, Peu. 2012. *Indian Government and Politics*. India: PHI Learning Pvt. Ltd.

Godbole, Madhav. 1997. 'Corruption, Political Interference and the Indian Civil Service'. In *Corruption in India: Agenda for Action*, edited by S. Guhan and Samuel Paul, pp. 60–87. India: Vision Books.

———. 2003. *Public Accountability and Transparency: The Imperatives of Good Governance*. India: Orient Longman.

Gould, N.E.S.J., and N. Eldredge. 1972. 'Punctuated Equilibria: An Alternative to Phyletic Gradualism. In *Models in Paleobiology*, edited by Thomas J.M. Schopf, pp. 82–115. San Francisco: Freeman, Cooper.

Government of India (GoI). 2011. *India Human Development Report 2011: Towards Social Inclusion*. New Delhi: Oxford University Press.

Haggard, Stephan. 1990. *Pathways from the Periphery: The Politics of Growth in the Newly Industrializing Countries*. New York: Cornell University Press .

Hall, P.A. 1986. *Governing the Economy: The Politics of State Intervention in Britain and France*. New York: Oxford University Press.

Hasan, Zoya. 2018. *Agitation to Legislation: Equity and Justice in Contemporary India*. New Delhi: Oxford University Press.

Heclo, Hugh. 1974. *Modern Social Politics in Britain and Sweden*. New Haven and London: Yale University of Press.

Hewitt, Vernon. 1994. 'The Prime Minister and the Parliament'. In *Nehru to the Nineties: The Changing Office of Prime Minister in India*, edited by James Manor, pp. 48–73. UK: C. Hurst & Co.

Huntington, Samuel P. 1968. *Political Order in Changing Societies*. New Haven and London: Yale University Press.

Jain, Srimandir Nath. 1982. *Official Secrecy and the Press*. Jointly published by Indian Law Institute and the Press Council of India. India: N.M. Tripathi Publishers.

Jenkins, Rob. 1999. *Democratic Politics and Economic Reform in India*. Cambridge: Cambridge University Press.

Kapur, Devesh, Pratap Bhanu Mehta, and Milan Vaishnav, eds. 2017. *Rethinking Public Institutions in India*. New Delhi: Oxford University Press.

Keck, M.E., and K. Sikkink. 1998. *Activists beyond Borders*. Ithaca and London: Cornell University Press.

Khagram, Sanjeev. 2005. *Dams and Development: Transnational Struggles for Water and Power*. India: Oxford University Press.

Khagram, Sanjeev, James V. Riker, and Kathryn Sikkink. 2002. *Restructuring World Politics: Transnational Social Movements, Networks, and Norms*. Minneapolis and London: University of Minnesota Press.

King, Gary, Robert O. Keohane, and Sidney Verba. 1994. *Designing Social Inquiry: Scientific Inference in Qualitative Research*. New Jersey: Princeton University Press.

Knoke, David. 1990. *Political Networks: A Structural Perspective*. Cambridge: Cambridge University Press.

Kochanek, Stanley, and Robert Hardgrave. 2007. *India: Government and Politics in a Developing Nation*. India: Cengage Learning.

Kohli, Atul. 1987. *The State and Poverty in India: The Politics of Reform*. New York: Cambridge University Press.

———. 1991. *Democracy and Discontent: India's Growing Crisis of Governability*. Cambridge: Cambridge University Press.

———. 2012. *Poverty Amid Plenty in the New India*. Cambridge: Cambridge University Press.

Kohli, Atul, and Prerna, Singh, eds. 2013. *Routledge Handbook of Indian Politics*. London and New York: Routledge.

Krishna, Anirudh. 2006. 'Politics in the Middle: Mediating Relationships between the Citizens and the State in Rural North India'. In *Patrons,*

Clients and Policies Patterns of Democratic Accountability and Political Competition, edited by Herbert Kitschelt and Steven I. Wilkinson. Cambridge: Cambridge University Press.

Lakshman, Narayan. 2011. *Patrons of the Poor: Caste Politics and Policymaking in India*. New Delhi: Oxford University Press.

Limaye, Madhu. 1994. *Janata Party Experiment: An Insider's Account of Opposition Politics 1975–77*, volume I. India: B.R. Publishing Corporation.

Maheshwari, Shriram. 1981. *Open Government in India*. New Delhi: Macmillan.

———. 1992. *The Indian Administrative Yearbook 1990*. India: Concept Publishing.

———. 2002. *A Dictionary of Public Administration*. New Delhi: Orient Longman.

Mahoney, James, and Kathleen Thelen. 2010. *Explaining Institutional Change: Ambiguity, Agency and Power*. Cambridge: Cambridge University Press.

March, J.G., and J.P. Olsen. 1989. *Rediscovering Institutions: The Organizational Basis of Politics*. New York: Free Press.

Mathur, Kuldeep. 2015. 'Evolution of RTI Regime in India: Broadening the Narrative'. In *Empowerment through Information: The Evolution of Transparency Regime in India*, volume 1, edited by Shamsul Bari, Vikram K. Chand, and Shekhar Singh, pp. 141–58. New Delhi: Transparency Advisory Group and Research Initiatives.

McAdam, Doug. 1982. *Political Process and the Development of Black Insurgency, 1930–1970*. Chicago: University of Chicago Press.

Mendel, Toby. 2008. *Freedom of Information: A Comparative Legal Survey*, second edition. Paris: UNESCO Publications.

Migdal, Joel S. 1988. *Strong Societies and Weak States: State–Society Relations and State Capabilities in the Third World*. Princeton, NJ: Princeton University Press.

———. 2001. *State in Society: Studying How States and Societies Transform and Constitute One Another*. Cambridge: Cambridge University Press.

Migdal, Joel S., Atul Kohli, and Vivienne Shue. 1994. *State Power and Social Forces: Domination and Transformation in the Third World*. Cambridge: Cambridge University Press.

Mirchandani, G.G. 1977. *Subverting the Constitution of India*. Columbia: South Asia Books.

Mitra, Subrata K. 1992. *Power, Protest and Participation: Local Elites and the Politics of Development in India*. London: Routledge.

Mukharji, G. 1967. *Access to Official Records and Information*. New Delhi: Indian Institute of Public Administration.

Mukherji, Rahul. 2006. 'Promoting Competition in India's Telecom Sector'. In *Reinventing Public Service Delivery in India*, edited by Vikram Chand, pp. 57–94. India: Sage Publications.

———. 2014a. *Globalization of Deregulation: Ideas, Interests, and Institutional Change in India*. New Delhi: Oxford University Press.

———. 2014b. *Political Economy of Reforms in India (Oxford India Short Introductions)*. New Delhi: Oxford University Press.

Naib, Sudhir. 2011. *The Right to Information Act 2005: A Handbook*. New Delhi: Oxford University Press.

———. 2013. *The Right to Information in India*. Oxford India Short Introductions. India: Oxford University Press.

Noorani, A.G. 1997. 'The Right to Information'. In *Corruption in India: Agenda for Action*, edited by S. Guhan and Samuel Paul, pp. 114–43. India: India Vision Books.

North, Douglass. 1990. *Institutions, Institutional Change and Economic Performance*. Cambridge: Cambridge University Press.

Pai, Sudha. 2007. *Political Process in Uttar Pradesh: Identity, Economic Reforms and Governance*. India: Pearson Education India.

Paul, Sohini. 2006. *The Right to Information and Panchayati Raj Institutions: Madhya Pradesh as Case Study*. New Delhi: CHRI.

Przeworski, Adam, and Teune Henry. 1970. 'Research Designs'. In *The Logic of Comparative Social Enquiry*, edited by Robert T. Holt and John E. Turner, pp. 31–46. New York: Wiley-Interscience.

Puddephatt, Andrew. 2009. *Exploring the Role of Civil Society in the Formulation and Adoption of Access to Information Laws: The Cases of Bulgaria, India, Mexico, South Africa, and the United Kingdom*. WBI Access to Information Working Paper Series. Washington, DC: World Bank (WB).

Rai, Udai Raj. 2011. *Fundamental Rights and Their Enforcement*. India: PHI Learning Pvt. Ltd.

Rao, M.S.A. 1989. 'Some Conceptual Issues in the Study of Caste, Class, Ethnicity and Dominance'. In *Dominance and State Power in Modern India: Decline of Social Order*, volume I, edited by Francine R. Frankel and M.S.A Rao, pp. 21–45. New Delhi: Oxford University Press.

Rau, Chalapati, M. 1980. 'Official Secrets and Freedom of Information in India'. In *Secrecy in Government*, edited by by T.N. Chaturvedi, pp. 109–14. New Delhi: Indian Institute of Public Administration.

RTI Assessment and Analysis Group (RaaG), and Transparency Advisory Group. 2015. 'Who Uses the RTI Act in India and for What?' In *Empowerment through Information: The Evolution of Transparency Regime in India*, volume II, edited by Shamsul Bari, Vikram K. Chand, and Shekhar Singh. New Delhi: Transparency Advisory Group and Research Initiatives.

Risse, Thomas-Kappen, Stephen C. Ropp, and Kathryn Sikkink. 1999. *The Power of Human Rights: International Norms and Domestic Change*. Cambridge: Cambridge University Press.

Roberts, A. 2006. *Blacked Out: Government Secrecy in the Information Age*. New York: Cambridge University Press.

Roy, Aruna, and the MKSS Collective. 2018. *The RTI Story: Power to the People*. New Delhi: Roli Books.

Rowat, Donald. C. 1980. 'Laws on Access to Official Documents'. In *Secrecy in Government*, edited by T.N. Chaturvedi, pp. 1–29. New Delhi: Indian Institute of Public Administration.

Sabatier, Paul A., and Hank C. Jenkins-Smith. 1993. *Policy Change and Learning: An Advocacy Coalition*. Boulder, CO: Westview Press.

Sankaran, S.R. 2002. 'Administration and the Poor'. In *Dalits and the State*, edited by Ghanshyam Shah, pp. 343–71. Centre for Rural Studies, Lal Bahadur Shastri National Academy for Administration (LBSNAA). New Delhi: Mittal Publications.

Sarkar, Siuli. 2010. *Public Administration in India*. New Delhi: PHI Learning Pvt. Ltd.

Sathe, S.P. 1991. *The Right to Know*. Bombay: N.M. Tripathi (Pvt.) Ltd.

Seervai, H.M. 1983. *Constitutional Law of India: A Critical Commentary*, third edition. Bombay: N.M. Tripathi Pvt. Ltd.

Shah, Ghanshyam. 2004. *Social Movements in India: A Review of Literature*, Second edition. India: Sage Publications.

———. 1977. *Protests Movements in Two Indian States*. India: Ajanta Publishers.

Sharma, Prashant. 2015. *Democracy and Transparency in the Indian State: The Making of Right to Information Act*. London and New York: Routledge.

Sheshadri, K. 1980. 'The Open Government and Its Enemies (with Apologies to Karl Popper)'. In *Secrecy in Government*, edited by T.N. Chaturvedi, pp. 96–108. New Delhi: Indian Institute of Public Administration.

Shreyaskar, Pankaj K.P. 2013. *RTI Act in India: Futures and Implications*. India: Mcgraw Hill Education (India) Private Limited.

Shrivastava, K.M. 2009. *The Right to Information: A Global Perspective*. New Delhi: Lancer Publishers.

Singh, Krishna Kumar. 2014. *The India and the World: Wonder of Shame and Uncertainty*. India: Partridge India.

———. 2007. 'Grassroots Initiatives'. In *The Right To Know: Transparency for An Open World*, edited by Ann Florini, pp. 19–53. Columbia University Press.

———. 2011. 'The Genesis and Evolution of the Right to Information Regime in India'. In *Transparent Governance in South Asia*, edited by Shekhar Singh, Prashant Sharma, Vikram K. Chand, Stephanie de Chassy, et al., pp. 43–124. Delhi: Indian Institute of Public Administration.

Skocpol, Theda. 1985. 'Introduction: Bringing the State Back In: Strategies of Analysis in Current Research'. In *Bringing the State Back In*, edited by Peter B. Evans, Dietrich Rueschemeyer, and Theda Skocpol, pp. 3–38. Cambridge: Cambridge University Press.

Sorabjee, Soli, J. 1976. *Press Censorship in India*. Bombay: N.M. Tripathi.

———. 1977. *The Emergency, Censorship, and the Press in India, 1975–77*. New Delhi: Central News Agency.

Swamy, Subramanian. 2011. *2G Spectrum Scam*. India: Har-Anand Publications Pvt. Ltd.

Tarrow, Sidney. 1994. *Power in Movement: Social Movements, Collective Action and Politics*. Cambridge: Cambridge University Press.

———. 2005. *The New Transnational Activism*. New York: Cambridge University Press.

———. 2011. *Social Movements and Contentious Politics*, third edition. Cambridge: Cambridge University Press.

Tilly, Charles. 1978. *From Mobilization to Revolution*. New York: Random House.

Thachil, Tariq. 2014. *Elite Parties, Poor Voters: How Social Services Win Votes in India*. New York: Cambridge University Press.

Thelen, Kathleen. 2004. *How Institutions Evolve: The Political Economy of Skills in Germany, Britain, the United States and Japan*. Cambridge: Cambridge University Press.

United Nations (UN). 1962a. 'Treaty Provisions and Information Concerning the Legal Status of the United Nations'. *United Nations Juridical Yearbook*. UN.

Weiner, Myron. 1978. *India at Polls: The Parliamentary Elections of 1977*. Washington DC: American Enterprise Institute for Public Policy Research.

Wilkinson, Paul. 1971. *Social Movements*. London: Pall Mall.

Articles (Journals, Papers, and Unpublished PhD Theses)

Acharya, Amitav. 2004. 'How Ideas Spread: Whose Norms Matter? Norm Localization and Institutional Change in Asian Regionalism'. *International Organization* 58(2): 239–75.

Ashraf, T. 2008. 'Empowering People through Information: A Case Study of India's Right to Information Act. *The International Information & Library Review*, 40(3), 148–52.

Auerbach, Adam M. 2017. 'Neighborhood Associations and the Urban Poor: India's Slum Development Committees'. *World Development* 96(C): 119–35.

Baker, Andrew. 2015. 'Varieties of Economic Crisis, Varieties of Ideational Change: How and Why Financial Regulation and Macroeconomic Policy Differ'. *New Political Economy* 20(3): 342–66.

Baxi, Upendra. 1985. 'Taking Suffering Seriously: Social Action Litigation in the Supreme Court of India'. *Third World Legal Studies* 4.

———. 2010. 'The Judiciary as Resource for Indian Democracy'. *Seminar Special Issue on the Constitution of India after 60 Years*: 615.

Béland, Daniel. 2007. 'Ideas and Institutional Change in Social Security: Conversion, Layering, and Policy Drift'. *Social Science Quarterly* 88(1): 20–38.

Bennett, Andrew, and Alexander L. George. 1997. 'Process Tracing in Case Study Research'. Paper presented at the MacArthur Foundation Workshop on Case Study Methods, Belfer Center for Science and International Affairs (BCSIA), Harvard University, 17–19 October.

Blyth, Mark. 2007. 'Powering, Puzzling, or Persuading? The Mechanisms of Building Institutional Orders'. *International Studies Quarterly* 51(4): 761–77.

———. 2013. 'Paradigms and Paradox: The Politics of Economic Ideas in Two Moments of Crisis'. *Governance*, 26(2): 197–215.

Boettke, Peter J., Christopher J. Coyne, and Peter T. Leeson. 2008. 'Institutional Stickiness and the New Development Economics'. *American Journal of Economics and Sociology* 67(2): 331–58.

Capoccia, Giovanni, and Daniel R. Kelemen. 2007. 'The Study of Critical Junctures: Theory, Narrative, and Counterfactuals in Historical Institutionalism'. *World Politics* 59(3): 341–69.

Carstensen, Martin B., and Vivien A. Schmidt. 2016. 'Power Through, over and in Ideas: Conceptualizing Ideational Power in Discursive Institutionalism'. *Journal of European Public Policy* 23(3): 318–37.

Chhibber, Pradeep, and Irfan Nooruddin. 2004. 'Do Party Systems Count? The Number of Parties and Government Performance in the Indian States'. *Comparative Political Studies* 37(2): 152–87.

Chopra, Deepta. 2011. 'Policy Making in India: A Dynamic Process of Statecraft'. *Pacific Affairs* 84(1): 89–107.

Crawford, Neta C. 2018. 'The Potential for Fundamental Change in World Politics'. *International Studies Review* 20(2): 232–8.

Culpepper, Pepper D. 2008. 'The Politics of Common Knowledge: Ideas and Institutional Change in Wage Bargaining'. *International Organization* 62(1): 1–33.

Deva, Satya. 1977. 'The Relevance of Max Weber's Ideas to Public Administration in Developing Societies'. *The Indian Journal of Political Science* 38(3): 345–56.

Elke, Krahmann. 2005. 'Security Governance and Networks: New Theoretical Perspectives in Transatlantic Security'. *Cambridge Review of International Affairs* 18(1): 15–30.

Finnemore, Martha, and Kathryn Sikkink. 1998. 'International Norm Dynamics and Political Change'. *International Organization* 52(4): 887–917.

Godbole, Madhav. 2000a. 'Right to Information: Write the Law Right'. *Economic and Political Weekly* 35(17): 1423–8.

———. 2000b. 'Unending Struggle for Right to Information'. *Economic and Political Weekly* 35(33): 2899–901.

Gould, Roger V. 1993. 'Collective Action and Network Structure'. *American Sociological Review* 58(2): 182–96.

Greif, Avner, and David D. Laitin. 2004. 'The Theory of Endogenous Institutional Change'. *American Political Science Review* 98(4): 633–52.

Haas, Peter M. 1992. 'Introduction: Epistemic Communities and International Policy Coordination'. *International Organization* 46(1): 1–35.

Hall, Peter A. 1993. 'Policy Paradigms, Social Learning, and the State: The Case of Economic Policymaking in Britain'. *Comparative Politics* 25(3): 275–6.

Jenkins, Rob. 2013. 'Land, Rights and Reform in India'. *Pacific Affairs* 86(3): 591–612.

Jenkins, R., and A.M. Goetz. 1999. 'Accounts and Accountability: Theoretical Implications of the Right-to-Information Movement in India'. *Third World Quarterly* 20(3): 603–22.

Jenkins-Smith, Hank C., and Paul A. Sabatier. 1994. 'Evaluating the Advocacy Coalition Framework'. *Journal of Public Policy* 14(2): 175–203.

Jha, Himanshu. 2018a. 'Emerging Politics of Accountability'. *Economic and Political Weekly* 53(10): 47–54.

———. 2018b. 'State Processes, Ideas, and Institutional Change: The Case of the Right to Information Act in India'. *Pacific Affairs* 91(2): 309–28.

———. 2019. 'Untangling the Global–Local Linkages: The Case of the Right to Information Act in India'. *India Review (Special Issue)* 18(1): 32–53.

Krasner, Stephen D. 1984. 'Approaches to the State: Alternative Conceptions and Historical Dynamics. Review Article'. *Comparative Politics* 16(2): 223–46.

Levitsky, Steven, and María Victoria Murillo. 2009. 'Variation in Institutional Strength'. *Annual Review of Political Science* 12: 115–33.

———. 2013. 'Building Institutions on Weak Foundations'. *Journal of Democracy* 24(2): 93–107.

Mander, Harsh, and Abha Singhal Joshi. 1998. 'The Movement for Right to Information in India: People's Power for the Control of Corruption'. Paper presented at the CHRI Conference, 'Pan-Commonwealth Advocacy for Human Rights, Peace and Good Governance in Africa', Harare, 21–4 January.

Milner, Helen. 1991. 'The Assumption of Anarchy in International Relations Theory: A Critique'. *Review of International Studies* 17(1): 67–85.

Mishra, Nilabh. 2003. 'People's Right to Information Movement: Lessons from Rajasthan'. *Discussion Paper Series 4*. Human Development Resource Centre, UNDP.

Muhar, P.S. 1965. 'Corruption in the Public Service in India'. *The Indian Journal of Political Science* 26(1): 1–18.

Mukherji, Rahul. 2013. 'Ideas, Interests, and the Tipping Point: Economic Change in India'. *Review of International Political Economy* 20(2): 363–89.

Mukherji, Rahul, and Himanshu Jha. 2017. 'Bureaucratic Rationality, Political Will, and State Capacity'. *Economic and Political Weekly* 52(49): 53–60.

Niles, Mark. C. 2002. 'On the Hijacking of Agencies (and Airplanes): The Federal Aviation Administration, "Agency Capture", and Airline Security'. *Journal of Gender, Social Policy & the Law* 10(2): 381–442.

Noorani, A.G. 1978. 'The Judiciary and the Bar in India during the Emergency'. *Law and Politics in Africa, Asia and Latin America* (Verfassung und Recht in Übersee) 11(4): 403–10.

———. 1990a. 'Article 19's Indictment'. *Economic and Political Weekly* 25(48/49): 2636.

———. 1990b. 'Press Freedom and Right to Privacy'. *Economic and Political Weekly* 25(18/19): 977.

———. 1996. 'The Press Council's Bill on Right to Information'. *Economic and Political Weekly* 31(51): 3283.

———. 1998. 'Law on Right To Information'. *Economic and Political Weekly* 33(45): 2826.

North, Douglass C., and Barry R. Weingast. 1989. 'Constitutions and Commitment: The Evolution of Institutions Governing Public Choice in Seventeenth-Century England'. *The Journal of Economic History* 49(4): 803–82.

Page, Scott E. 2006. 'Path Dependence'. *Quarterly Journal of Political Science* 1(1): 87–115.

Parry, John T. 2007. 'Terrorism and the New Criminal Process'. *William & Mary Bill of Rights Journal* 15(3): 765–835.

Peisakhin, L., and P. Pinto. 2010. 'Is Transparency an Effective Anti-corruption Strategy? Evidence from a Field Experiment in India'. *Regulation & Governance* 4(3), 261–80.

Pierson, Paul. 2000. 'The Limits of Design: Explaining Institutional Origins and Change'. *Governance: An International Journal of Policy and Administration* 13(4): 475–99.

Roberts, Alasdair. 2010. 'A Great and Revolutionary Law? The First Four Years of India's Right to Information Act'. *Public Administration Review* 70(6): 925–33.

Roy, Aruna, Nikhil Dey, and Shankar Singh. 2010. 'Prabhash Joshi and RTI Movement'. *Mainstream*, p. 48.

Ruparelia, Sanjay. 2013. 'India's New Rights Agenda: Genesis, Promises, Risks'. *Pacific Affairs* 86(3): 569–90.

Sabatier, Paul A. 1988. 'An Advocacy Coalition Framework of Policy Change and the Role of Policy-Oriented Learning Therein'. *Policy Sciences* 21(2/3): 129–68.

Sangiovanni, Mette Eilstrup. 2005. 'Transnational Networks and New Security Threats'. *Cambridge Review of International Affairs* 18(1): 7–13.

Sarangi, P. 2012. 'Can the Right to Information Help?' *Journal of Democracy*, 23(1): 149.

Shah, Manubhai, and Preeti Shah. 1991–2. 'A Study on the Access to Information: In US, Canada and UK'. *Consumer Confrontation* 1 and 2.

Singh, Shekhar. 2003. 'Social Mobilisation and Transparency: The Indian Experience'. *Working Paper Series*. Initiative for Policy Dialogue, Columbia University.

———. 2010. 'The Genesis and Evolution of the Right to Information Regime in India'. Paper presented at the regional workshop, 'Towards More Open and Transparent Governance in South Asia', New Delhi.

Singh, V.K. 2009. 'The Official Secrets Act 1923—A Troubled Legacy'. *Journal of the United Service Institution of India* 139(575): 139.

Srinivasan, Janaki. 2001. 'The Political Life of Information: "Information" and the Practice of Governance in India'. PhD thesis. University of California, Berkeley.

Srivastava, Manoj. 2010. 'Pro-poor Governance Reform Initiatives in Madhya Pradesh, India 1993–2010: An Introduction'. *Working Paper Series No. 10-119*. Development Studies Institute, London School of Economics and Political Science.

Quirk, Paul J. 1988. 'In Defense of the Politics of Ideas'. *The Journal of Politics* 50(1): 31–41.

Varshney, Ashutosh. 1998. 'Mass Politics or Elite Politics? India's Economic Reforms in Comparative Perspective'. *The Journal of Policy Reform* 2(4): 301–35.

Viswam, S. 1983. 'The Right to Information'. *India International Centre Quarterly* 10(2): 175–85.

Articles (Newspapers and News Magazines)

Abraham, A.S. 1989. 'Towards Open Government: Not Merely a Matter of Rules'. *The Times of India* (*ToI*). 11 December, p. 10.

Banerjee, Shoumojit. 2012. 'Mithilanchal Gets Back Its Lifeline'. *The Hindu*. 9 February.

Bhatia, P. 1965. 'Another Setback for Indian Government'. *The Guardian*. 4 March.

Bhattacharjea, Ajit. 1996. 'Right to Information Cannot Be Sidelined with Weak Reforms'. *Asian Age*. 16 December, p. 22.

———. 1997. Editorial article. *Dainik Hindustan*. 20 January.

Brandeis, Louis D. 1913. 'What Publicity Can Do'. *Harper's Weekly*. 20 December: 10–13.

Brelvi, S.A. 1948. 'Problem of Freedom of Information: Light or Decisions Made at Geneva Conference'. *ToI*. 23 May.

Business Standard. 2011. 'NAC Proposal on Land Acquisition, Rehab Rejected'. 12 June.

Chawla, Prabhu. 1987. 'Unresolved Controversy'. *India Today*. 15 April.

D'Monte, Darryl. 1989. 'The Right to Know: Need to Amend Laws'. *ToI*. 12 December, p. 12.

Economic Times. 2013. 'Sonia-Led NAC Dictates the Government Is a False Notion: Aruna Roy'. 3 June.

Gandhi, Moneisha. 1996. 'Extracting Information from Govt. Is a Formidable Task'. *ToI*. 22 July.

Girimaji, Pushpa. 1994. 'Secrecy Law Affects Accountability: Check-Out'. *ToI*. 7 September.

Hindustan Times. 2011. 'PM Rejects NAC Recommendation'. 5 January.

Katakam, Anumpa. 2010. 'House of Scandal'. *Frontline* 27(24). 20 November–3 December.

Kirpekar, Subhash. 1996a. '"Transparency Could Work Wonders for the Nation": Right to Information'. *ToI*. 6 July, p. 11.

———. 1996b. 'Sunshine Laws Elsewhere Could Serve as a Model for India: Right to Information'. *ToI*. 18 July, p. 18.

Lokayan Bulletin. 1999. 'Appeal, Jaipur Dharna: May 26 to July 14 1997'. p. 44.

Mander, Harsh. 1996. 'Position Misused: Giving and Taking Money Forms Only a Small Part of Corruption'. *Pioneer*. 10 May.

Mishra, Abhinandan. 2016. 'Pressure Builds to Release Report on Dawood's Political Links'. *Sunday Guardian Live*. September 18. Available at: https://www.sundayguardianlive.com/investigation/6515-pressure-builds-release-report-dawood-s-political-links (accessed 7 April 2020).

———. 2017. 'Report on Criminal, Political Nexus "Lost"'. *Sunday Guardian Live*. June 3. Available at: https://www.sundayguardianlive.com/investigation/9664-report-criminal-politician-nexus-lost (accessed 7 April 2020).

Nayar, Kuldip. 1997. 'The Right to Information, Human Rights Diary'. *The Hindu*. 18 January.

Roy, Aruna. 1996. 'From Bureaucracy to People's Movement'. *Lokayan Bulletin*. p. 51.

Roy, Bunker. 1999. 'The Politics of Waste and Corruption'. *Lokayan Bulletin*. p. 16.

Sawhney, Inder. 1990. 'Shekhawat a Proven Strategist'. *ToI*. 11 November.

Sebastian, Sunny. 1999. 'An Unusual Hearing in Desert Town'. *The Hindu*. 24 December.

Sharma, Tilak. 1995. 'Amend Official Secrets Act, Urge IAS Officers in U.P.'. *ToI*. 5 July, p. 9.

Sorabjee, Soli. 1989. 'Reflections, My First Clash with the Secrecy Syndrome'. *ToI*. 5 August, p. 11.

Subbaroyan, K. 1953. 'Raising Efficiency of Public'. *ToI*. 21 November.

Talwar, Ashwani. 1989. 'BJP to Back Devi's "Nyaya Yudh"'. 24 April, p. 13.

The Caravan. 2011. 'Dangerous Knowledge: Can India's Landmark Right to Information Act Ever Live Up to Its Promise?' 1 January.

The Guardian. 2010. 'Dying for Data: Indian Activist Killed for Asking Too Many Questions'. 27 December.

The Hindu. 2004. 'Common Minimum Programme'. 28 May.

The Indian Express. 2011. 'Rise in Number of RTI Applications with Increasing Awareness among Rurals'. 20 July.

———. 2013. 'Centre Sits on Most NAC Recommendations'. 1 October.

ToI. 1962a. 'Freedom of Information: U.N. Seminar in Delhi'. 20 February.

———. 1962b. 'Middle Course between Freedom and Censorship: Press Must Promote Unity, Says Radhakrishnan'. 21 February.

———. 1962c. 'Sanctity Must Be Preserved: Source of Information'. 26 February.

———. 1997a. 'Tamil Nadu on the Move'. 13 May.

———. 1997b. 'Govt. Is Keen on Passing Information Bill: Reddy'. 17 November.

———. 2011. 'Enforce Voluntary Disclosure, Says SIC'. 27 December.

Zaidi, Askari H. 1991. 'Panel for Changes in Secrets Act'. *ToI*. *15* August, p. 11.

ProQuest Historical References (The Times of India)

ToI. 1950. 'Validity of Order Challenged: Delhi Editor's Petition'. 11 April.

———. 1951a. 'Early Action on Constitution Amendment Bill: Mr. Nehru to Serve on Select Committee'. 16 May.

———. 1951b. 'Proposed Changes in Constitution: Mr. Nehru's Assurances in Parliament'. 17 May.

———. 1951c. 'First Amendment to 17-Month-Old Constitution Passed'. 3 June.

———. 1951d. '"Remove Restrictions on Freedom of Press": Re-Amendment of Constitution Urged By Mr. Gupta'. 24 June.

———. 1952. 'Need For Free Information: India's Support'. 27 October.

———. 1953. 'Need for Reform in Public Administration'. 13 May.
———. 1954. 'Organisation and Methods Branch'. 19 February.
———. 1956. 'Information on Govt. Activities: New Centre in Madras'. 4 July.
———. 1957. 'Scope of Official Secrets Act: Mr. Nehru's Views Focus Attention'. 26 October.
———. 1958. 'Centre's Refusal of Information'. 14 December.
———. 1963. 'Official Secrets Act Violated'. 29 March.
———. 1965a. 'Procedural Wrangle Over Secret Document'. 23 February.
———. 1965b. 'M.P. Can Quote from Secret Report Speaker: "Govt. Not Obliged to Disclose It"'. 27 February.
———. 1965c. 'Speaker's Ruling in Lok Sabha Makes Parliamentary History: MP's Right to Ferret Out Information Vindicated'. 1 March.
———. 1965d. 'Amendment Is Suggested'. 13 May.
———. 1965e. 'Parliament Briefs'. 4 September.
———. 1975. 'High Court Verdict Unseats Indira: Debarred from Elective Posts for 6 Years'. 13 June.
———. 1977. 'Rajasthan C.M.'s Call for Effective Administration'. 23 August.
———. 1979. 'Ensure Freedom of Press'. 15 January.
———. 1981. 'Court Order in Judges Case'. 3 November.
———. 1982a. 'NUJ for Freedom of Information Act'. 17 February.
———. 1982b. 'Plea to Modify Official Secrets Act'. 6 April.
———. 1984a. 'Freedom of Information Bill Introduced'. 5 May.
———. 1984b. 'Swamy's Bill on Free Information'. 5 May.
———. 1986a. 'No Repeal of Proviso of Secrets Act'. 19 July.
———. 1986b. 'Right to Information Upheld'. 21 October.
———. 1987a. 'Walk-Out Over Zail Letter to PM'. 14 March.
———. 1987b. 'Venkataraman Too Bars Discussion on Letter'. 21 March.
———. 1988a. 'Karnataka Bill on Press Freedom'. 7 February.
———. 1988b. 'Change in Official Secrets Act Urged'. 21 May.
———. 1988c. 'Govt Sinister or Stupid: V.P.'. 8 September.
———. 1989a. 'Politicians Mustn't Have Secrets'. 12 March.
———. 1989b. 'Mass Protest Planned over Thakkar Report'. 18 April.
———. 1989c. 'Official Secrets Act Outdated'. 9 May.
———. 1989d. JD Demonstration on Aug. 3 July.
———. 1990a. 'More Access to Official Secrets'. 10 February.
———. 1990b. 'Democracy Besieged by "Trinity of Tragedies"'. 3 March.
———. 1990c. 'Abolish Official Secrets Act'. 28 August.

———. 1990d. 'Right to Information Will Be Legalized'. 3 September.
———. 1992a. 'PM to Be Invited for Opposition Talks'. 21 May.
———. 1992b. 'Freedom of Information in Democracy Stressed'. 6 December.
———. 1993a. 'Review of Graft Legislation Urged'. 19 May.
———. 1993b. 'Call for Changes in Secrets Act'. 12 July.
———. 1993c. 'Sarkaria Calls for Openness'. 17 September.
———. 1993d. 'Gujarat Withdraws Secrets Act'. 19 October.
———. 2000. 'Collector to Collectives, Roy, Aruna'. 7 August.
The New York Times. 1953. 'Indian Government Praised in Survey'. 13 May.

Government Memoranda/Reports/Documents

Appleby, Paul H. 1953. *Public Administration in India: Report of a Survey*. New Delhi: Cabinet Secretariat, Organisation and Methods Division, GoI.
Centre for Good Governance (CGG). 2009. *Best Practices in Implementation of Right to Information*. Hyderabad, India: CGG.
Centre for Policy Research (CPR). 1990. *Report of the Workshop on Freedom of Information and Official Secrecy, held on March 21–22, 1990*. New Delhi: CPR.
CHRI. 1999. Comments and Recommendations on a Right to Information Law: Appraisal of Government of India's Working Group on Right to Information and Promotion of Open and Transparent Government, 1997.
———. 2009. *Compliance with the Right to Information Act: A Survey*. New Delhi, India: CHRI.
———. 2013. 'The Use of Right to Information Laws in India: A Rapid Survey'. New Delhi: CHRI, October.
Department of Personnel and Training (DoPT). 2013. *Right to Information: For Inclusion and Empowerment*. New Delhi: DoPT, Ministry of Personnel, Public Grievances and Pensions (MPPP), GoI.
Department-Related Parliamentary Standing Committee (DRPSC). 2005. *Third Report on the Right to Information Bill (2004)*. New Delhi: DRPSC on Personnel, Public Grievances, Law and Justice, 21 March.
Department-Related Parliamentary Standing Committee on Home Affairs (DRPSC-HA). 1999. 'Fifty-Fifth Report on the Demands for Grants (1999–2000) of the Ministry of Personnel, Public Grievances and Pensions', DRPSCHA, Point-17. Presented to Rajya Sabha on 19 April.

———. 2000. '78th Report on Freedom of Information Bill 2000', tabled in Rajya Sabha and Lok Sabha on 25 July, Parliament of India.

Deshmukh, B.G. 2009. 'Criminalisation and Accountability of Indian Bureaucracy'. In *Readings in Bureaucracy*, edited by Pradip Bhattacharya. West Bengal: Administrative Training Institute, Government of West Bengal.

Election Commission of India. 1954–5. *Election Law Reports*, Volume 10. Madras: Company Law Institute Press.

GoI. 1954. *Report of the Press Commission (Part I)*. New Delhi: GoI.

———. 1982. *Report of the Second Press Commission*. New Delhi: GoI.

Law Commission of India. 1971. *Forty-Third Report on Offences against the National Security*. New Delhi: Ministry of Law and Justice, GoI.

Mendel, Toby. 2004. *Legislation on Freedom of Information: Trends and Standards (English)*. PREM Notes, no. 93. Public Sector. Washington, DC: WB. Available at: http://documents.worldbank.org/curated/en/384751468320659644/Legislation-on-freedom-of-information-trends-and-standards (accessed 7 April 2020).

Nagaland Information Commission. 2013. *Annual Report 2012–13*.

Organisations and Methods Division (O&M Division). 1955. *Annual Report*. New Delhi: Cabinet Secretariat, GoI.

Planning Commission. 2002a. *Approach Paper to the Ninth Five Year Plan (1997–2002)*. New Delhi: GoI

———. 2002b. *Tenth Five Year Plan (2002–2007)*. GoI.

———. 2014. *Poverty Estimates on the Basis of Rangarajan Committee: Report of the Expert Group to Review the Methodology for Measurement of Poverty*. New Delhi: GoI.

Press Laws Enquiry Committee. 1948. *Report of the Press Laws Enquiry Committee*. New Delhi: GoI.

PricewaterhouseCoopers. 2009. *Final Report: Understanding the Key Issues and Constraints in Implementing the RTI Act*. New Delhi, India: PricewaterhouseCoopers.

Public Affairs Centre. 2009. *National Assessment of the Degree of Compliance to Suo Moto Disclosure Provisions of Right to Information Act 2005*. Bangalore, India: Public Affairs Centre.

RaaG, and National Campaign for People's Right to Information (NCPRI). 2009. *Safeguarding the Right to Information: Report of the People's RTI Assessment 2008*. New Delhi, India: RaaG and NCPRI.

Rajya Sabha Secretariat. 2001. 'Annexure III'. In '78th Report of the Department Related Parliamentary Standing Committee on Home Affairs: Freedom of Information Bill, 2000'. 25 July.

Santhanam Committee. 1964. *Report of the Committee on Prevention of Corruption*. New Delhi: Ministry of Home Affairs (MHA), GoI.

Second Administrative Reforms Commission. 2006. *The Right to Information: Master Key to Good Governance*. New Delhi: GoI.

Shakdher, S.L. (ed.) 1977. *The Sixth General Election to the Lok Sabha*. New Delhi: Lok Sabha Secretariat.

Society for Participatory Research in Asia (PRIA). 2007. *Tracking Right to Information in Eight States*. New Delhi, India: PRIA.

———. 2008. *Accessing Information under RTI: Citizens' Experiences in Ten States*. New Delhi, India: PRIA.

UN. 1962b. *UN Report of 1962 Seminar on Freedom of Information* (ST/TAO/HR/13). New Delhi: UN.

United Front's Policy Statement 1996. 1996. A Common Approach to Major Policy Matters and a Minimum Programme.

Working Group on Right to Information and Promotion of Open and Transparent Government. 1997. *Report of the Working Group on Right to Information and Promotion of Open and Transparent Government*. New Delhi: MPPP, GoI.

Internal Government Documents (Miscellaneous)

Circulars

Government of Maharashtra, Department of Urban Development. 1992. 'Inspection of Papers Relating to Development Permission by Environmental Action Group and Citizens'. Circular no. TPS/3692/1606/UD-11, 11 September.

Government of Maharashtra, Department of Urban Development. 1992. No.TPS.5692/1606/UD-11, 11 September (circulated to all the concerned departments).

Letters

From DoPT, MPPP, to all the Secretaries of GoI. 1997. D.O.No.34011/1(S)/97-Estt (B), 24 January 1997.

From Education Secretary, Abhimanyu Singh, Government of Rajasthan, to Gajanand Joshi, Deputy Director, Education Department, Udaipur. 1995. D.O.No.PS/ES/95/173. 15 February.

From Harsh Mander, Commissioner, Bilaspur Division, to Aruna Roy, MKSS. 1996. 31 December.

From Harsh Mander, IAS, Government of Madhya Pradesh to Addnl. Secretary, Department of Administrative Reforms and Public Grievances, GoI. 1997. D.O. Letter No 153/14/Steno/97, 28 March.

From Harsh Mander, Professor, Public Administration, to Nikhil Dey, MKSS. 1996. Letter No. D.O. No. HM/PA/RI/96, LBSNAA, 20 May.

From H.D. Shourie to Minister of Home Affairs L.K. Advani. 1998. 15 May.

From Joint Secretary, Ministry of Home Affairs to Director, MPPP. 1997. GOIG OI letter, No: D.O. No. II/21011/54/96-is/us.D.II. MHA, 11 February.

From Pritam Singh (IAS), Collector and District Management, Rajsamand District, Rajasthan. 1996. No. SHA/93/2033. Retrieved from the MKSS Papers, Manuscript Section, Nehru Memorial Museum and Library, New Delhi, India, 8 August.

From Professor V.S. Vyas, to Arun Kumar, Additional Chief Secretary, Government of Rajasthan. 1997. No. IDSJ/97, 16 May.

From Public and Rehabilitation Department, Government of Tamil Nadu, to DoPT. 2000. D.O.Letter No: 24675/99-33. 18 January.

From Secretary of DoPT, MPPP to the Secretaries of Various Ministries. 1997. 5 May.

From Secretary of MPPP to the Secratries of Various Ministers. 1997. 5 May.

From Sonia Gandhi (Chairperson of NAC) Addressed to the PM. 2005. No. 410/CP/NAC/2005. 14 January.

Memoranda

Cabinet Secretariat, GoM. 1998. Office Memo No. 501/3/1/97-Cab, 27 April 1998. GoM Constituted on 27 April, Cabinet Secretariat, GoI.

Cabinet Secretariat. 1999. Cabinet Secretariat Memo Note No. 501/3/1/97-Cab., 19 July 1999. Cabinet Secretariat, 29 October. GoI.

MPPP. 1997. Office Memorandum dated 2 January 1997, No. 34011/1(s)/97-Estt. (B). DoPT, GoI, 27 October.

MPPP. 2001. Office Memorandum, No. 34011/1(s)/97-Estt. (B). DoPT, MPPP, GoI, 6 February.

Ministry of Urban Affairs and Employment. 1998. Office Memorandum, 10 October.

Minutes

Extracts from the Minutes of the Cabinet. 2004. No.32/CM/2004. Cabinet Secretariat, GoI, 15 December.

Minutes of the Meeting of Committee of Secretaries. 1997a. Cabinet Secretariat Doc NO CD (CA.V)-97.1997. GoI, 21 August.

Minutes of the Meeting of Committee of Secretaries. 1997b. Cabinet Secretariat Doc NO CD (CA.V)-105.1997. GoI, 23 September.

Minutes of the Meeting of Committee of Secretaries. 1998. DOC. No. CD(CA.V)-33/1998. GoI, 25 June.

Minutes of the Meeting of Government of Ministers (GoM). 1997a. Government Document No. 34011/1(s)/97-Estt. (B). Held on 17 October. DoPT, MPPP, GoI.

Minutes of the Meeting of GoM. 1997b. Government Document No. 34011/1(s)/97-Estt. (B). Held on 28 October. DoPT, MPPP, GoI, 5 November.

Minutes of the Meeting of GoM. 1998a. GoI, 14 May.

Minutes of the Meeting of GoM. 1998b. Government Document No. 34011/1(s)/97-Estt. (B). Held on 18 December 1998. DoPT, MPPP, GoI, 28 December.

Minutes of the Meeting of GoM. 1999. DoPT Internal Document No. 34011/1 (s)/97-Estt. (B). Held on 22 November 1999. DoPT, MPPP, GoI, 26 November.

Minutes of the Working Group Meeting. 1996. Internal Papers of the NCPRI, 11 August.

Notes

Comments on the Draft Bill on the FoI by the MHA. 1997. Inter-ministerial communication. D.O, No.II/21011/54/96/ us.D.II. GoI, 11 February.

Communication from Addl. Secretary, Department of Administrative Reforms and Public Grievances to Secretary, Department of Legal Affairs. 1998. D.O.No.30411/1/(s)/97-Estt.(B) 3 July 1998. GoI, 3 July.

Communication from Cabinet Secretariat. 1998. D.O. No. 681/1/6/98-CA.III. GoI, 16 October.

DoPT Internal Note for the GoM. 1999. No. 34011/1(s)/97-Estt. (B). DoPT, MPPP, GoI, 24 December.

DoPT Note for the Cabinet. 2005. No. 34012/1(S)2005-Estt. (B). DoPT, MPPP, GoI, 3 May.

Government Background Note for the Group of Ministers. 1999. Ref: 34011/1(s)/97-Estt. (B), 12 November. DoPT, MPPP.

Government Communication Reply to H.D. Shourie by Secretary, MPPP. 1998. D.O. No.1920/Secy.(p)/98, 27 May.

Government Internal Note. 1997. Ref: CD-740/97. GoI, 17 October.

Internal Communication. 1998. D.O. No. Spl. Secy/203-S/98. Department of Urban Development, Ministry of Urban Affairs & Employment, GoI, 12 October.

Internal DoPT Note. 1998. No. K-13011/15/97-PG(CC), 30 December.

Internal DoPT Note to Rajya Sabha Secretariat. 2005. No. 3402/3(s)/2005-Estt. (B). DoPT, MPPP, GoI, 28 January.

Internal Government Communication. 1997. No. 34011/1(s)/97-Estt.(B). DoPT, MPPP, GoI, 16 January.

Internal Government Communication. 1998a. D.O. No. 30411/1/(s)/97-Estt. (B), 3 July.

Internal Government Communication. 1998b. D.O. No. 681/1/2/98-CAB.III, 10 October.

Internal Government Communication from Joint Secretary, DoPT. 2004. D.O. No. 1155/JS/AT&A/04, to Joint Secretary, Ministry of Finance. DoPT, MPPP, 31 March.

Internal Government Communication from Joint Secretary, Ministry of Finance. 2004. DO No.2/1/2003-FB-II. Ministry of Finance, GoI, 12 February.

Internal Government Communique Notifying the Constitution of GOM. 2005. No. 483/3/3/2004-Cab. Cabinet Secretariat, GoI, 5 January.

Internal Government Document. 2004. F. No.34011/6(s)/2004-Estt (B). DoPT, GoI.

Internal Government Note. 1997a. No. 34011/1(s)/97-Estt (B). MPPP, DoPT, 11 March.

———. 1997b. No. 34011/1(s)/97-Estt. (B). DoPT, MPPP, 13 March.

———. 1998. No. 34011/1(s)/97-Estt (B). DoPT, MPPP, 24 December.

Internal Government Note for the Cabinet, DoPT. 1998. No. 34011/1(s)/97-Estt (B). MPPP, GoI, January.

Internal Government Note to All Chief Secretaries. 1997. D.O. No. N-11011/42/95-PR (Pt.). From Secretary, N.C. Saxena, Department of Rural Development, Ministry of Rural Areas and Employment. 9 June.

Internal Government Notice of the Cabinet Secretariat. 1999. No. 501/3/1/97-Cab. Cabinet Secretariat, GoI, 10 December.

Internal Government Paper on Legislative Proposal for Freedom of Information and Amendments to Related Acts and Rules. 1997. No. 501/3/1/97-cab.. Cabinet Secretariat, GoI, 23 October.

Internal Note. 2005. D.O.No.21/CM/2005. Cabinet Secretariat, GoI, 5 May.

Internal Note for Committee of Secretaries. 1997. No. 34011/1(s)/97-Estt. (B). MPPP, DoPT, 25 July.

Internal Note for the GOM. 1997. No. 34011/1(s)/97-Estt. (B). MPPP, DoPT, 27 October.

———. 1998. No. 34011/1(s)/97-Estt. (B). MPPP, DoPT, 6 May.

———. 1999. No. 34011/1(s)/97-Estt. (B). MPPP, DoPT, 12 November.

Internal Note of the Cabinet Secretariat to DoPT. 2004. D.O.No.32/CM/2004. Cabinet Secretariat, GoI, 16 December.

Internal Note of DoPT. 2018. F. No: 4/9/2018-IR. DoPT (IR Division), MPPP, GoI.

Ministry of Home Affairs: Internal Note circulated to the GoM. 1997. F. No. II/21011/49/97-IS (US D.ii).

Note for the Cabinet. 1998. No. 34011/1/1(s)/97-Estt. (B). GoI, January.

Note from PMO to the Secretary, DoPT. 2005. PMO ID no. 600/40/C/5/04-ES-II, 27 January. PMO, GoI.

Note of Department of Legal Affairs, 27 October 1998.

Note of the Legislative Department for the GoM. 2000. No.1(57)/97-Leg.I. Legislative Department, Ministry of Law, Justice and Company Affairs. GoI, 11 January.

PMO Internal Note to DoPT. 2004. PMO.UO no. 600/40/CI-2004-Es.2, on follow up action on the National Common Minimum Programme. PMO, GoI.

P.S. Appu's Note on 'Corruption and Criminalization'. 1996. Shared with Harsh Mander, IAS, and Professor of Public Administration at LBSNAA. In Mander's Letter Addressed to Shankar Singh of the MKSS. D.O. No. HM/PA/RI/96, April.

Notifications

Rajasthan State Gazette, Notification. 1996. Department of Rural Development, Panchayati Raj, 30 December, Jaipur.

Government Notification. 2000. No DPAL 29 SHASANA 2000, Bangalore 25 August.

Orders

Government Order No.631/2/1/2004-Cab. 2004. Cabinet Secretariat, GoI, New Delhi, 31 May.

GoI. 1993. Order No. S/7937/SS(ISP)/93, 9 July.

Government of Karnataka Order Government Order D.O. No. UDD 443 MLR 97. 1997. *Related Transparency in the Local Bodies*, Government of Karnataka, 23 October.

Government of Madhya Pradesh Order by the Divisional Commissioner, Serial No. 8344/Samanya/Sa.Vi.Pra./96, Bilaspur. 1996. *Regarding the Right to Information in Matters of Public Distribution System*, 2 September.

Madhya Pradesh, Government Order, Bilaspur 26 November 1996

Order of the Government of Rajasthan No. F(4) Rural Development/law/1996. 1996. *Information related to Expenditure on Development Work undertaken in Rural Areas*, Government of Rajasthan, 6 April.

Proceedings

Proceedings of the First Meeting of the Working Group. 1997. Government Document No.34011/1(s)/97-Estt.(B). 'Right to Information and Promotion of Open and Transparent Government' held on 10 January 1997. DoPT, MPPP, GoI, 16 January.

Proceedings of the Second Meeting of the Working Group. 1997. Government Document No.34011/1(s)/97-Estt.(B). 'Right to Information and Promotion of Open and Transparent Government' held on 18 January 1997. DoPT, MPPP, GoI, 24 January.

Proceedings of the Third Meeting of the Working Group. 1997. Government Document No.34011/1(s)/97-Estt.(B). 'Right to Information and Promotion of Open and Transparent Government' held on 19 February 1997. DoPT, MPPP, GoI, 27 February.

Proceedings of the Fourth and Fifth Meeting of the Working Group. 1997. Government Document No.34011/1(s)/97-Estt.(B). 'Right to Information and Promotion of Open and Transparent Government' held on 14 March 1997 and 18 April 1997. DoPT, MPPP, GoI, 21 March and 24 April.

House Debates

Central Legislative Assembly Debates. 1923. Discussion on the Indian Official Secrets Bill, 14 February.

Rajya Sabha Debates. 1967. Indian Official Secrets (Amendment) Bill, 24 July.

———. 1982. Question Raised by Shiva Chandra Jha on Enactment of Freedom of Information Act, 1 March.

———. 1983. The Freedom of Information Bill, 22 December.
———. 1986. Question 2263 on Freedom of Information, 14 August.
———. 1987. Oral Answers to the Question on Busting of Pak Spy Network, 17 November.
———. 1991a. Question on Freedom of Information, 4 September.
———. 1991b. Discussion on Constitution (Amendment) Bill (Insertion of New Article 19A), by Chitta Basu, 13 September.
Lok Sabha Debates. 1967. Indian Official Secrets (Amendment) Bill, 12 August.
———. 1978. 'Question Raised by Jyotirmoy Basu on Amendment to the Official Secrets Act', 30 August.
———. 1984. 'Freedom of Information Bill', 4 May.
———. 1989. 'President's Address'. 20 December.
———. 2002. Discussion on Freedom of Information Bill, 2000, 13 December.
———. 2005. Discussion on Right to Information Bill, 2004, 10 May.
———. 2005. Discussion on Right to Information Bill, 2004. 11 May..
Lok Sabha Starred Question No: 557. 2015. Answered on 5 May 2015. GoI, MHA. Available https://mha.gov.in/MHA1/Par2017/pdfs/par 2015-pdfs/ls-050515/557.pdf (accessed 7 April 2020).
State Legislative Assembly Debates, 5 April 1995. 434–5.
Article 19. 1999. *The Public's Right to Know: Principles on Freedom of Information Legislation*. Global Campaign for Free Expression, June.

Legal Cases

Additional District Magistrate, Jabalpur vs *S.S. Shuka*.1976. The Supreme Court of India. 1976 AIR 1207. 28 April.
A.K. Gopalan vs *The State of Madras*. 1950. The Supreme Court of India. 19 May.
Bennett Coleman & Co. and Ors vs *Union of India and Ors*. 1972. The Supreme Court of India. 30 October.
Brij Bhushan and Anr. vs *The State of Delhi*. 1950. The Supreme Court of India. 2 March.
Dinesh Trivedi, MP and Ors vs *Union of India and Ors*. 1997. The Supreme Court of India. 20 March.
Dwarkadas Shrinivas of Bombay vs *The Sholapur Spinning & Weaving*. 1953. The Supreme Court of India. 18 December.

Express Newspapers (Private) vs *The Union of India and Ors.* 1958. The Supreme Court of India. 8 January.

Jamuna Prasad Mukhariya and Ors vs *Lacchi Ram and Ors.* 1954. The Supreme Court of India. 28 September.

Kedar Nath Singh vs *State of Bihar.* 1962. The Supreme Court of India. 20 January.

L.K. Koolwal vs *State of Rajasthan and Ors.* 1986. The Rajasthan High Court. 19 September.

M.C. Mehta and Anr. vs *Union of India and Ors.* 1986. The Supreme Court of India. 20 December.

M.C. Mehta vs *Union of India and Ors.* 1991. The Supreme Court of India. 22 November.

Maneka Gandhi vs *Union of India.* 1978. The Supreme Court of India. 25 January.

People's Union for Civil Liberties and Ors vs *Union of India and Ors.* 2003. The Supreme Court of India, 13 March.

People's Union for Civil Liberties vs *Union of India.* 2004. The Supreme Court of India. 6 January.

Romesh Thappar vs *The State of Madras.* 1950. The Supreme Court of India. 26 May.

S.P. Gupta vs *President of India and Ors.* 1981. The Supreme Court of India. 30 December.

Sakal Papers (P) Ltd. and Ors vs *The Union of India.* 1961. The Supreme Court of India. 25 September.

Sheela Barse vs *State of Maharashtra* 1987. The Supreme Court of India. 18 September.

Special Petition for Bombay Action Environmental Group vs *Pune Cantonment Board.* 1986. The Supreme Court of India (Spl.L.A (Civil) No. 11291).

State of Madras vs *V.G. Row. Union of India & State.* 1952. The Supreme Court of India. 31 March.

State of UP vs *Raj Narain and Ors.* 1975. The Supreme Court of India. 24 January.

Union of India vs *Association for Democratic Reforms and Ors.* 2002. The Supreme Court of India, 2 May.

Virendra vs *The State of Punjab and Anor.* 1957. The Supreme Court of India. 6 September.

Ramji Lal Modi vs *The State of UP.* 1957. The Supreme Court of India. 5 April.

Bills and Acts

Constitution (First Amendment) Act. 1951. 18 June.

The Freedom of Information Bill. 1983. Bill No. XXVIII of 1983, 22 December.

The Freedom of Information Bill. 1992. Bill No. XXIV of 1992, 31 March.

Right to Information Act. 2005.12 October.

The Right to Information (Amendment) Bill. 2019. 22 July 2019.

The Whistleblowers Protection Act. 2011. Ministry of Law and Justice, Legislative Department, The Gazette of India (Extraordinary), Part II Section 1. 12 May 2014.

Web Sources

ATI Monograph. 2005. *Readings in Public Administration-I*. India: Administrative Training Institute, Government of West Bengal. Available at: http://atiwb.gov.in/index_htm_files/READINGS%20IN%20%20PUBLIC%20ADMINISTRATION-I.pdf (accessed 7 April 2020).

Banisar, David. 2006. 'Freedom of Information Around the World 2006: A Global Survey of Access to Government Information Laws'. *Privacy International*. Available at: http://www.freedominfo.org/documents/global_survey2006.pdf (accessed 7 April 2020).

Baviskar, Amita. 2007. 'Is Knowledge Power? Right to Information Campaign in India'. Institute of Development Studies. Available at: https://www.ids.ac.uk/files/dmfile/IndiacaseOctober06final.doc (accessed 7 April 2020).

Bhattacharya, Sambit, and Raghbendra Jha. 2009. 'Economic Growth, Law and Corruption: Evidence from India'. *ASARC Working Paper*, Australian National University. Available at: https://crawford.anu.edu.au/acde/asarc/pdf/papers/2009/WP2009_15.pdf (accessed 7 April 2020).

BJP Election Manifesto. 1998. Available at: http://bjpelectionmanifesto.com/pdf/manifesto1998.pdf (accessed 7 April 2020).

Business Line (The Hindu). 2019. 'PM Modi, Ministers Spend Rs 393 Cr on Foreign, Domestic Travel in 5 Years'. 11 May 2019. Available at: https://www.thehindubusinessline.com/news/national/pm-modi-ministers-spend-rs-393-cr-on-foreign-domestic-travel-in-5-years/article27102663.ece (accessed 7 April 2020).

Central Information Commission. *Report on Monthly Disposal of Cases*. GoI. Available at: http://www.cic.gov.in/ (accessed 7 April 2020).

Civil Society Online. 2012 'Ratnauli's Wired Hero'. Available at: http://www.civilsocietyonline.com/pages/HOF_Details.aspx?185 (accessed 7 April 2020).

CUTS Briefing Paper. 1995. 'Access to the Constitution: A Neglected Right'. *Consumer Unity and Trust Society* . Available at: http://www.cuts-international.org/1-1995.pdf (accessed 7 April 2020).

CHRI. 2004. 'Detailed Analysis of the Indian Freedom of Information Act 2002 & Recommendations for Amendments'. Available at: http://www.humanrightsinitiative.org/programs/ai/rti/news/india_foi_act_analysis_for_mps.pdf (accessed 7 April 2020).

Department for International Development. 2012. *Challenges in Right to Information in South Asia*, Issue 5. Available at: http://r4d.dfi d.gov.uk/pdf/outputs/ids/Protifolon_5.pdf (accessed 7 April 2020).

Dey, Nikhil and Preeti Sampat. 2005. *Bare Acts and Collective Explorations: The MKSS Experience with the Right to Information*. Available at: http://preview.sarai.net/journal/05_pdf/08/02_preeti.pdf (accessed 7 April 2020).

Dutta, Priyadarshini. 2014. 'Dear Rahul: RTI Act Could have Come in 1983'. *Niti Central* . Available at: http://www.niticentral.com/2014/04/29/dear-rahul-rti-act-could-have-come-in-1983-itself-217750.html (accessed 7 April 2020).

First Post. 2012. '"Civil Society Is Not Only About Being Media Savvy": Aruna Roy'. Available at: http://www.firstpost.com/politics/civil-society-is-not-only-about-the-media-savvy-aruna-roy-173154.html (accessed 7 April 2020).

Gujaral, I.K. 1997. *Independence Day Speech*. Available at: http://www.india50.com/speecH1.html (accessed 7 April 2020).

Heinz, Carolyn Brown. 1999. 'The Maithil Brahmans: An Online Ethnography'. Available at: http://www.csuchico.edu/anth/mithila/ (accessed 7 April 2020).

India Today. 1980. 'Law: Supreme Controversy'. 15 April. Available at: http://indiatoday.intoday.in/story/serenity-of-supreme-court-jarred-by-letter-sent-by-justice-p.n.-bhagwati-to-indira-gandhi/1/409605.html (accessed 7 April 2020).

———. 1993. 'Home Secretary Madhav Godbole Quits in a Huff'. Available at: http://indiatoday.intoday.in/story/home-secretary-madhav-godbole-quits-in-a-huff/1/302023.html (accessed 7 April 2020).

———. 1994. 'Growing Number of Bureaucrats Rebel against Corruption'. Available at: http://indiatoday.intoday.in/story/growing-number-of-bureaucrats-rebel-against-corruption/1/294253.html (accessed 7 April 2020).

Kumar, Nitish. 2010. 'Good Governance Is Not a Favour to Citizens, We Are Elected to Serve'. *Governance Now.* Available at: http://www.governancenow.com/news/regular-story/good-governance-not-favour-citizens-we-are-elected-serve (accessed 7 April 2020).

Minocha, Naresh. 2014. 'Madam Soniaji, Please Check Facts & Take Back Your RTI Brag'. *NM Leo News*. Available at: http://nareshminocha.com/index.php/getting-started/120-polity/1620-madam-soniaji-please-check-facts-take-back-your-rti-brag (accessed 7 April 2020).

MyLaw.net. 2012. 'Interview of Justice (Retd.) and Former Chief Justice of India P.N. Bhagwati'. Available at: https://www.youtube.com/watch?v=7AdgzBgNki8 (accessed 7 April 2020).

Narrain, Siddharth. 2010. 'How Sedition Crept into the Constitution'. *The Hoot*. Available at: http://www.thehoot.org/web/freetracker/story.php?storyid=188&sectionId=13 (accessed 7 April 2020).

Nayak, Venkatesh. 2011. 'Classified: The Classifiers Until Now; The Indian Saga'. Available at: http://www.freedominfo.org/2011/07/classified-the-classifiers-until-now-an-indian-saga/ (accessed 7 April 2020).

NCPRI. 2004. 'Statement from NCPRI'. *Human Rights Initiative*. Available at: http://www.humanrightsinitiative.org/programs/ai/rti/news/statement_ncpri.pdf (accessed 7 April 2020).

NCPRI. 2019. Press Release, 1 August. Available at: https://mailchi.mp/da80512a770e/press-release-august-1-2019-police-detains-people-wanting-to-submit-petition-to-the-rashtrapati-bhawan-against-rti-amendments (accessed 7 April 2020).

Pande, Suchi. 2014. 'The Right to Know, the Right to Live: Grassroots Struggle for Information and Work in India'. Thesis submitted for the examination of D. Phil in Development Studies, University of Sussex. Available at: http://sro.sussex.ac.uk/id/eprint/47622/ (accessed 7 April 2020).

Paul H. Appleby Papers. Syracuse University Archives. Available at: http://archives.syr.edu/collections/fac_staff/sua_appleby_ph.htm (accessed 7 April 2020).

PRIA. 2007. *Tracking Right to Information in Eight States-2007*, Report by PRIA. Available at: https://cic.gov.in/sites/default/fi les/PRIA-Tracking-RTI-in-States.pdf (accessed 7 April 2020).

PUCL Bulletin. 1991. 'Freedom of Information and Expression in India'. Available at: http://www.pucl.org/from-archives/Media/freedom.htm (accessed 7 April 2020).

Ramon Magsaysay Award Foundation. n.d. 'Roy, Aruna—Biography'. Available at: https://www.rmaward.asia/awardees/roy-aruna/ (accessed 7 April 2020).

Rediff. 1997. 'The Rediff Interview/H.D. Shourie'. Available at http://www.rediff.com/news/jun/11fia.htm (accessed 7 April 2020).

Rediff. 2000. 'We Can't All Be Gandhi or Mao'. Available at: http://www.rediff.com/news/2000/jul/26award1.htm (accessed 7 April 2020).

———. *The Rediff Interview.* 'Interview of H.D. Shourie. Available at: http://www.rediff.com/news/jun/11fia.htm (accessed 7 April 2020).

Roy, Aruna, and Nikhil Dey. 2001. 'The Right to Information: Facilitating People's Participation and State Accountability'. *10th International Anti-Corruption Conference* . Available at: http://www.cccindia.org.in/cs54b.pdf (accessed 7 April 2020).

RTI Foundation India. 2013. 'PIO Asks RTI Applicant to Pay a Further Fee of Rs.1.34 Crores'. Available at: http://www.rtifoundationofindia.com/pio-asks-rti-applicant-pay-further-fee-rs-134-cror#.VbYIs3gxGqA (accessed 7 April 2020).

Transparency India International. 2017. *State Transparency Report 2017.* Available at: http://transparencyindia.org/wp-content/uploads/2019/05/State-Transparency-Report-2017-First-Edition.pdf (accessed 7 April 2020).

Index

About the Author

Himanshu Jha is with the Department of Political Science, South Asia Institute, at the Heidelberg University. Jha's most recent research explores the what, why, and how of institutional change. His current research interests lie in the area of institutional change, governance, distributive politics, state capacity, bureaucratic culture, and the politics of climate change. For his work, he relies on history and has a strong faith in field-based research.

He has widely published with reputed publishers and interdisciplinary journals, such as 'Ideas and Policy Paradigms: Explaining the Fall of Welfare Politics in West Bengal', with Rahul Mukherji, in *Indian Politics and Policy Journal* (2019), and 'The BJP's Puzzling Victory: Was It about Hindu Nationalism?' in *The Washington Quarterly* (2019); and has contributed chapters to several edited volumes, such as 'Emerging Politics of Accountability: Sub-national Reflections from Bihar' in *Including the Excluded in South Asia: Power, Politics and Policy Perspectives from the Region* (2019), edited by Madhushree Sekher and Radu Carciumaru, and 'The State, Social Policy and Welfare: Reflections on Andhra Pradesh and West Bengal', with Rahul Mukherji, in *The State in India: Ideas, Norms and Politics* (2019), edited by Vidhu Verma.

Besides his academic engagement, he loves to cook, eat, work out, and travel. Prior to academics, Jha was working in the developmental sector in India.